CONTENTS

Dedications

In memory of a much loved mother, Ella Jessie Scurfield, whose loving spirit and quiet courage will always be with me.

To Rong, my wife, whose support has been invaluable.

Acknowledgements

Our grateful thanks to all those who made this publication possible. In particular we wish to thank Kay Willmott for her help with typing the manuscript and our two editors, Sarah Mitchell and Kate Jarratt, for all their encouragement and support.

Bibliographic details

Elizabeth Scurfield graduated with a First Class Honours degree in Chinese from the School of Oriental and African Studies in London. She has nearly 25 years' experience of teaching Chinese to beginners successfully. She is currently Evening Programme Director and Principal Lecturer in Chinese at the University of Westminster in London.

Song Lianyi grew up and was educated in Beijing. He has taught Chinese as a foreign language for more than seven years, five of these in the UK. He is at present the Co-ordinator in Chinese at the Language Centre of the School of Oriental and African Studies. He is completing a PhD in language teaching techniques at the Institute of Education, University of London.

Beginner's CHINESE

AN EASY INTRODUCTION

Elizabeth Scurfield and Song Lianyi

TEACH YOURSELF BOOKS

For UK order queries: please contact Bookpoint Ltd, 39 Milton Park, Abingdon, Oxon OX14 4TD. Telephone: (44) 01235 400414, Fax: (44) 01235 400454. Lines are open from 9.00–6.00, Monday to Saturday, with a 24 hour message answering service. Email address: orders@bookpoint.co.uk

For U.S.A. & Canada order queries: please contact NTC/Contemporary Publishing, 4255 West Touhy Avenue, Lincolnwood, Illinois 60646–1975, U.S.A. Telephone: (847) 679 5500, Fax: (847) 679 2494.

Long renowned as the authoritative source for self-guided learning – with more than 30 million copies sold worldwide – the *Teach Yourself* series includes over 200 titles in the fields of languages, crafts, hobbies, sports, and other leisure activities.

British Library Cataloguing in Publication Data
A catalogue record for this title is available from The British Library.

Library of Congress Catalog Card Number: On file

First published in UK 1996 by Hodder Headline Plc, 338 Euston Road, London, NW1 3BH.

First published in US 1996 by NTC/Contemporary Publishing, 4255 West Touhy Avenue, Lincolnwood (Chicago), Illinois 60646–1975 U.S.A.

The 'Teach Yourself' name and logo are registered trade marks of Hodder & Stoughton Ltd.

Typeset by Graphicraft, Hong Kong
Printed in England by Cox & Wyman Ltd, Reading, Berkshire.

Impression number   13 12 11 10 9 8 7
Year   2002 2001 2000

About the course

Teach Yourself Beginner's Chinese is the right course for you if you are a complete beginner or feel that you need to start back at the beginning again to rebuild your confidence. It is a self-study course which will help you to understand and speak Chinese sufficiently well to function effectively in basic everyday situations, both business and social. The course will also offer you an insight into Chinese culture and there is even an opportunity for you to find out something about the Chinese writing system if you want to.

Which Chinese will you be learning?

In one form or another, Chinese is the language most spoken in the world. Although it has many different spoken forms they are all written in exactly the same way. More than 70% of Chinese people speak the northern dialect so the national language is based on this. More Chinese speakers can understand this national language than any other form of Chinese so it is what you will be learning in this book. In China it is called **Pǔtōnghuà** 'common speech', but it is sometimes referred to in the West as Modern Standard Chinese.

What is romanisation?

Chinese cannot be written using a phonetic alphabet in the way that European languages can. It is written in characters. You will find out more about characters in Unit 11. Various ways have been devised for representing Chinese sounds alphabetically. The standard form in use today is known as **pīnyīn** (literally 'spell sound') and is what we have used in this book. In 1958 **pīnyīn** was adopted as the official system of romanisation in the People's Republic of China.

How the course works

The book is divided into two main parts. Units 1 to 10 introduce you to the basic structures and grammatical points you'll need in everyday situations. These units should be taken in order as each builds on the previous ones.

Units 12 to 21 deal with everyday situations such as booking into a hotel, changing money, buying tickets, seeing a doctor, travelling and being entertained in a Chinese home. They give you the opportunity to put into practice and consolidate the language you have learnt in the first 10 units. You can take these units in any order, although the vocabulary does build up from unit to unit.

A few words about the cassette

This book can be successfully used on its own, but you are advised to obtain and use the accompanying audio cassette if at all possible. It will help you to pronounce Chinese correctly and to acquire a more authentic accent. The recorded dialogues and exercises will also give you plenty of practice in understanding and responding to basic Chinese. The Pronunciation Guide and the new words in the first few units plus items such as the days of the week, the months of the year and simple numbers are all recorded on the cassette. This will help you to speak Chinese correctly in the important early stages of your study. Readers without the cassette will find that there are some units which contain an exercise that cannot be done with the book alone but a written alternative is always provided.

About units 1–10

Each unit has approximately 12 pages, and starts by telling you what you are going to learn in that unit. The **Kāishǐ yǐqián** (*Before you start*) section prepares you for the unit ahead. Then there is an easy exercise **Shìshi** (*Let's try*) to get you speaking straight away.

Zhǔyào Cíhuì (*Key words and phrases*) contain the most important words and phrases from the unit. Try to learn them by heart. They will be used in that unit and in later units. There are various tips throughout the book to help you learn new words.

Duìhuà (*Dialogue*). Move onto the dialogues once you have read the new words a few times. The dialogues will show you how the new words are used and hopefully reinforce them. If you have the cassette listen to each dialogue once or twice without stopping or read through it without looking anything up. You don't have to understand every word to get the gist of it.

Now, using the pause button on your cassette recorder break the dialogue into manageable chunks and try repeating each phrase out loud. This will help you gain a more authentic accent. If you don't have the cassette use a ruler or a book mark to cover part of the dialogue so you can concentrate on a small bit at a time. The most important thing in either case is to **speak out loud** because this will help you gain confidence in speaking Chinese.

Learning tips give you advice on everything from how to master vocabulary to how to improve your listening and reading skills and develop confidence in speaking.

Jiěshì (*Explanations*). This section provides you with the nuts and bolts of the language. It goes over all the main grammar and structures for the units along with plenty of examples. Once you are confident about a particular grammar point try making up your own examples.

Liànxí (*Practice/Exercises*). Each exercise in this section helps you practise one or more of the points introduced in the **Jiěshì** section. For some exercises you will need to listen to the cassette. It is not essential to have the cassette to complete this course and most of these listening exercises can also be completed without it. However, listening to the cassette will make your learning easier and provide more variety.

Xiǎo cèyàn (*Mini test*), at the end of each unit, gives you the opportunity to test yourself on what you have learnt in that unit. In Unit 10 you are given the chance to test yourself on Units 1–10 with a **Dà cèyàn** (*Big test*) and to go back over anything you're not sure about.

Cultural tips are short notes in English which give you an insight into different aspects of Chinese culture and society and are usually linked to the situations being covered in that particular unit.

In each unit you will find at least one useful sign written in Chinese characters (**Hànzì**) so you can familiarise yourself with what they look like even though you haven't actually learnt any characters.

About units 12–21

These units give you the opportunity to practise what you have learnt in meaningful and useful situations. Each unit covers approximately 10 pages. The first page tells you what you are going to learn and under **Kāishǐ yǐqián fùxí** (*Revise before you start*) there is a check list of the structures you have already learnt which will reappear in that unit. This gives you the opportunity to look at some, or all, of these again and to go over them so you feel fully confident before beginning the unit. You will find that some structures come up time and time again so that you will not find it necessary to revise them after a while. You will also find a short text in Chinese (except for Unit 13 which is in English) about the topics in each unit followed by a comprehension exercise.

Cartoons (*Mànhuà*) and **proverbs** (*Chéngyǔ*). You will find cartoons in some of the units which will give you an insight into Chinese humour and hopefully make you laugh! We have also included some proverbs (written in Chinese characters and in **pīnyīn**) which have some relevance to the topic and add some cross-cultural interest. These are short phrases which have their origins in classical Chinese.

Xiǎo cèyàn (As in Units 1–10)

Dá'àn (*Key to the exercises*).

The answers to the **Liànxí**, **Shìshi**, **Xiǎo cèyàn**, **Dà cèyàn** can all be found at the back of the book. Do remember that variations are possible in some of the answers but we couldn't include them all.

Unit 11 – Let's look at Chinese characters!

Contrary to what most people believe, Chinese is not a difficult language to speak – particularly at beginner's level. Pronunciation and grammar are generally straightforward even if they require you to do a few things you're not used to. Even tones are not intrinsically difficult and can be fun, though they do involve a lot of time and practice.

Nobody can say, however, that learning to read and write Chinese characters is easy – fascinating yes, but not easy. That is why we have written this book in **pīnyīn**, so that the learner can get straight down to speaking Chinese without the barrier of an unknown form of writing.

Unit 11 is a special unit designed to give you the chance to find out something about the origin of Chinese characters and to have a taste of what's involved in reading and writing them. This unit is designed as a 'one-off' so that those of you who would rather concentrate solely on listening and speaking can miss it out without it affecting your understanding of other units.

At the back of the book

At the back of the book is a reference section which contains:

Dá'àn (*Key to the exercises*).
A Chinese–English Vocabulary list containing all the words in the course.
An English–Chinese Vocabulary list with the most useful words you'll need when expressing yourself in Chinese.

____ How to be successful at ____ learning Chinese

1 **Little and often** is far more effective than a long session every now and then. Try to do 20–30 minutes a day if you can. If you can't manage that, then set yourself a minimum of 2–3 times a week. Try to make it at roughly the same time each day – when you get up, or at lunchtime, or before you go to bed for instance. This will make it easier for you to get into the habit of studying regularly.

2 **Revise and test yourself regularly.** Find a balance between moving through the book and revising what you have already learnt. If you move forward too quickly you will find later units difficult and you will get discouraged. Try to avoid this.

3 **Hear yourself speak!** If at all possible find yourself a quiet place to study where you can speak out loud. You need to build up your speaking and listening skills and your confidence, so make it as easy and as comfortable for yourself as you can.

4 **Find opportunities to speak Chinese.** You don't have to go to China to do this. Join a Chinese class to practise your Chinese with other people, find a Chinese native speaker to help

you (but make sure he or she speaks **Pǔtōnghuà**) and find out about Chinese clubs, societies, and so on.

5 **Don't be too harsh on yourself!** Learning a language is a gradual process – you have to keep at it. Don't expect to remember every item of vocabulary and every new structure all at once. The important thing is to get your meaning across. Making mistakes in Chinese will not stop a Chinese person understanding you.

But most of all remember that learning and using a foreign language is fun, particularly when you find you can use what you have learnt in real situations.

—— Symbols and abbreviations ——

🔲	This indicates that the cassette is needed for the following section. (But often there is an alternative way of completing the section if you don't have the cassette.)
🗨	This indicates dialogue.
☑	This indicates exercises – places where you can practise using the language.
🔑	This indicates key words and phrases.
⚙	This indicates grammar or explanations – the nuts and bolts of the language.
✳	This draws your attention to points to be noted.
→ P.	This refers you to another page giving further information on a point.

(sing)	singular	(lit.)	literally
(pl)	plural	(MW)	measure word

——————— Punctuation ———————

Chinese punctuation is very similar to that of English but a pause-mark (、) is used in lists instead of a comma, even if the list only has two items in it. A comma is used for longer pauses.

Use of hyphens

We have used hyphens to show you how words are built up in Chinese:

Zhōngguó *China* + **rén** *person* → **Zhōngguó-rén** *a Chinese person*

Déguó *Germany* + **rén** → **Déguó-rén** *a German person*

A hyphen is also used to link a verbal suffix or verbal complement to the verb. This will encourage you to say it together with the verb as it should be said:

Wǒ chī-**guo** Yìndù fàn.	*I've eaten Indian food.*
Tā méi qù-**guo** Zhōngguó.	*He's never been to China.*
Nǐ shuō-**de** hěn màn.	*You speak very slowly.*
Tāmen xiě-**de** bú kuài.	*They don't write quickly.*

In general we have written 'words' separately except where they are seen as being one idea:

hǎo	*good*	but **hǎo deduō**	*much better*
		or **hǎo duōle**	
tā	*he, she, it*	but **tāde**	*his, hers, its*
xīngqī	*week*	but **xīngqīyī**	*Monday*
yuè	*month*	but **yīyuè**	*January*
běn	measure word for books	but **běnzi**	*notebook*

However, verb-objects and so on are separate for clarity:

shuō huà	*to speak* (speech)
(verb) (object)	
shuō Fǎyǔ	*to speak French*

PRONUNCIATION GUIDE

——————— Chinese Sounds ———————

Vowels

Here is the list of the Chinese vowels with a rough English equivalent sound and then one or two examples in Chinese. There are single vowels, compound vowels or vowels plus a nasal sound which will be listed separately.

	rough English sound	Chinese examples
a	father	baba, mama
ai	bite	tai, zai
ao	cow	hao, zhao
e	fur	che, he, ge
ei	play	bei, gei, shei, fei
i	tea	didi, feiji, ni
i (after z, c, s, zh, ch, sh and r only)		zi, ci, shi

The 'i' is there more or less for cosmetic reasons – no syllable can exist without a vowel. Say the consonant and 'sit on it' and you have the sound.

ia	yarrow	jia, xia
iao	meow	biao, piao, yao
ie	yes	bie, xie, ye
iu	yo-yo	liu, jiu, you

y replaces i at the beginning of a word if there is no initial consonant.

| o | more | moyimo, mapo |
| ou | go | dou, zou |

u	moo	bu, zhu
ua	suave	gua, hua
uo	war	shuo, cuo, wo
uai	swipe	kuai, wai
ui	weigh	dui, gui, zui

w replaces **u** at the beginning of a word if there is no initial consonant.

| ü | pneumonia | ju, qu, lü, nü |
| üe | pneumatic + **air** (said quickly) | yue, xue, jue |

Note that **ü** and **üe** can occur only with the consonants **n, l, j, q** and **x**. As **j, q** and **x** cannot occur as j+u, q+u or x+u, the umlaut (··) over the 'u' in **ju, qu** and **xu** has been omitted. **N** and **l**, however, can occur as both **nu** and **nü, lu** and **lü** so the umlaut (··) has been kept.

And **yu** replaces **ü**, and **yue** replaces **üe** if there is no initial consonant.

Here are the **vowels with a nasal sound** formed with vowels followed by **n** or **ng**. Speak through your nose when you pronounce them and listen carefully to the cassette.

	rough English sound	Chinese examples
an	man	fan, man
ang	bang	zhang, shang
en	under	ren, hen
eng	hung	deng, neng
in	bin	nin, jin, xin
ian	yen	tian, nian, qian
iang	**Yang**tse (River)	liang, xiang
ing	finger	ming, qing, xing
iong	**Jung** (the psychoanalyst)	yong, qiong, xiong
ong	Jung	tong, cong, hong
uan	wangle	wan, suan, huan
un	won	wen, lun, chun
uang	wrong	wang, huang, zhuang
üan	pneumatic + **end** (said quickly)	yuan, quan, xuan
ün	'une' in French	yun, jun, qun

Note that **ian** is pronounced as if it were i<u>en</u>.

The same rules about **y** replacing **i** and **w** replacing **u** at the beginning of a word if there is no initial consonant also apply to vowels with a nasal sound.

Yuan replaces **üan** and **yun** replaces **ün** if there is no initial consonant.

Consonants

Here is a list of the Chinese consonants some of which are quite similar to English sounds, others less so. Those that are very different from the nearest English sound are explained.

	rough English sound	Chinese examples
b	**b**ore	**b**ai, **b**ei
p	**p**oor	**p**ao, **p**ang
m	**m**e	**m**a, **m**ei, **m**ing
f	**f**an	**f**an, **f**eng
d	**d**oor	**d**a, **d**ou, **d**uo
t	**t**ore	**t**a, **t**ai, **t**ian
n	**n**eed	**n**a, **n**ü, **n**ian
l	**l**ie	**l**ai, **l**ei, **l**iang
z	ad**ds**	**z**i, **z**ai, **z**uo
c	i**ts**	**c**i, **c**ai, **c**uo
s	**s**ay	**s**i, **s**ui, **s**uan

The next four consonants are all made with the tongue loosely rolled in the middle of the mouth.

zh	**j**elly	**zh**ao, **zh**ong, **zh**u
ch	**ch**illy	**ch**e, **ch**i, **ch**ang
sh	**sh**y	**sh**i, **sh**ei, **sh**eng
r	**r**azor	**r**e, **r**i, **r**ong

The next three consonants are all made with the tongue flat and the corners of the mouth drawn back as far as possible.

j	**g**enius	**j**ia, **j**iao, **j**ian
q	**ch**eese	**q**i, **q**ian, **q**u
	(as said in front of the camera!)	
x	**sh**eet	**x**iao, **x**in, **x**ue
	(rather like a whistling kettle)	

Arch the back of the tongue towards the roof of the mouth for the last three consonants.

g	**g**uard	**g**e, **g**ei, **g**ui
k	**c**ard	**k**ai, **k**an, **k**uai
h	lo**ch**	**h**e, **h**ai, **h**ao

Tones

Chinese is a tonal language. Every syllable in Chinese has its own tone. **Pǔtōnghuà** has four distinct tones plus a neutral tone. This means that syllables which are pronounced the same but have different tones will mean different things. For example, **tang** pronounced in the first tone means *soup* but pronounced in the second tone means *sugar*! But don't worry – all the four tones fall within your natural voice range. You don't have to have a particular type of voice to speak Chinese.

The four tones are represented by the following marks which are put over the vowel such as **nǐ** *you* or over the main vowel of a syllable where there are two or three vowels eg. **hǎo** *good*, but **guó** *country*:

— 1st tone, high and level

╱ 2nd tone, rising

∨ 3rd tone, falling – rising

╲ 4th tone, falling

The diagrams below will help to make this clearer.

Think of **1** as being at the bottom of your voice range and **5** at the top.

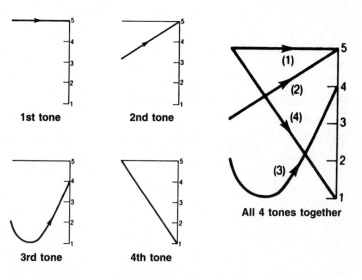

1st tone   2nd tone

3rd tone   4th tone

All 4 tones together

1st tone: Pitch it where **you** feel comfortable. Say 'oo' as in 'zoo' and keep going for as long as you can. You should be able to keep it up for maybe half a minute. When you have got used to that, change to another vowel sound and practise that in the same way and so on.

2nd tone: Raise your eyebrows every time you attempt a second tone until you get used to it. This is infallible!

3rd tone: Drop your chin onto your neck and raise it again. Then practise the sound doing the movement at the same time.

4th tone: Stamp your foot gently and then accompany this action with the relevant sound.

Neutral tones: Some syllables in Chinese are toneless or occur in the neutral tone. This means they have no tonemark over the vowel. They are rather like unstressed syllables in English, such as *of a* in 'two of a kind'.

Tone changes

Occasionally syllables may change their tones.

(*a*) Two 3rd tones, one after another, are very difficult to say. Where this happens, the first one is said as a 2nd tone. We have still marked it as a 3rd tone in the book otherwise you may think that it is always a 2nd tone which it isn't:
Nǐ hǎo! (*How do you do?*) is said as **Ní hǎo**.

(*b*) If three 3rd tones occur together, the first two are normally said as 2nd tones:
Wǒ yě hǎo. (*I'm OK too.*) is said as **Wó yé hǎo**.

(*c*) Note that in the phrase **yí ge rén** (*one* measure word *person*), the **ge** is said without a tone although it is actually 4th, but it still carries enough weight to change the **yì** into a 2nd tone.

You will find a few other tone changes in the book. These will be pointed out to you when they occur for the first time.

1

NǏ HǍO! NǏ HǍO MA?
Hello! How are you?

In this unit you will learn:

- how to say *hello* and *goodbye*
- how to exchange greetings
- how to say *please* and *thank you*
- how to make a simple apology
- how to observe basic courtesies

Kāishǐ yǐqián (Before you start)

Read about the course on ➡️🅿️ 1–7. This gives useful advice on how to make the best of this course.

Everybody learns differently. You need to find the way which works best for you. You will find some useful learning tips in each unit marked with the symbol ✳️.

Make sure you have your cassette handy as you will need it to listen to the Pronunciation Guide and Dialogues.

If you don't have the cassette, use the Pronunciation Guide ➡️🅿️ 8–12 to help you with the pronunciation of new words and phrases.

It's a good idea to listen through the Pronunciation Guide and to practise the Chinese tones before starting Unit 1. This way you can make the most of the dialogues. More advice on ➡️🅿️ 18.

✳️ Remember that studying for 20 minutes regularly is much more effective than occasionally spending two hours in one go.

Try following this study guide and adapt it to your needs as you go along:

1 Listen to the **Duìhuà** (*Dialogues*) once or twice without the book (read them if you haven't got the cassette).

2 Go over each one, bit by bit, in conjunction with the **Zhǔyào cíhuì** (*Key words and phrases*) and **Xuéxí jìqiǎo** (*Learning tips*) underneath the dialogues.

3 Study the section **Jiěshì** (*Explanations*) very carefully and make sure that you understand it.

4 Make sure you understand the *Learning tips* on how to pronounce and how to learn.

5 Read the *Cultural tips*.

6 Go back to the **Duìhuà** and **Zhǔyào cíhuì** and listen and study for as long as it takes you to grasp them. This time use the pause button on the cassette. Try reading a new word or phrase aloud after the cassette, then rewind and play it again to check your progress.

7 Do the **Liànxí** (*Exercises*) and check your answers in **Dá'àn** (*Key to the Exercises*) at the back of the book. Test yourself with the **Xiǎo cèyàn** (*Mini test*).

Now you are ready to start!

Rùkǒu
Entrance

Zhǔyào cíhuì
(*Key words and phrases*)

bù	not
bú yòng xiè	not at all (*lit.* no need thank)
bú zài	not at; to be not at / in

duìbuqǐ	excuse me
hǎo	good, well
. . . hǎo ma?	How is / are . . . ?
hěn	very
jīntiān	today
lái	to come
lǎoshī	teacher
ma	(*question particle*)
míngtiān	tomorrow
míngtiān jiàn	see you tomorrow
nǐ	you (*sing*)
Nǐ hǎo! (sing)	Hello!
nǐmen	you (*pl*)
Nǐmen hǎo! (pl)	Hello!
Qǐng jìn!	Please come in.
Qǐng wèn, . . . ?	May I ask . . . ?
Qǐng zuò!	Please sit down.
tā	she / he
tàitai	Mrs; wife
xiānsheng	Mr; husband; gentleman
xiǎo	little, young, small
xièxie	thank you; to thank
zài	at; to be at / in
zàijiàn	goodbye

✴ *Xuéxí jìqiǎo* (Learning tips)

Read the words and expressions aloud. Concentrate on the pronunciation. Turn back to the Pronunciation Guide ➡️🄿 8–12 and check anything you need to. Especially check out the four tones and the neutral tone. They're quite easy to get the hang of after a little practice.

If you have a cassette, listen to the words and repeat them after you hear them using the pause button.

🔊 ——— Duìhuà (*Dialogues*) ———

Listen to the cassette and listen to people saying *hello*, *thank you* and *goodbye* in Chinese. Press the pause button after each person has spoken and repeat aloud.

🎞 *Duìhuà 1 Saying hello*

Mr Wang is a tourist guide. He prefers to be called **Xiǎo Wáng** (lit. *little Wang*) as he is only 28 years old, though his full name is Wáng Jìjūn. When Mr and Mrs Green see Xiǎo Wáng, they greet him in Chinese.

Mrs Green Nǐ hǎo, Xiǎo Wáng!
Mr Green Xiǎo Wáng, nǐ hǎo!
Xiǎo Wáng Gélín xiānsheng, Gélín tàitai, nǐmen hǎo!
Mrs Green Nǐ tàitai hǎo ma?
Xiǎo Wáng Tā hěn hǎo, xièxie.

Try saying two 3rd tones together. Difficult isn't it? Both **nǐ** (*you*) and **hǎo** (*good*) are 3rd tones but when said together **ni** is a 2nd tone. This was explained more fully in the Pronunciation Guide ➡️🄿 12.

Neutral tones

Some syllables or words in Chinese are toneless or have what is called a neutral tone. The **-sheng** of **xiānsheng**, the **-men** in **nǐmen**, and the question particle **ma** in the **Duìhuà** above are good examples of this.

🎞 *Duìhuà 2 Saying goodbye*

When Mr and Mrs Green have finished their visit, they thank Xiǎo Wáng and say goodbye to him.

Mr Green Xiǎo Wáng, xièxie nǐ.
Mrs Green Xièxie nǐ, Xiǎo Wáng.
Xiǎo Wáng Bú yòng xiè.
Mr Green Zàijiàn.
Xiǎo Wáng Zàijiàn.
Mrs Green Zàijiàn.

How to pronounce q

This is not at all like a **q** in English as in *queen*. **Q** in Chinese is pronounced like the **j** in *jeans* but with air behind it. It is rather like the **ch** in *cheetah* but with the corners of the mouth drawn back as far as they can go. Refer back to the Pronunciation Guide for more help.

📷 *Duìhuà 3*

Mr Green comes to see his Chinese visitor. He knocks at the door.

Lǐ   Qǐng jìn.
Green *(enters the room)*
Lǐ   Gélín xiānsheng, nǐ hǎo!
Green Nǐ hǎo, Lǐ xiānsheng.
Lǐ   Qǐng zuò.
Green Xièxie.
Lǐ   Gélín tàitai hǎo ma?
Green Tā hěn hǎo. Xièxie.

📷 *Duìhuà 4*

Frank goes to the teachers' office to look for his teacher.

Frank   Qǐng wèn, Zhāng lǎoshī zài ma?
Lǐ lǎoshī Duìbuqǐ, tā bú zài.
Frank   Tā jīntiān lái ma?
Lǐ lǎoshī Bù lái. Tā míngtiān lái.
Frank   Xièxie nǐ.

Lǐ lǎoshī Bú yòng xiè. Míngtiān jiàn.
Frank Míngtiān jiàn.

How to practise tones

1   When you are practising words individually pay attention to the tone and try to reproduce it. Go back and look at Tones ➡ P. 11–12 where you will find some useful hints on how to say each of the four tones.

2   When you are repeating phrases or sentences as in the **Duìhuà** pay more attention to the shape of the whole sentence and copy that rather than each individual tone.

3   Don't worry if you find the idea of tones rather daunting at first – you will soon get used to them!

Jiěshì
(Explanations)

1   Mr and Mrs

In Chinese the surname or family name always comes first. Traditionally this is the most important thing about your identity. The Chinese have always placed much emphasis on the family. Your title appears after your surname:

Gélín xiānsheng   *Mr Green*
Gélín tàitai   *Mrs Green*
Wáng lǎoshī   *Teacher Wang*

2   Greetings

Nǐ hǎo can be used at any time to say *Hello* or *How do you do?*. You will come across other greetings which refer specifically to the morning or the evening, such as when wishing somebody good night.

3   Asking somebody to do something

Qǐng is used when you want to ask somebody to do something. You use the verb **qǐng** (*to invite/request*) plus the word for whatever you want them to do. Of course **qǐng** could be translated as **please** in such cases.

| **Qǐng** jìn. | *Please come in.* |
| **Qǐng** zuò. | *Please sit down.* |

You use the verb **wèn** (*to ask*) when you want to ask a question.

| **Wèn** wèntí | *Ask (a) question(s)* |
| Qǐng **wèn** | *May I ask . . . ?* |

4 *Hǎo* Adjective or verb?

The answer is both! **Hǎo** is both an adjective (a word that describes a noun) and a verb (a word that tells you what a person, animal or thing does, or is). However, Chinese adjectives can also act as verbs so: **hǎo** means *to be good, to be well,* as well as *fine, good, OK*:

| Nǐ **hǎo**. | *How do you do. / How are you?* |
| Tā hěn **hǎo**. | *He/she is (very) well. / He/she is (very) good.* |

But:

| **hǎo** tàitai | *a good wife* |
| **hǎo** lǎoshī | *a good teacher* |

The use of **hěn** in **hěn hǎo** is *not* optional. If you do not use it, a comparison is implied. **Hěn** carries a lot less weight than the English 'very' unless you stress it.

5 You like me? I like you!

Pronouns (words used in place of nouns to refer to a person) are very easy in Chinese: **Wǒ** means *me* as well as *I*. **Tā** means *him, her, it* as well as *he/she,* or *it*. To make them plural you simply add **-men**. The table below will make this clearer:

wǒ	*I, me*	**wǒmen**	*we, us*
nǐ	*you* (sing)	**nǐmen**	*you* (pl)
tā	*he, she, it him, her*	**tāmen**	*they, them*

Although *he, she* and *it* are all pronounced **tā**, each of them is written with a different character. This only affects the written language (see Unit 11), so there is absolutely nothing to worry about.

6 Simple questions with ma?

To make a question from any statement you just put **ma** at the end of it.

Tā míngtiān lái.	*She will come tomorrow.*
Tā míngtiān lái ma?	*Is she coming tomorrow?*
Wáng lǎoshī zài.	*Teacher Wang is around.*
Wáng lǎoshī zài ma?	*Is Teacher Wang around?*

7 How to say no!

To make a verb negative in Chinese all you have to do is put **bù** in front of it. There is only **one** exception to this rule which you will meet in Unit 2. (The tone change on **bù** is explained on ➡️💡 27.)

Nǐ hǎo.	*You're well/good.*
Nǐ bù hǎo.	*You are not well/not good.*
Tā zài.	*He/she's here.*
Tā bú zài.	*He/she's not here.*

8 Word order that's different but not difficult!

Basic Chinese word order is the same as in English,

I	**like**	**you**
Subject	Verb	Object

but in English, you say: *He is coming tomorrow.* Whereas in Chinese, you say:

Tā míngtiān lái.	*He tomorrow comes.*

To sum up, time words like *today, tomorrow, Wednesday, 6 o'clock* come **before** the verb in Chinese. Other words that come before the verb are the negative **bù**, and words such as **yě** (*also*) and **hěn** (*very*).

———————— **Cultural tips** ————————

Greetings

Traditionally the Chinese neither shake hands nor kiss when they meet or say goodbye. The custom was to clasp your hands together at

chest height and as you move them very slightly backwards and for-
wards you bow your head over them. The lower you bow your head,
the higher the status of the other person. With the growing influence
of the West, however, shaking hands is becoming more common.

Please and thank you

Qǐng (*please*) and **xièxie** (*thank you*) are used much less frequently
in Chinese than in English, but it is always better to use them too
much rather than too little!

✓ ———— **Liànxí (*Exercises*)** ————

1   What do you say? Choose the most appropriate response for (*a*)
    from the first four boxes. Do the same for (*b*) and (*c*).

   (*a*) When you greet a friend, you say:

Nǐ hǎo	Zàijiàn	Bú yòng xiè	Xièxie

   (*b*) When you thank someone, you say:

Zàijiàn	Nǐ hǎo	Xièxie	Bú yòng xiè

   (*c*) When someone thanks you for your help, you respond by
        saying:

Nǐ hǎo	Bú yòng xiè	Zàijiàn	Xièxie

2   Responding to a Chinese person. To help you out the first letter
    of the correct response is already put in.
    Example: Qǐng jìn. – Xièxie.

   (*a*) Nǐ hǎo!   N_____ _____!

   (*b*) Xièxie nǐ.   B_____ _____ _____.

   (*c*) Qǐng zuò.   X_____.

   (*d*) Zàijiàn!   Z_____!

3   This time you begin and the Chinese person responds. And
    you're on your own.

   (*a*) ___ ___.   Nǐ hǎo!

   (*b*) Lǐ tàitai ___ ___?   Tā hěn hǎo. Xièxie nǐ.

   (*c*) Lǐ xiānsheng ___ ___?   Duìbuqǐ, tā bú zài.

   (*d*) _____ _____.   Bú yòng xiè.

4 What would you put in each of the gaps to make them into words or phrases?

Example: Duì__qǐ. – Duìbuqǐ.

(*a*) Xiè___.

(*e*) Qǐng ___.

(*b*) __ ___ xiè.

(*f*) ___ zuò.

(*c*) ___ jiàn!

(*g*) __ ___ hǎo.

(*d*) _____ jiàn!

(*h*) __ hǎo __?

5 Match the sentences on the left to those on the right.

(*a*) Tāmen hěn hǎo.

(*i*) They won't be in tomorrow.

(*b*) Tāmen jīntiān bú zài.

(*ii*) They will come today.

(*c*) Tāmen jīntiān lái.

(*iii*) They are not in today.

(*d*) Tāmen míngtiān bú zài.

(*iv*) They are very well.

🖉 *Xiǎo cèyàn* (Mini test)

Now you've arrived at the end of Unit 1. What would you say in the following situations:

(*a*) You meet your Chinese friend, Mr Li, and you want to say hello.

(*b*) Then you ask how his wife is.

(*c*) You are a little bit late and you say you are sorry.

(*d*) Thank your friend (for his/her help).

(*e*) When he/she thanks you, say *You are welcome*.

(*f*) When you take your leave, what do you say?

You'll find the answers to **Xiǎo cèyàn** (*Mini test*) in **Dá'àn** (*Key to the exercises*) at the end of the book. If you've got them correct you are ready to move on to Unit 2. If you found the test difficult, spend more time revising this unit.

欢迎 **huānyíng**

再见 **zàijiàn**

再见

zàijiàn

2

NǏ JIÀO SHÉNME?
What's your name?

In this unit you will learn:

- how to say who you are
- how to make simple introductions
- how to ask who other people are
- how to address people correctly
- how to deny something

Kāishǐ yǐqián

There is a lot of practice with asking questions in this unit. Try to learn some of the questions by heart as they will be very useful. Remember what was said about tones in Unit 1 in the section How to practise tones.

☑ Shìshi (Let's try)

A Chinese visitor has knocked on the door of your office.

(a) What would you call out?

(b) How would you greet him when he comes through the door?

(c) How would you ask him to sit down?

(d) At the end of your talk you show him to the door. What do you say to him? (You have arranged to see him again tomorrow.)

✳ *Xuéxí jìqiǎo*

Here are some hints for learning vocabulary. See which one works best for you:

1 Practise saying the words aloud as you read them.

2 Cover up the English and see if you can remember what any of the Chinese words mean.

3 Cover up the Chinese and see if the English words jolt your memory.

4 Listen to the cassette over and over again.

5 Write the words out several times.

6 Study the new words from beginning to end then start from the bottom and work back up again.

7 Group the words in a way that will help you to remember them, such as all the verbs together, all the countries and the language which is spoken in each one.

8 Copy the words with their tone marks on to one side of a small card with their English equivalent on the other. Go through them looking at the Chinese first and giving the English word and then vice versa. If you get any one wrong put it back in the pile and have another go at it. You can also mix up the English and Chinese.

Zhǔyào cíhuì

dāngrán	of course
guì	expensive, honourable
Nín guì xìng?	What's your (*honourable*) name?
háizi	child / children
huì	can, to be able to
jiào	to call / be called
méi	no, not, (have not)
méi guānxi	it's OK / it doesn't matter
míngzi	name
nà	that
nán	male
Nǐ ne?	And you?
nín	you (*polite form*)

péngyou	friend
piàoliang	beautiful
rènshi *shéi*	recognise, know (*people*)
shénme	what
shì	to be
shéi	who
shuō	to speak, to say
wǒ	I, me
wǒde/nǐde/nínde/tāde	my, your, his / her
xiǎojie	miss
xìng	surname
yě	also
yìdiǎn(r)	a little
Yīngwén	English (*language*)
yǒu	to have
zhè	this
zhēn	real / really
Zhōngwén	Chinese (*language*)

Nǐ/tā jiào shénme (míngzi)?	What is your / his / her name?
Wǒ/tā jiào . . .	I / he / she is called . . .
Wǒ/nǐ/tā (bú) shì . . .	I / you / he / she am / are / is (not) . . .
Zhè/nà (bú) shì . . .	This / that is (not) . . .
Tā shì shéi?	Who is he / she?
Tā shì bu shi . . . ?	Is he / she . . . (or not)?

Common Chinese surnames

Zhāng	Wáng	Lǐ	Zhào	Liú
张	王	李	赵	刘

Chén	Lín	Wú	Guō	Zhèng
陈	林	吴	郭	郑

✳ Xuéxí jìqiǎo

1 Refer back to the Pronunciation Guide to help you pronounce the surnames above. Repeat them aloud several times.

2 If you have the cassette, listen to the names and repeat them after the recording.

Duìhuà

Duìhuà 1

Listen to or read the dialogue and see how you ask what another person's name is in Chinese.

Jane Nín guì xìng?
Chén Wǒ xìng Chén. Nín ne?
Jane Wǒ xìng Lord. Zhè shì nínde háizi ma?
Chén Bú shì. Wǒ méi yǒu háizi. Zhè shì Lǐ tàitai de háizi.
Jane (*to the boy*) Nǐ jiào shénme míngzi?
Child Wǒ jiào Pàn Pan.

Duìhuà 2   At a conference

White Zhèng xiānsheng, nǐ hǎo!
Cháng Wǒ xìng Cháng, bú xìng
Zhèng. Wǒ jiào Cháng
Zhèng.
White Duìbuqǐ, Cháng
xiānsheng.
Cháng Méi guānxi. White
xiānsheng, nǐ yǒu mei
yǒu Zhōngwén míngzi?

White Yǒu. Wǒ jiào Bái Bǐdé.
Cháng Bái xiānsheng, nǐ huì bu huì shuō Yīngwén?
White Dāngrán huì. Cháng xiānsheng, nǐ yě huì shuǒ Yīngwén
   ma?
Cháng Huì yìdiǎnr.

Tone of bù

Bù (*not*) is normally a 4th tone, but it becomes a 2nd tone before another 4th tone. When this happens it is marked as such in the book, such as **bú xìng not bù xìng**. It is toneless in such expressions as **huì bu huì** (see **Duìhuà 2**).

Duìhuà 3

How do you introduce yourself and somebody else? Find out in this **Duìhuà**.

Bái Tā shì shéi? Nǐ rènshi bu rènshi tā?
Wú Rènshi. Tā shì Guō xiǎojie.
Bái Tā zhēn piàoliang. (*walks over to the girl*)
Bái Nǐ hǎo! Wǒ jiào Bái Bǐdé. Nǐ ne?
Guō Nǐ hǎo! Wǒ jiào Guō Yùjié. (*A man walks over to her and hands her a drink.*)
Guō Zhè shì wǒde nán péngyou. Tā jiào Liú Wénguāng. Zhè shì Bái xiānsheng.
Liú Bái xiānsheng, nǐ hǎo!
Bái O, nǐ hǎo!

 —————————————— **Jiěshì** ——————————————

1 How to be courteous

In Chinese, when you don't know somebody very well (or at all) and you wish to show respect, you use **nín** instead of **nǐ**. It is, however, used less frequently than it used to be. It cannot be used in the plural. This means that the plural form of both **nǐ** and **nín** is **nǐmen**.

2 You and yours!

Nǐ means *you* (sing). If you add the little word **de** to it, it means *your* or *yours*:

nǐ**de** háizi	*your child*
wǒ**de** xiānsheng	*my husband*
zhè shì nǐ**de**	*this is yours*
Lǐ tàitai **de** háizi	*Mrs Li's child*

In close personal relationships: **nǐ tàitai** (*your wife*), **wǒ māma** (*my mum*) the **de** may be omitted (Dialogue 1, ➡️🄿 16 where Mrs Green asks Xiǎo Wáng, **Nǐ tàitai hǎo ma?**)

3 How to say No with Yǒu!

To say *do not have* in Chinese you put **méi** in front of the verb **yǒu** *to have*.

All other verbs are negated by putting **bù** in front of them ➡️🄿 20.

Wǒ **méi yǒu** háizi.	*I have no children.*
Tā **méi yǒu** Zhōngwén míngzi.	*She doesn't have a Chinese name.*

4 Another way of asking questions

If you put the positive and negative forms of the verb together (in that order) you can make a question:

Nǐ **yǒu mei yǒu** háizi?	*Do you have children?*
Nǐ **shì bu shì** lǎoshī?	*Are you a teacher?*

This is a popular alternative to the question form with **ma** ➡️🄿 20. The negative form of the verb is normally unstressed when it is used to make a question in this way. It **is** stressed, however, if the question is said slowly or with emphasis.

5 Yes and No?

Yes and *no* don't exist as such in Chinese. If you are asked a question the answer is either the positive form of the verb (to mean yes) or the negative form of the verb (to mean no):

Nǐ yǒu méi yǒu háizi?	*Do you have children?*
Yǒu.	*Yes, I do.*
Méi yǒu.	*No, I don't.*

Nǐ rènshi tā ma?	*Do you know her?*
Rènshi.	*Yes, I do.*
Bú rènshi.	*No, I don't.*

6 To be or not to be?

Shì, the verb *to be* in English, is used much less in Chinese than in English. This is because adjectives in Chinese can also act as verbs as you saw in Unit 1, ➡P 19. For example, **hǎo** means *to be good* as well as *good* so there is no need for the verb *to be*.

Zhè **shì** nǐde háizi ma?	*Is this your child?*
Bú **shì**. Zhè **shì** Lǐ tàitai de háizi.	*No, it's Mrs Li's.*
Tā **shì** nǐde nǚ péngyou ma?	*Is she your girlfriend?*
Bú **shì**. Tā **shì** wǒ tàitai.	*No, she is my wife.*

7 Who and what?

In Chinese, question words such as **shéi** (*who*) and **shénme** (*what*) appear in the sentence in the same position as the word or words which replace them in the answer:

Nǐ jiào **shénme** míngzi?	*What are you called?*
	(*lit.* You are called what?)
Wǒ jiào **Pàn Pan**.	*I'm called* Pàn Pan.
Nà shì **shéi**?	*Who is that (young lady)?*
	(*lit.* That [young lady] is who?)
Tā shì **wǒ (de) péngyou**.	*She is my friend.*

This is different from the word order in English where the question word is at the beginning of the sentence.

8 Follow-up questions

To avoid having to ask a question in full or to repeat the same question you can use the little word **ne?** at the end of a phrase to take a short cut!

Nǐ jiào shénme míngzi?	*What's your name?*
Wǒ jiào Wú Zébì. Nǐ **ne**?	*I'm called/My name is Wu Zebi.*
	What about you?
	(*ie.* what's your name?)

Wǒ jiào Bái Bǐdé. Tā **ne**?   *My name's Peter White.*
What's hers?

────────── **Cultural tips** ──────────

As you saw in Unit 1, the surname or family name comes before
your title in Chinese. This means that your given name (Christian
name) comes after your surname:

Cháng (family name) **Zhèng** (given name)
Bái (family name) **Bǐdé** (given name)

The use of first names is generally reserved for family members.
Colleagues or people in your peer group are addressed on an informal basis by their surnames prefaced by **lǎo** (*old*) or **xiǎo** (*young*),
largely depending on whether the person in question is older or
younger than you.

────────── **Liànxí** ──────────

1   Complete the following exchanges by filling in the blanks in the
    sentences below:

    (*a*) Tā jiào _____ míngzi?   Tā _____ Fāng Yuán.

    (*b*) Nǐ _____ shuō Zhōngwén ma?   Huì. Wǒ huì _____
        yìdiǎnr.

    (*c*) Tāde nán péngyou _____ shéi?   Wǒ bú _____ tā.

2   Look at the pictures and answer the following questions in
    Chinese:

        (*a*) Tāmen shì shéi?
    ← (*b*) Tā jiào shénme?
            (*c*) Tā xìng Yīng ma? →
    ← (*d*) Tā yě xìng Yīng ma?
        (*e*) Nǐ rènshi tāmen ma?

Lǐ Jīnshēng   **Yīng Zǐpéng**

────── **30** ──────

3 Listen to the cassette and answer the following questions about the Chinese woman in the passage. If you don't have the cassette, read the passage below and then answer the questions.

(a) What's her surname?
(b) What's her first name?
(c) How much English does she speak?
(d) What is her occupation?
(e) Does she know you?
(f) What does she look like?
(g) Does she have a boyfriend?

Wǒde Zhōngwén lǎoshī jiào Wáng Lányīng. Tā hěn piàoliang. Tā yǒu nán péngyou. Tāmen bú rènshi nǐ. Tāmen huì shuō yìdiǎnr Yīngwén.

4 Who is who? State the names and the occupation of each person pictured below. You can get more practice if you use both of the patterns given in the example:

Tā jiào Yán Lóng. Tā shì xuésheng (*student*).
Zhè/nà shì Yán Lóng. Tā shì xuésheng.

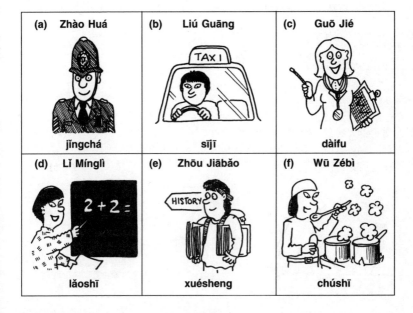

(a) Zhào Huá	(b) Liú Guāng	(c) Guō Jié
jǐngchá	sījī	dàifu
(d) Lǐ Mínglì	(e) Zhōu Jiābǎo	(f) Wū Zébì
lǎoshī	xuésheng	chúshī

5 According to the pictures in **Liànxí 4**, are the following statements true or false? If it's *true*, say **duì** meaning *correct*. If it's not true, say **bú duì**, meaning *not correct*. Tick the right box in each case.

Example   Zhào Huá xìng Huá. (bú duì)

duì/bú duì?

(a) Zhào Huá shì lǎoshī.   ☐ ☐
(b) Liú Guāng bú shì sījī.   ☐ ☐
(c) Nà ge dàifu jiào Wú Zébì.   ☐ ☐
(d) Zhōu Jiābǎo xìng Jiābǎo.   ☐ ☐
(e) Lǐ lǎoshī jiào Lǐ Míng.   ☐ ☐
(f) Wú Zébì shì chúshī.   ☐ ☐

6 You have learned two ways to ask questions. With each set of words use these different question forms to make up two questions. The example will make this clear.

Example   Tā/huì shuō/Fǎwén (*French*)
      – Tā huì shuō Fǎwén ma?
      – Tā huì bú huì shuō Fǎwén?

(a) Nǐ/huì shuō/Yīngwén
(b) Nǐmen/shì/lǎoshī

(c) Xiǎo Zhèng/zài

(d) Lǐ xiānsheng/jīntiān/lái
(e) Wáng Fāng/yǒu/Yīngwén míngzi
(f) Lín lǎoshī/jiào/Lín Péng

☑ *Xiǎo cèyàn*

How would you say the following?

(a) Ask what a person's surname is.
(b) Say *My name is xxx*.
(c) Say that you haven't got a Chinese name.
(d) Say that you don't know her.
(e) Say *That's OK* when someone apologises to you.
(f) Say that your friend is not a teacher.

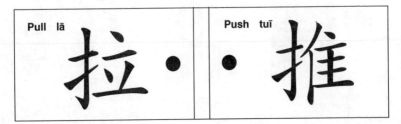

Pull   lā   拉

Push   tuī   推

3

NǏ SHÌ NǍ GUÓ RÉN?
Where are you from?

In this unit you will learn:

- how to say where you come from and what nationality you are
- how to ask for and give an address
- the numbers from 0 to 10
- how to ask for, and give, a telephone number
- how to fill out a form

Kāishǐ yǐqián

Talking about where you come from, what nationality you are, where you live and what your telephone number is in Chinese is straight-forward with the necessary vocabulary and a few of the basic rules about word order. Chinese numbers are very easy as you will dis-cover in this unit.

It is important to have short-term goals to encourage yourself. In this unit keep practising how to ask other people where they come from, where they live and what their telephone number is. Make sure you can answer these questions yourself! Aim at answering them without thinking.

Shìshi

You are at a party where you hardly know anyone.

(a) How do you introduce yourself and how do you ask somebody his/her name?

(*b*) If you find out that one of the guests is married, how do you ask if they have any children?

Zhǔyào cíhuì

diànhuà	telephone (*lit.* electric speech)
duì	yes, correct
Dōngchéng (Qū)	Eastern City (District)
duōshao?	what's the number of?
fàndiàn	hotel
fángjiān	room
fēijī	plane
Guǎngdōng	Canton (*province*)
guó	country
hào	number
hàomǎ	number (*often used for telephone, telex, fax numbers and car registration plates*)
hépíng	peace
jǐ hào?	which number?
lù	road, street
Lúndūn	London
míngpiàn	namecard
nǎr?	where?
piào	ticket
qū	district
rén	person
Xīchéng (Qū)	Western City (District)
xǐhuan	to like
yìsi	meaning
zhù	to live
zhù zài	to live in / at a place

✳ Xuéxí jìqiǎo

1   Try pronouncing the names of the countries ➡️🄿 37. Repeat them aloud over and over again.

2   Every time you stumble over the pronunciation of a word or syllable go back to the Pronunciation Guide and check it out. ➡️🄿 8–12.

3   Foreign names, such as the names of countries and cities, can be expressed in Chinese in three main ways:

(a) Based on the original sound, such as **Yìdàlì** (*Italy*)
(b) Based on the meaning, such as **Niújīn** (*Oxford*) (*lit.* ox/cow ford)
(c) A mixture of the orginal sound and its meaning, such as **Xīn** (*new*) **Xīlán** (*New Zealand*).

Duìhuà

Duìhuà 1

Mr Peter White (Bái Bǐdé) meets a Chinese person, Lín Jiànmù, at a conference.

Lín Nín shì nǎ guó rén?
Bái Wǒ shì Yīngguó-rén. Zhè shì wǒde míngpiàn.
Lín Xièxie. O, Bái xiānsheng, nín zhù zài Lúndūn?
Bái Duì. Nín shì Zhōngguó-rén ba?
Lín Shì, wǒ shì Guǎngdōng-rén.

Duìhuà 2

Bái xiānsheng comes to collect his plane ticket at a Chinese travel agency.

Assistant Zhè shì nínde fēijī piào.
Bái Xièxie. Wǒ zhù zài shénme fàndiàn?
Assistant Nín zhù zài Hépíng Fàndiàn.
Bái Hépíng shì shénme yìsi?
Assistant Hépíng shì '*peace*' de yìsi.
Bái Hěn hǎo. Wǒ xǐhuan hépíng.

Shùzì líng dào shí (Numbers from 0 to 10)

líng	zero	**liù**	six
yī	one	**qī**	seven
èr	two	**bā**	eight
sān	three	**jiǔ**	nine
sì	four	**shí**	ten
wǔ	five		

| yī | èr | sān | sì | wǔ | liù | qī | bā | jiǔ | shí |

- Practise saying 1 to 5: **yī èr sān sì wǔ**. Then say 6 to 10: **liù qī bā jiǔ shí**. Then put them altogether: **yī èr sān . . . jiǔ shí**.
- Now say: **yī sān wǔ qī jiǔ**. Then say: **èr sì liù bā shí**.
- Now try this: **yī èr sān, sān èr yī, yī èr sān sì wǔ liù qī**.

Duìhuà 3

Mr White and Mr Lin decide to further their business association.

Lín Nǐ zhù zài nǎr?
Bái Wǒ zhù zài Hépíng Fàndiàn.
Lín Jǐ hào fángjiān?
Bái Wǔ-líng-bā hào fángjiān. Nǐ zhù zài nǎr?
Lín Wǒ zhù zài Píng'ān Lù qī hào.
Bái Píng'ān Lù zài nǎr?
Lín Píng'ān Lù zài Xīchéng Qū.
Bái Hépíng Fàndiàn yě zài Xīchéng Qū shì bu shi?
Lín Bú zài. Zài Dōngchéng Qū.
Bái Nǐde diànhuà hàomǎ shì duōshao?
Lín Wǔ-wǔ-èr jiǔ-sān-èr-sì. Nǐde ne?
Bái Wǒde shì liù-qī-sān bā-bā-sān-líng.

Jiěshì

1 Where are you from?

To give your nationality you say the name of the country and then add -**rén** *person* after it:

Zhōngguó	*China, Chinese*
Zhōngguó-rén	*Chinese person*
Měiguó	*America (US)*
Měiguó-rén	*American*

Look at the two maps and the table between them to see exactly how this works.

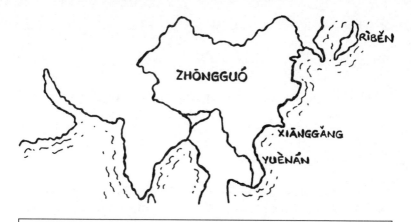

Country	Nationality	Country	Nationality
Zhōngguó	Zhōngguó-rén	(Xiānggǎng)	(Xiānggǎng-rén)
Yīngguó	Yīngguó-rén	Rìběn	Rìběn-rén
Fǎguó	Fǎguó-rén	Wēi'ěrshì	Wēi'ěrshì-rén
Déguó	Déguó-rén	Sūgélán	Sūgélán-rén
Yuènán	Yuènán-rén	Ài'ěrlán	Ài'ěrlán-rén

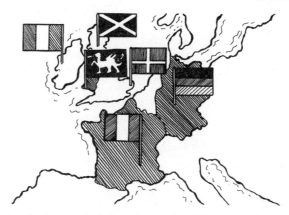

You do exactly the same thing when you wish to say which province or town you come from:

Wǒ shì Lúndūn-rén.	*I'm a Londoner.*
Nǐ shì Luómǎ-rén ma?	*Are you from Rome?*
Tā shì bu shì Běijīng-rén?	*Is he from Beijing?*
Wǒmen shì Fújiàn-rén.	*We're from Fujian province.*
Tāmen shì Guǎngdōng-rén.	*They're from Canton province.*

2 Ba

Ba is placed after a verb or phrase to make a suggestion or to ask for confirmation of a supposition:

Nǐ shì Zhōngguó-rén **ba**?   *You're Chinese, I take it?*
Hǎo **ba**?   *Is that all right then?*

3 Hépíng de yìsi

You have to reverse the word order in Chinese to translate a phrase such as: *the meaning of peace*. The two words **hépíng** (*peace*) and **yìsi** (*meaning*) are linked by the little word **de**.

hépíng **de** yìsi   *the meaning of* hépíng

Some people call this the possessive **de** to distinguish it from another **de** you will meet in Unit 8.

Look carefully at the following examples:

Fàndiàn **de** yìsi shì *hotel*.   *The meaning of fandian is hotel.*

Bái xiānsheng **de** diànhuà hàomǎ   *Mr White's telephone number*

Mǎ tàitai **de** háizi   *Mrs Ma's child*

4 Room 508

Room 508 is said as *508 Room* in Chinese (the reverse of English word order) with the addition of the word **hào** (*number*) after 508. More examples of this are given below:

10 (shí) **hào**   *No 10*
5 (wǔ) **hào** fángjiān   *Room 5*

Room numbers up to 100 are generally said as one number. You will meet numbers from 10 to 100 in the next unit.

Numbers over 100 are broken down into single digits:

374 (sān-qī-sì) hào fángjiān   *Room 374*
896 (bā-jiǔ-liù) hào fángjiān   *Room 896*

5 Shì bu shi?

Making a question by putting **shì bu shi** at the end of a sentence in Chinese conveys the idea of *Am I right?* or *Is it true?*:

Hépíng Fàndiàn yě zài
  Xīchéng Qū **shì bu shi?**

The Peace Hotel is also in the Western City District, isn't it?

Nǐ shì Yīngguó-rén **shì bu shi?**

You're English/British, aren't you?

6 Telephone numbers

Telephone numbers are often made up of seven or eight digits each of which is usually said separately:

551 8274   wǔ-wǔ-**yāo** bā-èr-qī-sì
228 9436   èr-èr-bā jiǔ-sì-sān-liù

Yāo is used instead of **yī** when telephone numbers or large numbers for rooms, buses, trains, and so on, are broken down into single digits. This avoids any confusion with **qī** (seven).

✳ Xuéxí jìqiǎo

1 Have imaginary conversations with yourself in Chinese using the material in the dialogues and the structures you have covered.

2 Think of somebody and say everything you can about them in Chinese: what their name is, what nationality they are, where they live, what their telephone number is, whether they have children, if you like them, and so on. Then do the same thing with somebody else, and so on, until you can go through the whole routine without hesitation.

3 **Don't worry about making mistakes!**
Anybody who has successfully learnt a foreign language knows that the way to make progress is to listen and speak as much as possible. Don't worry if you don't understand a lot of what is said to you in the beginning – just respond to what you do understand.

You will find the following two sentences very useful. Practise them over and over again:

Qǐng nǐ shuō màn yìdiǎn.   *Please speak more slowly.*
                           (*lit.* invite you say slow a little)
Qǐng nǐ **zài** shuō yí biàn.   *Please say it again.*
                           (*lit.* invite you again say one time)

This **zài** is not the **zài** which means *to be in/at*; it is the **zài** which means *again* as in **zàijiàn** (*goodbye*) (*lit.* again see). Words like **zài** (*again*) are called adverbs. They come before the verb in Chinese.

Cultural tip

Chinese people are very direct with their questions. It is not considered rude to ask how old you are, how much you earn, how much your house cost to buy or what the rent is, how much the clothes you are wearing cost, and so on.

Even questions as to why you are so fat or so thin or why you haven't married or why you got divorced (have you got a bad temperament?!) are all considered perfectly legitimate. Things are changing, however, as those people who have increasing contact with Westerners realise that the latter are uncomfortable with such questions.

Liànxí

1   Answer the following questions. If you don't know, say **Wǒ bù zhīdao** (*lit.* I not know.):

  (*a*) Nǐ shì Měiguó-rén ma?
  (*b*) Nǐ māma (*mum*) shì Fǎguó-rén ma?
  (*c*) Nǐde lǎoshī shì Zhōngguó-rén ba?
  (*d*) Nǐ bàba (*dad*) bú shi Déguó-rén ba?
  (*e*) Dèng Xiǎopíng shì Zhōngguó-rén ma?
  (*f*) Shāshìbǐyà (*Shakespeare*) shì bu shì Yīngguó-rén?

2   You are going to hear three people introducing themselves. Listen to the cassette twice and take notes while you are doing so. Then fill in as many details about each of the three speakers

as you can. Listen again paying particular attention to the bits you have not been able to catch. Listen for a fourth time to check what you have written.

	Speaker 1	Speaker 2	Speaker 3
Surname:			
Given name:			
Nationality:			
Telephone no:			
Address:			
– city:			
– street:			
– number:			

If you're still not sure of what you've heard, have a look at what the three people say in the *Key to the exercises* ➡️ P. 242.

NB: Chinese addresses are written in the reverse order to the way addresses are written in English. In English you give the number of your flat/house first, then the street or road and then the town or city. In Chinese it is city, street, number, as you can see from the chart above.

3 (*a*) Follow the same pattern as the passage you heard in Exercise 2 and say something about yourself. Fill in your details on the chart below as you did in Exercise 2. You can do this exercise even if you don't have the cassette.

(*b*) Think of one of your friends and fill in his/her details.

(*c*) If you are doing this with another person, ask him/her questions and fill in his/her details.

	Yourself	Friend A	Friend B
Surname:			
Given name:			
Nationality:			
Telephone no:			
Address:			
– city:			
– street:			
– number:			

4 You often see Chinese addresses written in English as in the following examples. How would these addresses be said (or written) in Chinese?

(a) Mingli Li (Lecturer)
2, Chaoyang Lu
BEIJING

(b) Mr. Hua Zhao,
Room 384, Dongfang Hotel,
9 Longhai Ln,
Suzhou

(c) Miss Jiabao Zhao,
5, Heping Ln,
Xicheng Qu
Nanjing

5 Match the words in the left-hand column with the ones on the right to make words you've already seen. (We've done one for you.)

(a)	fēijī	(i)	Fàndiàn
(b)	Lúndūn	(ii)	jiàn
(c)	Hépíng	(iii)	piào
(d)	èr-líng-wǔ	(iv)	Qū
(e)	míngtiān	(v)	fángjiān
(f)	Dōngchéng	(vi)	hàomǎ
(g)	diànhuà	(vii)	rén

☑ *Xiǎo cèyàn*

(a) You meet someone you don't know. How do you ask your friend who he is?
(b) How do you ask someone where he/she lives?
(c) Tell someone that you don't live in London.
(d) Ask someone to give you his/her telephone number.
(e) Ask what the meaning of **diànhuà** is.
(f) Say to the Chinese air hostess that this is your (plane) ticket.

You'll find the answers in **Dá'àn**. How have you done? If most of them are correct you will be ready to go on to Unit 4. Congratulations! Before you do so, spend some time revising Units 1, 2 and 3. Regular revision will help to consolidate what you have learnt and give you more confidence.

4

NǏ YǑU XIŌNGDÌ JIĚMÈI MA?
Do you have brothers and sisters?

In this unit you will learn how to:

- talk about yourself and your family
- ask other people about their family
- ask someone if they are married and/or have children
- say how old you are
- ask how old somebody is
- count up to 100

Kāishǐ yǐqián

You'll find that speaking about yourself and your family in Chinese is very easy. Remember how to say *I have* or *I don't have* (**wǒ yǒu, wǒ méi yǒu**)? Using this and the basic vocabulary you will learn in this unit you have all you need!

You will also be able to count up to 100 by the end of this unit. Having mastered 1 to 10 in Unit 3 you will be surprised how easy it is. 11 is 10 + 1, 12 is 10 + 2, 20 is 2 × 10, 30 is 3 × 10, all the way up to 99 which is 9 × 10 + 9. There is a special word **bǎi** for *hundred* so 100 is **yìbǎi**.

✔ Shìshi

You have just been introduced to a Chinese business associate who is on a week's visit to London.

(*a*) Ask her which hotel she is staying in and what the number of her room is.

(*b*) What do you say when you give her your card?

 ——— **Zhǔyào cíhuì** ———

bú kèqi	you are welcome (*lit.* not polite)
dà	big
. . . duō dà?	How old . . . ?
. . . duō dà niánjì?	How old . . . ? (*respectful*) (*lit.* how old year record)
gè	(*measure word*)
hé	and
jié hūn	marry
. . . jǐ suì?	How old . . . ? (*for children*)
. . . jié hūn le ma?	. . . married?
jīnnián	this year
liǎng	two (*of anything*)
. . . suì	. . . years old; age
xiàng	(*to look*) like
** bú xiàng**	not to look (*like*) it
xiǎo	small
yí ge . . . yí ge	one . . . , the other
zhēnde	really

 ——— **Family members** ———

bàba	dad, father
māma	mum, mother
érzi	son
nǚ'ér	daughter
gēge	elder brother
jiějie	elder sister
dìdi	younger brother
mèimei	younger sister
xiōngdì	brothers
jiěmèi	sisters
dà dìdi	the older one of the younger brothers
xiǎo dìdi	younger one of the younger brothers

📠 *Shùzì shíyī dào yìbǎi* (Numbers from 11 to 100)

shíyī	11	shíliù	16	sānshí	30	bāshí	80
shí'èr	12	shíqī	17	sìshí	40	jiǔshí	90
shísān	13	shíbā	18	wǔshí	50	yìbǎi	100
shísì	14	shíjiǔ	19	liùshí	60		
shíwǔ	15	èrshí	20	qīshí	70		

👂 —————————— Duìhuà ——————————

📠 *Duìhuà 1*

Dīng Fèng is carrying out a family planning survey and Liú Fúguì (from the Miáo national minority) has agreed to answer a few questions:

Dīng Nín jiào shénme míngzi?
Liú Wǒ jiào Liú Fúguì.
Dīng Liú xiānsheng jié hūn le ma?
Liú Jié hūn le.
Dīng Yǒu mei yǒu háizi?
Liú Yǒu liǎng ge, yí ge érzi, yí ge nǚ'ér.
Dīng Tāmen jǐ suì?
Liú Érzi liǎng suì, nǚ'ér wǔ suì.

✳ *Xuéxí jìqiǎo*

Practise saying 11 to 15: **shíyī, shí'èr, shísān, shísì, shíwǔ**. Then say 16 to 20 **shíliù, shíqī, shíbā, shíjiǔ, èrshí**. Then put them together: **shíyī, shí'èr, shísān, . . . èrshí**. Do the same for 21 to 25, 26 to 30, and so on.

Tones on yī

Yī (*one*) is a 1st tone when it is part of a number, such as **yī** (*one*), **shíyī** (*eleven*), **èrshíyī** (*twenty-one*). When it occurs before a measure word it is normally a 4th tone, for example **yì tiān** (*one day*), **yì běn shū** (*one book*), but it turns into a 2nd tone before another 4th tone, for example **yí suì** (*one year old*), such as **yí gè háizi** where **gè** is essentially a 4th tone though, as it sounds toneless, no tonemark is written on it.

Suì (*year of age*), tiān (*day*) and nián (*year*), all act as measure words – see and nouns combined (refer to ➡️🄿 47 for an explanation of what a measure word is). Note that yìbǎi is *one hundred*.

 Duìhuà 2

Dīng Fèng asks Liú Fúguì some more questions. By reading/listening to the dialogue can you find out whether Liú Fúguì has any brothers or sisters? How old are they?

Dīng Nín yǒu xiōngdì jiěmèi ma?
Liú Yǒu liǎng ge dìdi、 yí ge mèimei. Méi yǒu gēge hé jiějie.
Dīng Nín dìdi、 mèimei duō dà?
Liú Dà dìdi èrshíliù, xiǎo dìdi èrshísì.
Dīng Mèimei ne?
Liú Mèimei èrshíbā.
Dīng Hěn hǎo, xièxie nín.
Liú Bú kèqi.
Dīng Zàijiàn.
Liú Zàijiàn.

Duìhuà 3

Wú and Lù are looking at a photo of Lù's family.

Wú Nǐ bàba、 māma duō dà niánjì?
Lù Bàba wǔshísān, māma sìshíjiǔ.

Wú Bú xiàng, bú xiàng. Zhè shì nǐ mèimei ba. Tā zhēn piàoliang.
Lù Tā jīnnián èrshí'èr.
Wú Zhēnde? Tā jié hūn le ma?
Lù Méi yǒu. Kěshì yǒu nán péngyou le.
Wú O.

 ———————————— **Jiěshì** ————————————

1 Sentences ending in . . . le

If you put the little word **le** at the end of a sentence it shows that something has happened or has already taken place:

Wǒ jié hūn **le**.   *I'm married*
Wǒ qǐng tā **le**.   *I invited him.*
Wǒ wèn tā **le**.   *I asked her.*

If you want to make a question simply add **ma** or **méi you** to the end of a sentence. **Yǒu** is unstressed.

Nǐ jié hūn le **ma**?   *Are you married?*
Nǐ jié hūn le **méi you**?   *Are you married?*

If you want to say something has not happened you use **méi yǒu** (*not have*) plus the verb:

Wǒ **méi yǒu** jié hūn.   *I'm not married.*
Wǒ **méi** qǐng tā.   *I didn't invited him.*
Wǒ **méi** wèn tā.   *I haven't asked her.*

The **yǒu** can be omitted.

2 One or two

In Chinese something called a measure word (MW) or classifier has to be used between a number and the noun following it.

In English you can say:
  two children
  three daughters
  four books

But in Chinese you have to put the measure word/classifier in between the number and the item:

two measure word/classifier children
three measure word/classifier daughters
four measure word/classifier books

liǎng **ge** háizi	*two children*
sān **ge** nǚ'ér	*three daughters*
sì **běn** shū	*four books*

Different measure words are used with different categories of nouns. For example, **běn** is used for books and magazines whereas **zhāng** is used for rectangular or square, flat objects such as tables, beds, maps and so on, but it is not a true measure as to length or anything else:

wǔ **běn** zázhì	*five magazines*
liù **zhāng** zhuōzi	*six tables*
qī **zhāng** chuáng	*seven beds*

Gè is by far the most common measure word. It is used with a whole range of nouns which do not have their own specific measure word. When in doubt use **gè**! The noun accompanying the number and measure word is often omitted when it is clear from the context what this is:

| Nǐ yǒu mei yǒu háizi? | *Have you any children?* |
| Yǒu liǎng **ge** (háizi), yí **ge** érzi, yí **ge** nǚ'ér. | *Two, a son and a daughter.* |

3 Two for tea!

Liǎng meaning *two of a kind* is used with measure words instead of **èr** (*two*), so *two children* is **liǎng ge háizi** and not **èr ge háizi**.

4 How old are you?

When asking small children how old they are you use **jǐ** (*how many*) when you are expecting a small number (generally less than 10) as an answer plus the word for years (of age) **suì**:

| Háizi **jǐ suì**? | *How old is/are the children?* |
| Tā wǔ **suì**. | *He/she's five years old.* |

Note that no verb is necessary in such sentences. When asking teenagers or young adults how old they are you use **duō** (*how*) together with **dà** (*old/big*):

Nǐ **duō dà**?　　*How old are you* (of teenager/young adult)?
Wǒ èrshí suì.　　*I'm twenty.*

Again, note that no verb is necessary.

When asking older(!) adults how old they are, the phrase **duō dà niánjì** (*lit.* how big year record) is used:

Nǐ bàba, māma **duōdà niánjì**?　　*How old are your Mum and Dad?*
Bàba wǔshísān, māma sìshíjiǔ.　　*Dad is 53, Mum is 49.*

Bàba (*dad*) comes before **māma** (*mum*) in Chinese word order, as does **fùqin** (*father*) before **mǔqin** (*mother*)!

5 Punctuation – when is a comma not a comma?

When it's a pause-mark! In Chinese, if two or more items are listed together, a pause-mark 、 is used between the items and not a comma. A comma is reserved for longer pauses:

Wǒ yǒu liǎng ge dìdi、
　yí ge mèimei.

I have two younger brothers and a younger sister.

Nǐ bàba, māma duō dà niánjì?

How old are your Mum and Dad?

6 Brothers and sisters

The collective term for *sisters* (without saying whether they are older or younger) is **jiěmèi**, combining half of **jiějie** with half of **mèimei**. Similarly there is a collective term **xiōngdì** for *brothers*, although in this case a more literary term for elder brother is used:

Wǒ méi yǒu xiōngdì jiěmèi.　　*I don't have any brothers or sisters.*

7 Polite Talk

In Unit 1, when Mrs Green thanked Xiǎo Wáng he responded by saying:

Bú yòng xiè (*lit.* not need/use thank) *Don't mention it, not at all.*

He could also have said **Bú xiè**.

An equally appropriate response to thanks would be:

Bú kèqi. (*lit.* not guest air) *It's nothing, not at all.*

Chinese people tend to say thank you rather less than in the West so they feel obliged to respond when somebody says thank you to them.

✷ Xuéxí jìqiǎo

Create opportunities to speak Chinese as much as you can.

1 Try to find other learners of Chinese to practise with. Find out about classes in your local area or where you work. (Your public library will usually be able to help you.)

2 If you have the cassette listen to it as much as you can – in the car, on public transport.

3 Advertise a language exchange in your local newspaper – offer to give English conversation lessons in return for Chinese ones. Make sure that you say you are learning Modern Standard Chinese (or Mandarin as it is called by many overseas Chinese) as many Chinese people in the UK are Cantonese speakers who have come from Hong Kong.

———— Cultural tip ————

The Chinese zodiac

The Chinese zodiac works in a 12-year cycle rather than in months as the Western one does. You probably know whether you are a

Capricorn or a Leo or whatever but do you know which **Animal Year** you belong to? The order is as follows:

Rat	1996	(1948, 1960, 1972, 1984)
Ox	1997	(1949, 1961, 1973, 1985)
Tiger	1998	(1950, 1962, 1974, 1986)
Rabbit/Hare	1999	(1951, 1963, 1975, 1987)
Dragon	2000	(1952, 1964, 1976, 1988)
Snake	2001	(1953, 1965, 1977, 1989)
Horse	2002	(1954, 1966, 1978, 1990)
Sheep/Ram	2003	(1955, 1967, 1979, 1991)
Monkey	2004	(1956, 1968, 1980, 1992)
Cockerel	2005	(1957, 1969, 1981, 1993)
Dog	2006	(1958, 1970, 1982, 1994)
Pig	2007	(1959, 1971, 1983, 1995)

Can you work out which animal you are?! For instance if you were born in 1976 you are a dragon, if you were born in 1971 you are a pig. Each Animal Year is said to possess certain characteristics. It might be fun to get hold of a book on Chinese astrology and read up on your particular animal. Such books are now relatively easy to obtain at any reputable bookshop.

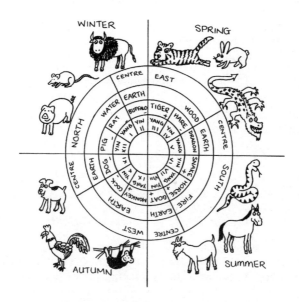

Liànxí

1 Choose the right number:

(a) Which is the smallest number?
- wǔshíbā
- èrshíjiǔ
- sìshíliù

(b) Which is the odd one out?
- qīshíyī
- bāshíbā
- jiǔshíjiǔ

(c) Which number is the largest?
- sānshí'èr
- èrshísān
- sānshíyī

2 Now try the following calculations. Find the number to replace the question marks and say it aloud in Chinese.

(a) $7 \times 3 = ?$ (c) $10 + ? = 76$
(b) $? - 40 = 30$ (d) $98 \div 2 = ?$

You can also say equations in Chinese:

+ **jiā** (*plus*)
− **jiǎn** (*minus*)
× **chéng** (*times*)
÷ **chú** (*divide*)

What would you say to fill these blanks?

(e) Shíwǔ chéng èr shì ___.
(f) ___ jiǎn wǔshí shì shí.
(g) Èrshí jiā ___ shì sānshíwǔ.
(h) Jiǔshíjiǔ chú sān shì ___.

3 Listen to the cassette (or read the passage below if you haven't the cassette) and say or write down the names and ages of Dīng's children. If you're still not sure of what you've heard, check it out in the *Key to the exercises* ➡️ 🄿 242.

Dīng Fèng jié hūn le. Tā yǒu liǎng ge háizi, yí ge érzi, yí ge nǚ'ér. Érzi jiào Dīng Níng, jīnnián shí'èr suì. Nǚ'ér jiào Dīng Yīng, jīnnián shísì suì.

4 You are an only child and you are neither married nor have any children. Your father is a doctor (**yīsheng**), and your mother a teacher. How would you answer the following questions in Chinese?

(*a*) Nǐ yǒu gēge ma?
(*b*) Nǐ jié hūn le ma?
(*c*) Nǐ bàba shì lǎoshī ma?
(*d*) Nǐ yǒu jǐ ge háizi?
(*e*) Nǐ dìdi jiào shénme?

5 Match the questions in the left-hand column with the answers on the right.

(*a*) Nǐ jié hūn le ma?	(*i*) Wáng Yìfū.
(*b*) Tā jǐ suì?	(*ii*) Tā méi yǒu nǚ'ér.
(*c*) Wáng lǎoshī jiào shénme míngzi?	(*iii*) Tā wǔ suì.
(*d*) Nǐmen yǒu háizi ma?	(*iv*) Wǒ jié hūn le.
(*e*) Lǐ tàitai yǒu nǚ'ér ma?	(*v*) Wǒmen méi háizi.

6 The following is what Hēnglì (Henry) said about himself, his brother and his sister. Imagine you are Hēnglì's sister and talk about yourself and your brothers.

Wǒ jiào Hēnglì, jīnnián èrshí suì. Wǒ méi yǒu gēge, méi yǒu jiějie. Wǒ yǒu yí ge dìdi, yí ge mèimei. Wǒ dìdi jiào Bǐdé (*Peter*). Tā shíwǔ suì. Wǒ mèimei jiào Mǎlì (*Mary*). Tā jīnnián shíqī suì. Wǒmen dōu shì xuésheng (*student*).

☑ Xiǎo cèyàn

You see a little Chinese girl and say the following to her:

(*a*) Hello!
(*b*) What's your name?
(*c*) How old are you?
(*d*) Have you got any brothers and sisters?
(*e*) Thank you.
(*f*) Goodbye!

5

JǏ DIǍN LE?
What time is it now?

In this unit you will learn:

- the days of the week
- the months of the year
- how to tell the time
- how to ask what time it is
- some useful expressions of time
- how to give the date
- how to make arrangements

Kāishǐ yǐqián

In China, or any Chinese-speaking environment, you'd need to be able to find out when shops and banks are open. You also need to be able to recognise the Chinese characters for opening times **Yíngyè shíjiān** 营业时间 and the numbers one to 12 (plus the characters for *o'clock*) and the days of the week. You will be able to do all this by the end of the unit.

☑ *Shìshi*

1 You are at a reception where you meet a Chinese acquaintance of a friend of yours. He does not speak any English so you take the opportunity to try out your Chinese. You know he is called Chén. Think of at least 10 questions you can ask him in Chinese. Go back to Units 1 to 4 if you need to review vocabulary.

2 Revise the following numbers and say them aloud. 64 – 29 – 57
– 38 – 12 – 95 – 40 – 2 – 73 – 10. Check your answers with the
numbers ➡️🅿️ 45.

Zhǔyào cíhuì

bàn	half
bāng	to help
chà	lacking, short of
Chūnjié	the Spring Festival
dào	to
diǎn	o'clock
dōu	all, both
fēn(zhōng)	minute
guān (mén)	to close (*door*)
hái	still
hái yǒu	still have, there are still
huì	meeting
huǒchē	train
jǐ?	how many? (*usually less than 10*)
-jǐ diǎn	what time?
-(Xiànzài) jǐ diǎn le?	What time is it now?
Jiànqiáo	Cambridge
jiù shì	to be precisely; to be nothing else but
kāi huì	to have a meeting
kāi (mén)	open (*door*)
kāishǐ	to start
kàn(yi)kàn	to have a look
míngnián	next year
Niújīn	Oxford
qù	to go
shàng	on
shàngwǔ	morning
shíjiān	time
wǎnshang	evening
xiànzài	now
xiàwǔ	afternoon
xīngqī	week
xīngqī jǐ?	what day is it?
yǐjīng	already
yíkè	a quarter (*time*)
yǐwéi	to think, to assume
yuè	month
zǎoshang	morning

[handwritten annotations: shēngrì 生日 Birthday; kě xī – it's a pity]

zhàntái	platform
zhīdao	to know
zhōumò	weekend
zhù (nǐ)	wish (*you*)
Zhù nǐ yílù píng'ān	Have a safe journey!
Jǐ yuè jǐ hào?	What's the date? (*lit.* how many months, how many numbers?)

1997

一月 yīyuè Jan	二月 èryuè Feb	三月 sānyuè Mar	四月 sìyuè Apr
五月 wǔyuè May	六月 liùyuè June	七月 qīyuè July	八月 bāyuè Aug
九月 jiǔyuè Sept	十月 shíyuè Oct	十一月 shíyīyuè Nov	十二月 shí'èryuè Dec

Liǎng diǎn bàn | **Sān diǎn yí kè** | **Chà wǔ fēn sì diǎn** | **Chà yí kè liù diǎn Wǔ diǎn sān kè**

❋ *Xuéxí jìqiǎo*

1 Months of the year are very easy to say in Chinese. You already know the numbers 1 to 12. All you then need is the word for **yuè** 月 (*moon*). January is **yī-yuè**, February is **èr-yuè** and so on. Be careful not to confuse **yí ge yuè** *one month* with **yīyuè** *January*, **liǎng ge yuè** *two months* with **èryuè** *February*.

yīyuè	January	**qīyuè**	July
èryuè	February	**bāyuè**	August
sānyuè	March	**jiǔyuè**	September
sìyuè	April	**shíyuè**	October
wǔyuè	May	**shíyīyuè**	November
liùyuè	June	**shí'èryuè**	December

2 Days of the week are also easy to say in Chinese. They all start with **xīngqī** 星期 (*week*) (*lit.* star period) and then you use the numbers 1 to 6 for Monday to Saturday. Sunday is special! You add the word **rì** 日 (*sun*) or **tiān** 天 (*day*) to **xīngqī** to make it into Sunday.

xīngqīyī	Monday	**xīngqīwǔ**	Friday
xīngqī'èr	Tuesday	**xīngqīliù**	Saturday
xīngqīsān	Wednesday	**xīngqītiān**	} Sunday
xīngqīsì	Thursday	**xīngqīrì**	

3 Repeat the days of the week and the months of the year several times out loud until you have mastered them or listen to them on the cassette and say them after the recording.

Duìhuà

Duìhuà 1

A customer is ringing a shop to find out the opening hours.

营业时间

Yíngyè Shíjiān
Opening hours

Customer Qǐng wèn, nǐmen jǐ diǎn kāi mén?
Assistant Shàngwǔ bā diǎn dào xiàwǔ wǔ diǎn bàn.
Customer Zhōngwǔ guān mén ma?
Assistant Bù guān.
Customer Zhōumò kāi bu kai?
Assistant Xīngqīliù kāi, xīngqītiān bù kāi.

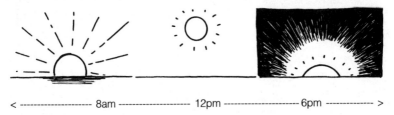

早上　上午　中午　下午　晚上

< -------------------- 8am -------------------- 12pm -------------------- 6pm ------------- >

zǎoshang　　**shàngwǔ**　　**zhōngwǔ**　　**xiàwǔ**　　**wǎnshang**

📼 *Duìhuà 2*

Two colleagues, Xiǎo Xú and Lǎo Wàn, are in the office when Xiǎo Xú suddenly remembers something.

Xiǎo Xú Xiànzài jǐ diǎn le?
Lǎo Wàn Liǎng diǎn yí kè le. 2:15
Xiǎo Xú O, huì yǐjīng kāishǐ le.
Lǎo Wàn Shénme huì? Nǐ bú shì míngtiān kāi huì ma?
Xiǎo Xú Jīntiān xīngqī jǐ?
Lǎo Wàn Xīngqīsān.
Xiǎo Xú O, wǒ hái yǐwéi shì xīngqīsì ne.

ASSUMED, THOUGHT

────── Cultural tip ──────

In Chinese-speaking environments, other than in China, you may well hear the word **lǐbài** 礼拜 used instead of **xīngqī**. So Monday would be **lǐbàiyī** instead of **xīngqīyī**, Tuesday would be **lǐbài'èr** and so on. The word **lǐbài** has certain Christian connotations as to go to church is **zuò** (*do*) **lǐbài**.

Duìhuà 3

> **Departure**
> OXFORD
> Platform 6
>
> 15.15
> 16.20

At a train station, Jane sees a Chinese person looking at the departure and arrivals board, obviously very perplexed. She decides to help him if she can.

Jane Nǐ qù nǎr? *Where going?*
Chinese Wǒ qù Niújīn.
Jane Jǐ diǎn de huǒchē? *what of Time Train?*
Chinese Wǒ bù zhīdao. Piào shang méi yǒu shíjiān. *No Time on Tix*
Jane Wǒ bāng nǐ kànkan. (*looks at the notice board*) *Help look*
Ah, sān diǎn yī kè, zài dì liù zhàntái. *It 6 Platform*
Chinese Xiànzài sān diǎn chà wǔ fēn, hái yǒu èrshí fēnzhōng. *20 Minutes*
Jane Zhù nǐ yílù píng'ān. *zhong feng / wind / behind you*
Chinese Xièxie nǐ. Zàijiàn.

Duìhuà 4

Ann wants to find out whether her birthday happens to fall on Chinese New Year. Read the dialogue and see if you can find the answer.

Ann Míngnián Chūnjié shì jǐ yuè jǐ hào?
Friend Èryuè shí'èr hào.
Ann Zhēn kěxī. Wǒde shēngrì shì èryuè shíyī hào.
Friend Méi guānxi. Yīngguó shíyī hào de wǎnshang jiù shì Zhōngguó shí'èr hào de zǎoshang.

 ——————— **Jiěshì** ———————

1 Telling the time

Xiànzài jǐ diǎn (zhōng) le?　　*What time is it/now?* (*lit.* now how many points clock)

To reply to this question you use the 12-hour clock in Chinese. **Zhōng** is normally left out except when asking the time or (as in English) on the hour where it is optional. The use of **xiànzài** is also optional.

(*a*) (Xiànzài) shíyī diǎn (zhōng) le. **11.00**
(*b*) (Xiànzài) shíyī diǎn (líng) wǔ fēn le. **Líng** (*zero*) is optional. **11.05**
(*c*) Shíyī diǎn shí fēn. **11.10**
(*d*) Shíyī diǎn shíwǔ fēn *or* shíyī diǎn yí kè (*one quarter*). **11.15**
(*e*) Shíyī diǎn èrshí fēn. **11.20**
(*f*) Shíyī diǎn èrshíwǔ fēn. **11.25**
(*g*) Shíyī diǎn sānshí *or* shíyī diǎn bàn (*half*). **11.30**

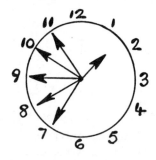

(*h*) Yì diǎn sānshíwǔ *or* chà (*lack*) èrshíwǔ (fēn) liǎng diǎn. **1.35**
(*i*) Yì diǎn sìshí *or* chà èrshí (fēn) liǎng diǎn. **1.40**
(*j*) Yì diǎn sìshíwǔ fēn *or* yì diǎn sān kè (*three quarters*) *or* chà yí kè liǎng diǎn *or* liǎng diǎn chà yí kè. **1.45**
(*k*) Yì diǎn wǔshí fēn *or* chà shí fēn liǎng diǎn. **1.50**
(*l*) Yì diǎn wǔshíwǔ fēn *or* chà wǔ fēn liǎng diǎn. **1.55**

Formal announcements of time are given using the 24-hour clock.

2 Dates

Months of the year, days of the week and parts of the day are easy ➡️ 🄿 57–8 but you still need to learn dates. In Chinese the order for a date is the reverse of that used in English:

It is year, month, day, time of day (morning, afternoon, etc.) hour.

In Chinese you move from the general to the particular.

The year is read as single numbers followed by the word **nián** 年 (*year*):

yī-jiǔ-yī-sì nián	*1914*
yī-jiǔ-sì-wǔ nián	*1945*

You ask what the date is by saying: **Jǐ yuè jǐ hào?** (*lit.* how many months how many numbers).

Jīntiān jǐ yuè jǐ hào?	*What's the date today?*
Jīntiān bāyuè shí hào.	*Today's August 10th.*
Xīngqīsān jǐ hào?	*What's the date on Wednesday?*
(Xīngqīsān) èrshíbā hào.	*It's 28th (on Wednesday).*

You can now work out how to say 12 noon on Tuesday, July 23rd 1989:

Yī-jiǔ-bā-jiǔ nián qīyuè èrshísān hào xīngqī'èr zhōngwǔ shí'èr diǎn.

Note that when you're telling the time and giving dates no verb is necessary. You have already met this in Unit 3 when dealing with ages.

3 Another type of le

You will have noticed the little word **le** appearing after **Xiànzài jǐ diǎn?** and **Liǎng diǎn yí kè** in **Duìhuà** 2. It is used to indicate that a new state of affairs or situation has appeared. It is used at the end of such sentences as:

Nǐmen yǐjīng hěn dà **le**.	*You're already pretty grown up (whereas previously you weren't).*

Nǐ xiànzài hěn piàoliang **le**. *You're very good looking now (whereas previously you weren't!).*

The Chinese stretch this idea of a change of state to its limits by often using it with questions and answers about age and time:

Háizi jǐ suì **le**? *How old is the child? (lit.* child how many years become)

Xiànzài jǐ diǎn **le**? *What time is it? (lit.* now how many o'clock become)

4 Jǐ diǎn de huǒchē?

This is the same **de** you looked at in Unit 3, ➡️🔲 38. The main idea – what you are talking about – comes after the **de**, and what describes this main idea or tells you more about it, comes before the **de**:

Jǐ diǎn **de** huǒchē? *The train at what time?*
Xīngqītiān kāi **de** shāngdiàn *Shops which open on Sundays*
Zài Lúndūn kāi **de** huì *The meeting held in London*

5 Ticket on – on the ticket

Piào shang (*lit.* ticket on) *on the ticket*. Again the reverse of the English word order. Do the Chinese do everything back to front, you may be tempted to ask? No wonder they used to write from top to bottom and from right to left (and still do in Taiwan and Hong Kong)! Thus in Chinese you say:

shāngdiàn **lǐ** *inside the shop*
lù **shàng** *on the road*
huǒchē **xià** *underneath the train*

Words such as **lǐ**, **shàng** and **xià** are normally unstressed when used in this way.

6 Kànkan!

Repeating the verb has the effect of softening the suggestion, question or statement. Thus the repeated verb is often unstressed. It conveys the idea of *having a little go* at doing the action of the verb in both the sense of a trial and in not making a big fuss about doing something. Verbs of one syllable often have **yi** inserted in the middle when they are repeated.

Kànyikàn.   *Have a little look.*
Shuōyishuō.   *Try saying.*

Verbs of two syllables cannot have **yi** inserted in this way; so you cannot say **rènshi**ᵧ**rènshi** or **kāishǐ**ᵧ**kāishǐ**.

7   First or second

To make the numbers one, two, and so on into *the first, the second,* and so on, you only have to put the word **dì** in front of the number. **Èr** does not change into **liǎng** in such cases as there are not two seconds! An expression which used to be very common in China when any form of competition was involved is:

Yǒuyì **dì** yī, bǐsài dì èr.   *Friendship first, competition second.*

✳ Xuéxí jìqiǎo

Have fun while you're learning!

1   What have you learnt about the Chinese language so far? How is it different from any other language you've learnt? Take some time to reflect on this and jot down your thoughts. See if your ideas change as you learn more.

2   Tongue-twisters are fun in any language. Try the following. Repeat them until you can say them off by heart:

Sì shì sì.   *4 is 4.*
Shí shì shí.   *10 is 10.*
Sì bú shì shí.   *4 is not 10.*
Shí yě bú shì sì.   *10 is not 4 either.*

Shísì bú shì sìshí.   *14 is not 40.*
Sìshí yě bú shì shíshì. *40 is not 14 either.*

The last one is the hardest of all:

Sìshísì shí shīzi   *44 stone lions*

Liànxí

1 Can you say the dates of the following festivals (**jié**) in Chinese?

(*a*) New Year's Day (**Xīnnián**)
(*b*) Christmas Day (**Shèngdàn jié**)
(*c*) International Women's Day (**Guójì Fùnǔ jié**)
(*d*) National Day of China (**Zhōngguó de Guóqìng jié**)
(*e*) National Day of your country (**X X Guóqìng jié**)

2 Give the birthdays of five people using the following structures:

Sòng lǎoshī de shēngrì shì sìyuè shísì hào.
Sìyuè shísì hào shì Sòng lǎoshī de shēngrì.

You can use these structures to talk about dates when you have learned more words such as those in Exercise 1.

3 On the cassette, you will hear some dates and times. Repeat them and write them down. If you haven't got the cassette, read the dates and times below and write them down in English.

(*a*) jiǔyuè jiǔ hào
(*b*) xīngqītiān shàngwǔ
(*c*) shíyīyuè èrshíbā hào xīngqīsì
(*d*) xīngqīliù shàngwǔ shí diǎn sìshíwǔ
(*e*) qīyuè liù hào xīngqīwǔ xiàwǔ sān diǎn bàn
(*f*) shí'èryuè sānshíyī hào xīngqīyī shàngwǔ shíyī diǎn

4 Based on the assumption that the time is now 5.05 in the afternoon (**wǔ diǎn líng wǔ fēn**), please answer the following questions in Chinese:

(*a*) What will the time be in 10 minutes?
(*b*) What time was it 10 minutes ago?
(*c*) How long is it before it is 5.45?
(*d*) What time is it in 12 hours' time?
(*e*) The train is leaving in two minutes. What time is the train scheduled to leave?

5 Please answer the following questions in Chinese based on the day of the week it is when you are doing this exercise.

(*a*) What day is it tomorrow?
(*b*) And yesterday?

(c) Five days from today?

(d) How many days is it before next Tuesday?

6   We don't know the answers to the following questions, but you do:

(a) Which months are Spring in the part of the world you are living in?

(b) When is Summer (i.e. what months)? Autumn? Winter?

(c) How many months is it before your next birthday?

(d) How many months is it before the New Year? (**Hái yǒu x ge yuè.**)

☑ *Xiǎo cèyàn*

Answer the following questions in Chinese according to the information on the board.

(a) What's the date today?

(b) What day is it today?

(c) What's the time now?

(d) When does the train from Oxford arrive? At which platform?

Thursday March 30th 16.27	
Departure	**Arrival**
CAMBRIDGE	OXFORD
Platform 1	Platform 3
16.50	16.45

(e) When does the train to Cambridge leave? At which platform?

6

NǏ JĪNTIĀN XIĂNG ZUÒ SHÉNME?

What do you want to do today?

In this unit you will learn:

- how to say what you want to do
- how to understand and ask for advice
- how to express similarities
- how to compare and contrast

Kāishǐ yǐqián

Word order is very important in Chinese so there's plenty of help with some the basic rules in this unit. You'll also learn different ways of making comparisons.

✅ *Shìshi*

1 It is often very difficult to get train tickets in China. You are in Běijīng and want to go to Tiānjīn in a couple of days' time. A Chinese friend offers to get your ticket for you as he knows you are very busy. Tell him you want a train ticket for the 9.30 a.m. train on Thursday.

2 Say the following dates in Chinese:

    (*a*) 6 January 1997
    (*b*) 21 March 2000 (líng = *zero*)
    (*c*) 15 August 1943

3 When is your birthday?

4 When were your parents born?

Zhǔyào cíhuì

Běihǎi Gōngyuán	Beihai Park
bǐ	compared to
bù yídìng	not necessarily
chē	vehicle, (*bus*, *bike*, *car*)
dǎ tàijíquán	to do Tai Chi
diànyǐng	film, movie
dìng (piào)	to book (a ticket)
dōngxi	thing, object
fúwùyuán	assistant, housestaff (*lit.* service person)
gěi	for; to give
gēn	and
gōngjīn	kilogram
háishi	or (*used in question forms*)
huàn qián	to change money
jīngjù	Peking opera
kàn	to watch, look at
mǎi	to buy
nàme	in that case, then
nán	difficult
qián	money
róngyì	easy
ránhòu	afterwards
shénme shíhou?	when?
tīng yīnyuèhuì	to attend a concert
wèntí	question, problem
méi wèntí	no problem
Xīfāng	the West, Western
xiān	first
xiǎng	would like to; to think
xiūxi	to rest, rest
yào	to want, to need; will
yínháng	bank
yīnyuè	music
yīnyuèhuì	concert
yíyàng	same
yǒu yìsi	interesting (*lit.* have meaning)
zài	(*indicating continuing action*)
zájì	acrobatics
Zǎoshang hǎo!	Good morning!
Zhōngguó Yínháng	Bank of China
zuò	to do
zuò qìgōng	to do qigong
-zuò chē	to take the bus (*lit.* sit vehicle)

A bǐ B nán/róngyì	A is more difficult / easier than B.
A gēn B (bù) yíyàng	A is the same as (different from) B.
Nǐ xiǎng zuò shénme?	What do you want to do?
Tā zài zuò shénme?	What's he/she doing?
Tài hǎo le!	Excellent!

❊ Xuéxí jìqiǎo

1   Go back to the Pronunciation Guide and read the notes there. The best way of learning this selection of sounds is in pairs, as follows:

b and **p**	*zh* and *ch*
d and **t**	*j* and *q*
z and **c**	*g* and *k*

2   Take a sheet of A4 paper and hold it vertically in front of you. Say **b** ... If you are saying it correctly the sheet will not move. Then say **p** and the top of the sheet should be blown away from you. The same should happen with **d** and **t**, i.e. the sheet should not move when you say **d** but it should move with **t**! Repeat this with each remaining pair. The sheet should not move with **z**, **zh**, **j** and **g** but it should move with **c**, **ch**, **q** and **k**.

👂 ──────── Duìhuà ────────

▣ Duìhuà 1

Frank is attending a conference in China. Today he is free. His Chinese host, Xiǎo Wú, is asking him about his plans. Listen to or read the dialogue and note down his plans:

Frank's plans

shàngwǔ:
xiàwǔ:
wǎnshang:

Xiǎo Wú Jīntiān xiūxi. Nǐ xiǎng zuò shénme?
Frank Wǒ xiǎng qù mǎi dōngxi. Kěshì wǒ yào xiān huàn qián.
Xiǎo Wú Hǎo. Wǒmen xiān zuò chē qù Zhōngguó Yínháng
huàn qián, ránhòu qù shāngdiàn mǎi dōngxi.
Frank Hǎo. Xiàwǔ wǒ xiǎng qù Běihǎi Gōngyuán.
Xiǎo Wú Méi wèntí. Wǎnshang ne? ᴧᴄᴿᴏ⳽ᴀ⳥ S
Frank Wǎnshang wǒmen qù kàn zájì hǎo bu hǎo?
Xiǎo Wú Tài hǎo le. Wǒ qǐng fúwùyuán gěi wǒmen dìng piào.

📼 Duìhuà 2

Frank has changed his money, done the shopping and been to
Beihai Park. Unfortunately there are no tickets for the acrobatics this evening. So Frank and Xiǎo Wú are planning what to do
instead.

Xiǎo Wú Jīntiān wǎnshang nǐ
xiǎng kàn diànyǐng
háishi kàn
jīngjù?
Frank Wǒ bù xǐhuan jīngjù.
Xiǎo Wú Nàme wǒmen kàn
diànyǐng ba.
Diànyǐng bǐ jīngjù
yǒu yìsi.
Frank Yǒu mei yǒu yīnyuèhuì?
Xiǎo Wú Nǐ xiǎng tīng Zhōngguó yīnyuè háishi tīng Xīfāng
yīnyuè?
Frank Zài Zhōngguó dāngrán tīng Zhōngguó yīnyuè.

上午 8:00
上下 10:15
下午 1:30
下午 4:00
晚 7:30 Sold out! **Kè mǎn**
客满

📼 Duìhuà 3

A whole range of activities goes on in Chinese parks in the early
morning. Tai Chi is especially popular. Frank decides to go and see
for himself.

Frank Zǎoshang hǎo!
Passer-by Zǎoshang hǎo!
Frank (*pointing to someone doing Tai Chi*) Tā zài zuò
shénme?
Passer-by Tā zài dǎ tàijíquán.

北海公园   Běihǎi Gōngyuán

Frank   Nèi ge rén yě zài dǎ tàijíquán ma?
Passer-by Bù. Tā zài zuò qìgōng.
Frank   Qìgōng gēn tàijíquán yíyàng ma?
Passer-by Bù yíyàng.
Frank   Qìgōng bǐ tàijíquán nán ma?
Passer-by Bù yídìng. Wǒ shuō qìgōng bǐ tàijíquán róngyì.

Jiěshì

1 Word order again!

In some ways the Chinese language is much more logical than English in its word order. In English you can say:

> *First* I want to change some money. *or*
> I want to change some money *first*.

In Chinese the position of **xiān** (*first*) is not changeable. It comes after **Wǒ yào** (*I want*) but before **huàn diǎnr qián** (*change some money*):

> Wǒ yào **xiān** huàn diǎnr qián.

This is because **xiān** is connected with what you want to do, not with what you want; and adverbs like **xiān** precede the verb to which they refer.

2 Time before manner before place (T.M.P.)

In Chinese you say:

I *tomorrow at 9 a.m.* (time) *by plane* (manner) go *to China* (place).

You can't say:

I'm going to China by plane at 9 a.m. tomorrow.
or I'm going by plane to China at 9 a.m. tomorrow.

In Chinese the word order is logical: first you establish *when* you're going to do it, then *how* you're going to do it, and then *where* you're going to do it. So the rule to remember is **Time (T)** comes before **Manner (M)** and **Manner (M)** comes before **Place (P)**; T.M.P. for short:

Wǒmen xiān **(T)** zuò chē **(M)** qù Zhōngguó Yínháng **(P)** huàn qián.	*We'll go to the Bank of China in the car to change money first (lit. we first sit car go China Bank change money).*
Wǒmen shí'èr diǎn zhōng **(T)** zài Hépíng Fàndiàn **(P)** chī wǔfàn.	*We'll have lunch at the Peace Hotel at 12.*

As you can see from the second example sometimes only two out of the three elements (T.M.P.) are present but the rule still applies.

3 Either or?

Do you want to go to a film *or* to the opera?

To express the *or* in the sentence above you use **háishi** in Chinese. Of course, you don't have to reverse the subject/verb order to make a question as in English.

All you do is put **háishi** between two statements thereby making them alternatives from which the listener must choose *one*:

Nǐ xiǎng kàn diànyǐng **háishi** kàn jīngjù?	*Would you like to go to a film or to the Peking opera? (lit. you fancy see film or see Peking opera).*
Nǐ xiǎng tīng Zhōngguó yīnyuè **háishi** (tīng) Xīfāng yīnyuè?	*Would you like to listen to Chinese music or Western music?*

If the subject or object in both halves is the same you don't need to repeat it (this holds true for any two clauses, not just ones using **háishi**, and is a feature of Chinese), but there should be a verb in both halves even if it is the same one. However, in colloquial Chinese the second verb is sometimes left out if it is the same as the first one. This is shown in the two examples above.

An exception to this rule is if the verb is **shì** (*to be*). In this case, the second **shì** may be left out. Here is an example of this:

Tā shì nǐde péngyou   *Is he your friend or your teacher?*
 háishi nǐde lǎoshī?

Try saying **háishi shì** and you'll understand why!

4 To be in the middle of doing something

To show that an action is in progress the word **zài** is put in front of the verb:

Tā **zài** dǎ tàijíquán.   *He's doing Tai Chi.*
Wǒ **zài** zuò qìgōng.   *I'm doing qigong.*
Nǐ **zài** kàn diànshì.   *You're watching TV.*

You will sometimes find the words **zhèng** or **zhèng zài** used in exactly the same way instead of **zài**. They are simply alternatives. **Ne**, at the end of a sentence, can also convey the idea that the action is in progress; or you might find **ne** occurring with any of the above. Here are a few examples to illustrate this:

Xiǎo Liú **zhèngzài tīng**   *Xiao Liu is listening to music.*
 yīnyuè (**ne**).
Tāmen **zhèng** chī wǔfàn **ne**.   *They're in the middle of lunch.*
Wǒmen kāi huì **ne**. Qǐng nǐ   *We're in the middle of a*
 míngtiān zài lái.   *meeting. Please come again*
          tomorrow.

Note that this action in progress can take place in the past, present or future and it is the use of time-words (plus context) which tells us when the action actually takes place:

Míngtiān shàngwǔ tā yídìng   *She'll certainly be swimming*
 zài yóuyǒng (**ne**).   *tomorrow morning.*
Zuótiān wǎnshang wǒ **zài**   *I was at the theatre yesterday*
 kàn xì (**ne**).   *evening.*

5 The same or not the same?

In Chinese, to express that one thing is the same as another, or *A is the same as B* you say **A gēn** (*with*) **B yíyàng** (*the same*).

A **gēn** B **yíyàng** gāo.
A is as tall as B.

Wáng tàitai **gēn** Lǐ xiǎojie **yíyàng** gāo.
Mrs Wang is as tall as Miss Li.

Zhāng xiānsheng **gēn** tā jiějie **yíyàng** pàng.
Mr Zhang is as fat as his elder sister.

To say that A is *not* the same as B you simply put bù in front of yíyàng:

A gēn B **bù** yíyàng gāo.
A is not as tall as B.

6 Making comparisons

To say that something is *more . . . than* use **bǐ**:

A **bǐ** B nán.	*A is more difficult than B.*
Qìgōng **bǐ** tàijíquán nán.	*Qigong is more difficult than Tai Chi.*
Kàn diànyǐng **bǐ** kàn jīngjù yǒu yìsi.	*Going to the cinema* (lit. see/ watch film) *is more interesting than watching Peking Opera.*

It is important to note that **bù bǐ** does not mean *less . . . than*. Look carefully at the following examples:

Tā **bù bǐ** wǒ dà.	*He is no older than I.*
Wǒ jiějie **bù bǐ** nǐ gāo.	*My elder sister is no taller than you.*

7 Helping verbs

Verbs such as *want, ought to, must, can* occur before action verbs or verbal expressions:

Nǐ **xiǎng** zuò shénme?	*What would you like to do?*
Wǒ **xiǎng** qù mǎi dōngxi.	*I'd like to go shopping.*
Wǒ **gāi** qù.	*I ought to go.*
Tā **yào** zǒu.	*She wants to leave.*
Nǐ **huì** shuō Hànyǔ ma?	*Can you speak Chinese?*
Tāmen **xǐhuan** mǎi dōngxi.	*They like shopping.*

Note the difference between **xiǎng** (*would like to do, fancy doing, something*) and **xǐhuan** (*like*).

Unlike other types of verbs which can take endings to indicate for example that something has taken place or to show direction, these 'helping' or auxiliary verbs cannot have anything added to them.

8 To give or not to give

Gěi basically means *to give*, but it can be used with a noun or pronoun (referring to a person or living thing) *before* the verb to mean *to do something for someone or something*.

Wǒ **gěi** nǐ kànkan.	*I'll take a look for you.*
Tā **gěi** wǒ kāikai.	*He opened up for me.*
Wǒ qǐng fúwùyuán **gěi** wǒmen dìng piào.	*I'll ask the attendant to book tickets for us.*

─────── **Cultural tips** ───────

- Chinese traditional music sounds very different from Western music. If you ever have the chance to see Peking Opera do take it. You may decide never to go again but it is certainly worth trying once, just for the experience! The make-up and costumes are very elaborate and give you all sorts of information about the characters being portrayed so try to go with somebody who knows something about Peking opera. Most people enjoy the battles and the acrobatics if not the singing!

- You might have heard of **tàijí** (often written **Tai Chi** in the West) or of **qìgōng** which are forms of exercise practised for hundreds of years in China. Some forms of **qìgōng** are thought to be beneficial to cancer sufferers and people are encouraged to go to regular classes (usually in the local park early in the morning around 6 a.m.) as part of their treatment and recovery programme.

Why not try out a **tàijí** or **qìgōng** class yourself? Ask at your local library for information. You are likely to meet other people in the class who are interested in learning Chinese and with whom you can practise, chat and exchange ideas.

 ──────────────── **Liànxí** ────────────────

1 Tā/tāmen zài zuò shénme?
   (*What is he/she doing? What are they doing?*)
   Look at the pictures overleaf and say what the people are doing using the pattern above.

(a) **mǎi dōngxi**   (b) **kàn zájì**   (c) **huàn qián**

(d) **dǎ tàijí**   (e) **kàn diànyǐng**   (f) **tīng yīnyuè**

2 Look at the pictures in **Liànxí 1**. Suppose these are the things you plan to do at the weekend. Draw up a plan and say when you are going to do what. Expressions of time can either occur before the verb, or at the beginning of the sentence if you want to give them more emphasis. Look at these examples:

Xīngqīliù shàngwǔ wǒ yào qù zuò qìgōng.
Xīngqītiān wǎnshang wǒ xiǎng qù kàn diànyǐng.

3 Tāmen yíyàng ma?

gāo	tall
dà	old
xiǎo	young (*used when comparing ages*)
zhòng	heavy

Answer the following questions using **yíyàng** or **bù yíyàng**.

Qǔ   Hú   Xǔ

(*a*) Qū gēn Xǔ yíyàng gāo ma?

(*b*) Xǔ gēn Hú yíyàng dà ma?

(*c*) Qū gēn Hú yíyàng zhòng ma?

(*d*) Xǔ gēn Hú yíyàng gāo ma?

(*e*) Qū gēn Xǔ yíyàng zhòng ma?

(*f*) Hú gēn Qū yíyàng dà ma?

AGE 70   AGE 25   AGE 25
60 kg   76 kg   60 kg
1.66 m   1.75 m   1.76 m

4 According to the information in **Liànxí 3** are the following statements true or false. If true, say **duì**. If false say **bú duì** and say what is true.

	duì/bú duì?
(*a*) Hú bǐ Xǔ gāo.	☐ ☐
(*b*) Hú bù bǐ Qū zhòng.	☐ ☐
(*c*) Xǔ bǐ Hú dà.	☐ ☐
(*d*) Qū bǐ Xǔ dà.	☐ ☐
(*e*) Hú gēn Xǔ bǐ Qū xiǎo.	☐ ☐

5 The following is what Mr Jones has put in his diary. Answer the questions below according to what is written in the diary.

Monday evening – learn Chinese
Tuesday morning – meeting
Wednesday morning – go to a concert
Thursday afternoon – meet a friend
Friday evening – see a film
Saturday – shopping – change money
Sunday – learn Tai Chi

(a) Qióngsī xiānsheng xīngqīliù háishi xīngqītiān xué tàijíquán?
(b) Tā shénme shíhou qù kàn péngyou?
(c) Tā xīngqīsān wǎnshang qù tīng yīnyuèhuì háishi xīngqīsì wǎnshang?
(d) Tā xīngqī'èr shàngwǔ kāi huì háishi xiàwǔ kāi huì?
(e) Tā shénme shíhou qù mǎi dōngxi?

☑ *Xiǎo cèyàn*

(a) Ask your Chinese friend what she would like to do tomorrow.
(b) Say Xiǎo Mǎ and her elder sister are as tall as each other.
(c) Say you find acrobatics more interesting than Peking opera.
(d) Ask Xiǎo Zhào where he would like to go this evening.
(e) Ask Miss Lǐ whether she would like to see a film or go to a concert.

The following signs should come in useful.

Gentlemen

男 厕 所

Nán Cèsuǒ

Ladies

女 厕 所

Nǚ Cèsuǒ

7

DUŌSHAO QIÁN?
How much is it?

In this unit you will learn:

- how to ask for things (in shops)
- how to ask the price
- how to state quantities
- numbers from 100 to 1,000
- how to express the distance between two points

Kāishǐ yǐqián

You will get to grips with Chinese money in this unit and be able to comment on the prices of things. You will also master basic colours and learn how to make more complex comparisons.

☑ Shìshi

Tomorrow evening it is your turn to entertain the Chinese visitors to your bank.

(a) You don't know whether to take them to a concert or to a play (**kàn xì**) so what do you ask them?

(b) They want to go to a concert. How do you ask them whether they like Western music?

(c) They assure you that in the West they want to listen to Western music so what do **they** say to you?

Zhǔyào cíhuì

bǎi	hundred
bǐ	to compare,
búcuò	pretty good, not bad
cái	not . . . until, only then
cǎoméi	strawberry
dào	to arrive
deduō	much . . .
duō cháng?	how long?
duō yuǎn?	how far?
duōle	much more than
duōshao?	how much? how many?
jǐ	crowded
jiàn	(*measure word for clothes*)
jīn	half a kilogram
jìn	near, close
jiù	just; only
Kěyǐ ma?	Can I . . . ? Is it allowed . . . ?
kuài	(*unit of money*)
lí	distance from
mài	to sell
máoyī	woollen pullover
něi/nǎ?	which?
nèi/nà	that
píngguǒ	apple
pútao	grapes
shénme yánsè (de)?	what colour?
shìhé	to suit
shìchǎng	market
shìshi	to try
tài . . . le!	too . . . !
tián	sweet
xiāngjiāo	banana(s)
xīnxiān	fresh
Xíng ma?	Is it OK? Can I . . . ?
yuǎn	far
zánmen	we/us (*including listener*)
zhàn	(bus) stop, station
zhèi/zhè	this
zhèr	here, this place
zhème (guì)	so (*expensive*)
zìyóu	free, freedom
zǒu lù	to walk, on foot
zuì	the most
Nín mǎi shénme?	What would you like (*to buy*)?
Wǒ yào . . .	I want . . .

X zěnme mài?	How much is X?
Duōshao qián yì jīn? ⎫ **Yì jīn duōshao qián?** ⎭	How much is it for half a kilo?
A lí B duō yuǎn?	How far is A from B?
A lí B hěn jìn/yuǎn.	A is close to/far from B

Yánsè Biǎo (lit. colour table)

hóng (sè) (de)	red	**lán(sè) (de)**	blue
huáng (sè) (de)	yellow	**bái(sè) (de)**	white
lǜ(sè) (de)	green	**hēi(sè) (de)**	black

✳ *Xuéxí jìqiǎo*

Here are two more pairs: **lu** and **lü**, **nu** and **nü**.

Go back to the Pronunciation Guide and read the notes there. You will need a mirror for the next exercise.

First of all push out your lips and say *oo*. Then tighten them and say *you*. Repeat this but put l in front of the *oo*. Now you have the sound **lu**. To say **lü** say the word *lewd* without the d. For **nu** and **nü** say the *noo* of *noodles* and the *nu* of *nude*! Now look in the mirror and say the sounds again. What do you notice about your lips when you say the two different sounds?

You have to tighten them to say the **ü** sound don't you? For those of you who know a little French or German the **ü** in Chinese is like the *u* in *tu* (French) or the *ü* in *über* (German).

Ju, **qu** and **xu** are also pronounced as though they were written with ü. Don't confuse them with **zhu**, **chu**, and **shu** where the u is the *oo* sound.

 *Shùzì yìbǎi dào yìqiān* (Numbers from 100 to 1,000)

100	**yìbǎi**	300	**sānbǎi**
200	**èrbǎi**	308	**sānbǎi líng bā**
202	**èrbǎi líng èr**	410	**sìbǎi yīshí**
210	**èrbǎi yīshí**	794	**qībǎi jiǔshísì**
225	**èrbǎi èrshíwǔ**	1,000	**yìqiān**

Think of a number as being made up of units, tens and hundreds. If there is a zero in the tens column, you have to say **líng** (*zero*) in Chinese.

10 is **shí** in Chinese but when it occurs with one hundred, two hundred, and so on you have to say one ten: **yīshí**, so 110 is **yìbǎi yīshí**.

Duìhuà

Duìhuà 1

百货商店
Bǎihuò Shāngdiàn

It may not be easy to get what you want in a shop despite the polite service you get. This customer knows what she wants and what she doesn't want as this **Duìhuà** shows:

(*at the information point*)
Customer Qǐng wèn, zài nǎr mǎi máoyī?
Assistant Zài èr lóu.

(at knitwear counter)

Assistant Nín mǎi shénme?
Customer Wǒ xiǎng mǎi yí jiàn máoyī.
Assistant Yào něi jiàn? Nín xǐhuan shénme yánsè de?
Customer Nèi jiàn hóngsè de gěi wǒ kànkan xíng ma?
Assistant Zhèi jiàn hěn hǎo.
Customer Nn, tài dà le. Nèi jiàn huángsè de wǒ shìshi kěyǐ ma?
Assistant Zhèi jiàn yě búcuò.
Customer O, tài xiǎo le.
Assistant Zhèi jiàn lánsè de hěn shìhé nǐ.
Customer Tài hǎo le. Duōshao qián?
Assistant Wǔbǎi kuài.
Customer Nn, tài guì le. Duìbuqǐ, xièxie nǐ.
Assistant ... ...

Cultural tip

In Chinese the ground floor is **yī lóu**, (*lit.* one floor), the first floor is **èr lóu** (*lit.* two floor), the second floor **sān lóu** (*lit.* three floor), the third floor **sì lóu** (*lit.* four floor) and so on.

📼 Duìhuà 2

If you can't get what you want in one shop, you can try somewhere else. This is what Xiǎo Fāng is suggesting to Ann.

Fāng Wōmen qù zìyóu shìchǎng kànkan ba.
Ann Hǎo. Zìyóu shìchǎng lí zhèr duō yuǎn?
Fāng Hěn jìn. Zuò chē liǎng、sān zhàn jiù dào le.
Ann Chē tài jǐ le. Zánmen zǒu lù qù ba.
Fāng Kěshì zǒu lù tài yuǎn le.
Ann Zǒu lù yào duō cháng shíjiān?
Fāng Zǒu lù èr、sānshí fēnzhōng cái néng dào.
Ann Hǎo ba. Nàme zánmen zuò chē qù ba.

Duìhuà 3

There are markets throughout China where you can probably bargain. This is what you might hear at a fruit stall.

Buyer Píngguǒ zěnme mài?
Seller Sì kuài yì jīn.
Buyer Zhēn guì! Tāmende píngguǒ sān kuài bā yì jīn.
Seller Kěshì wǒde píngguǒ bǐ tāmende dà yìdiǎnr.
Buyer Pútao duōshao qián yì jīn?
Seller Sì kuài liǎng máo wǔ yì jīn.
Buyer Zhème guì! Tāmen de sì kuài yì jīn.
Seller Kěshì wǒde pútao bǐ tāmende tián duōle.
Buyer Cǎoméi yì jīn duōshao qián?
Seller Bā kuài èr.
Buyer Tài guì le!
Seller Kěshì wǒde cǎoméi bǐ tāmen de xīnxiān deduō.
Buyer Nǐde dōngxi zuì guì.
Seller Kěshì wǒde dōngxi zuì hǎo!

斤斤计较 **Jīn jīn jìjiào** (Chinese proverb)
Haggle over every ounce, quibble over small differences

Jiěshì

1 More on measure words

You have already met in Unit 4 the measure words **běn** (for books and magazines) and **zhāng** (for rectangular or square flat objects), together with the most common measure word of all **gè**.

Some measure words like **jīn** (*half a kilogram*) and **bēi** (*cup*) are actually indicators of quantity. The table below lists some of the more common of these:

Pinyin	Category	Examples
bǎ	objects with a handle, chairs	*knife, umbrella toothbrush, chair*
bāo	parcel, packet	*cigarettes, noodles*
bēi	cup, glass	*tea, coffee, wine*
běn	volume	*book, dictionary*
fēng		*letter*
gè	people, things which do not fall into other categories; substitute MW	*person, student*
jiàn	piece, article	*clothes, luggage*
jīn	indicator of quantity (0.5 kilogram)	*fruit, vegetables*
kuài	piece	*soap, land*
lǐ	indicator of length ($\frac{1}{3}$ mile)	*road*
liàng	things with wheels	*car, bicycle*
píng	bottles, jars	*beer, wine, jam*
tiáo	long and winding; carton (e.g. 200)	*towel, trousers, fish; cigarettes*
wèi	people (*polite*)	*teacher, lady, gentleman*
zhāng	flat, rectangular objects	*ticket, blanket, table, paper, map*

Note that **gōngjīn** (*lit.* public pound) is a *kilogram*, **gōnglǐ** (*lit.* public li) is a *kilometre* and **yīnglǐ** (*lit.* English li) is a *mile*.

2 Money, money, money...!

Chinese money operates the decimal system and the currency in China is known as **rénmínbì** (*the people's currency*). Foreign currency is known as **wàibì** (*lit.* external/outside currency).

The largest single unit is the **yuán** 元 (written as ¥ in many transactions). There are 10 **jiǎo** 角 in one **yuán** and 10 **fēn** 分 in one **jiǎo**. These are the words (and Chinese characters) used in the written language and printed on banknotes, tickets, and so on so it is important to recognise them.

Look carefully at the facsimiles below and see if you can pick out the characters for **jiǎo** and **fēn**. You saw how the characters for 1 to 10 were written in Unit 3. Don't be put off by the more complex characters you will see on Chinese banknotes. This also goes for the character 元 which is written 圆 on banknotes. These prevent confusion (and forgery!) when numbers are being written out in financial transactions.

In spoken Chinese, **kuài** 块 piece/lump is used for **yuán** and **máo** 毛 for **jiǎo** but **fēn** remains unchanged.

RMB	Spoken	Written
0.01 yuán	yì fēn (qián)	yì fēn
0.1 yuán	yì máo (qián)	yì máo
1.00 yuán	yí kuài (qián)	yì yuán
5.5 yuán	wǔ kuài wǔ *or* wǔ kuài bàn	wǔ yuán wǔ jiǎo
14.32 yuán	shísì kuài sān máo èr	shísì yuán sān jiǎo èr fēn
30.09 yuán	sānshí kuài líng jiǔ fēn	sānshí yuán líng jiǔ fēn

If a sum of money involves **kuài** and **fēn** but no **máo** the absence of **máo** is marked by a **líng** (*zero*).

When two or more different units of currency are used together, the last one is often omitted:

sì kuài liù	rather than	sì kuài liù máo	¥4.60
bā máo qī	rather than	bā máo qī fēn	¥0.87

3 Too much?

Tài (*too*) is almost always with **le**:

tài xiǎo **le**	*too small*
tài guì **le**	*too expensive*
tài hǎo **le**	*excellent, great*

It is probably better just to accept this as a rule rather than to try to analyse it!

4 How far is A from B?

To say A is a long way from B, where A and B are fixed points, use:
A **lí** (*separate*) B hěn **yuǎn** (*far*)

If you don't use **hěn** (*very*), some sort of comparison is implied, i.e. A is a long way from B (but near to C). Thus in Chinese **hěn** is very weak!

Lúndūn **lí** Àidīngbǎo hěn **yuǎn**.　　*London is a long way from Edinburgh.*

To say A is near B use: A **lí** B hěn **jìn** (*near*).

Niújīn **lí** Lúndūn hěn **jìn**.　　*Oxford is close to London.*

To say exactly how far A is from B use: A **lí** B **yǒu** + the distance.

Yǒu (*to have*) can also have the meaning *there is/there are*.

Jiànqiáo (*Cambridge*) lí Niújīn　　*Cambridge is 180 kilometres*
　yǒu yìbǎibāshí gōnglǐ.　　*from Oxford.*

A and B can also be fixed points in time. To say how far A is from B *in time* use: A **lí** B **yǒu** + time difference.

Nǐde shēngrì lí jīntiān hái
yǒu sì tiān.

*There are still four days to go to
your birthday (lit. your birthday
separate today still have four
days).*

5 Approximate numbers

If you want to say two or three (people) in Chinese you put the
words for two (of a pair) and three one after another with a pause-
mark in between them:

liǎng、sān ge rén   *two or three people*
wǔ、liù běn shū   *five or six books*

20 or 30 is **èr、sānshí**: the **shí** is only said *once*.

45 or 46 is **sìshíwǔ、liù**: the **sìshí** is only said *once*.

6 We including you!

Both **zánmen** and **wǒmen** mean *we* and *us*. The difference is that
zánmen specifically includes the listener(s) in what is being said.

A says to his sister:

Zánmen bàba、māma duì
wǒmen hěn hǎo shì bu shi?

*Our Mum and Dad were very
good to us, weren't they?*

Zánmen here has a more intimate feel to it than **wǒmen**.

7 More on comparisons

You have already met **bǐ** in Unit 6, ➡️ **P.** 73:

Chī fàn **bǐ** hē jiǔ yǒu yìsi.   *Eating is more interesting than
consuming alcohol.*

To say that A is *much* more ... than B use:

A **bǐ** B adjective/verb **duōle**.
   or
A **bǐ** B adjective/verb **deduō**.

Zhè jiàn máoyī **bǐ** nèi jiàn
  dà **duōle**.
Cǎoméi **bǐ** píngguǒ guì
  deduō.

This sweater is much bigger
* than that one.*
Strawberries are much more
* expensive than apples.*

To say that A is a little more . . . than B use: A **bǐ** B adjective/verb
yìdiǎnr.

Wǒde shuǐguǒ (*fruit*) **bǐ** tāde
  shuǐguǒ xīnxiān **yìdiǎnr**.

My fruit is a little fresher
* than his.*

8 Be the best!

You only have to put the little word **zuì** (*most*) in front of **hǎo** to
make it into *the best*! Look carefully at the following examples using
zuì:

    zuì hǎo   *the best* (*lit.* most good)
    zuì guì   *the most expensive*
    zuì tián   *the sweetest*

You can put **de** + noun after the examples to make such phrases
as:

    zuì hǎo **de** pútao   *the best grapes*
    zuì guì **de** cǎoméi   *the most expensive strawberries*
    zuì tián **de** píngguǒ   *the sweetest apples*

9 Cái and jiù

Both **cái** and **jiù** are adverbs indicating something about time. **Cái**
indicates that something takes place later or with more difficulty
than had been expected. **Jiù**, on the other hand, indicates that something takes place earlier or more promptly than expected:

Tā sì diǎn zhōng **cái** lái.

He didn't come until four
(though I had asked him to
come at 3.15).

Tāmen liù diǎn bàn **jiù** lái le.	*They were there by 6.30* (though we had invited them for seven).

Cái often translates as *not . . . until*. **Jiù** usually has a **le** at the end of the sentence to convey a sense of completion whereas **cái** does not. **Jiù** will sometimes have **zǎo** (*early*) in front of it as well as **le** at the end.

Both **cái** and **jiù** must come immediately before the verb whatever else there is in the sentence. Look carefully at the following examples:

Zuò chē liǎng、sān zhàn **jiù** dào **le**.	*It's only two or three stops on the bus.*
Zǒu lù èr、sānshí fēnzhōng **cái** néng dào.	*It will take as much as 20 or 30 minutes on foot* (if we walk).
Zuótiān hěn lěng dànshi jīntiān **cái** xià xuě.	*Yesterday was very cold but it didn't snow until today.*
Wǒ xiànzài **cái** zhīdao Fǎguó dōngxi guí.	*It's only now that I know things in France are expensive.*
Wǒ **zǎo jiù** zhǐdao **le**.	*I knew ages ago* (that things in France are expensive).

Xuéxí jìqiǎo

What do you do if you don't understand?

1 Don't panic and don't give up listening.

2 Try to concentrate on what you do understand and guess the rest. If there comes a point where you really feel you can't understand anything, isolate the phrase or word(s) that is causing you problems and say to the speaker:

. . . . shì shénme yìsi?	*What does . . . mean?*

Hopefully he or she will say it in another way that you will be able to understand. Remember the two useful sentences you learnt in Unit 3:

Qǐng nǐ zài shuō yí biàn.	*Please say it again.*
Qǐng nǐ shuō màn yìdiǎn.	*Please speak more slowly.*

Cultural tip

Most Chinese people are expert bargainers. A lot of selling is done from street stalls or with articles laid out on a piece of cloth on the ground. In these circumstances it is possible to bargain. If you are interested in buying something point to it and say:

Zhè ge duōshao qián?　　　*How much is this?*

Having got a price, one way is to start by halving it and to say:

Wǒ zhǐ néng gěi nǐ X kuài.　　*I can only give you X kuai.*

And then the fun starts with the two of you negotiating a price that you both find acceptable. It is a good policy to decide from the outset how much you are prepared to pay for something so that you have that in mind when bargaining. If neither of you can agree on a price you can finish the bargaining by saying:

Xièxie, wǒ bù mǎi le.　　*Thank you, I won't buy it then.*

and walking away. Sometimes if you are lucky the vendor will rush after you and offer it to you for the last price you offered or one very similar.

Fruit and vegetables sold from stalls are normally offered at a certain price and if you think it's too expensive you just don't buy them. Don't buy from anyone whose prices are not shown until you have ascertained how much they are. The Chinese are very good at charging fellow-Chinese one price and foreigners another (naturally more expensive). Unfortunately it is very hard to check whether they are giving you the correct weight as they often use a pole with weights on one end and a pan (to hold the purchased fruit on) on the other. There is no bargaining in ordinary shops and department stores.

 ———————————— **Liànxí** ————————————

1 Say the following prices in Chinese.
   Example: ¥ 4.03 sì kuài líng sān fēn

   (*a*) ¥ 0.52   (*c*) ¥ 12.76   (*e*) ¥ 205.54
   (*b*) ¥ 2.25   (*d*) ¥ 99.99   (*f*) ¥ 8.07

2 **Duōshao qián?**

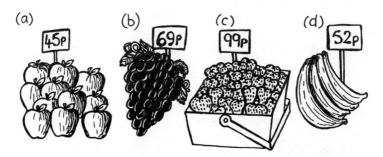

Tell your Chinese friend how much these fruits cost in your local town. You need to know the words **bàng** (*a pound in weight*) and **biànshì** (*pence*).

   Example: Píngguǒ yí bàng wǔshísì biànshì.
               Pútao liùshí biànshì yí bàng.

3 You want to buy the following vegetables in a Chinese market, but they are not priced. Ask the greengrocer the prices by filling in the blanks in the questions below:

   xīhóngshì (*tomato*)   ¥ 0.65 a jin
   báicài (*Chinese leaves*)   ¥ 0.42 a jin
   tǔdòu (*potato*)   ¥ 0.28 a jin

(*a*) **You**   __ __ mài?
 Greengrocer Liù máo wǔ yì jīn.
(*b*) **You**   __ yì jīn __ qián?
 Greengrocer Yì jīn sì máo èr.
(*c*) **You**   __ __ qián yì jīn?
 Greengrocer Liǎng máo bā yì jīn.

4 Listen to the cassette and write down the items mentioned and their prices. We've done the first for you. If you get really stuck look at what is said in the *Key to the exercises*.

(a) yú (*fish*)	¥ 7.09
(b)	¥
(c)	¥
(d)	¥
(e)	¥

5 What would you say in the following situations?
 Example: Situation – It's freezing today.
     You could say – **Jīntiān tài lěng** (*cold*) **le.**

(*a*) You've tried on a pullover and found it too big.
(*b*) It is 30°C today. (**rè** = *hot*)
(*c*) She's got too much money!
(*d*) The ticket to a match costs £150.
(*e*) You have studied French for years and still cannot speak it. (*i.e. French is too difficult*).

6 Make comparisons with the information given using the pattern
 A bǐ B adjective
 or
 A bǐ B adjective (yìdiǎnr, deduō or duōle):
 Example: cǎoméi ¥8.50/jīn, pútao ¥6.30/jīn
     Cǎoméi bǐ pútao guì duōle.

(*a*) Nǎ ge guì? (bǐ)   Píngguǒ ¥ 4.00/jīn; Pútao
         ¥ 4.10/jīn
(*b*) Tāmen shéi gāo? (yìdiǎnr) Xiǎo Wáng 1.73m; Lǎo Lǐ
         1.70m
(*c*) Nǎ ge dìfang rè? (duōle) Běijīng 29°C; Lúndūn 17°C
(*d*) Tāmen shéi dà? (deduō) Bái xiānsheng 58; Bái tàitai
         48

7 Use either **cái** or **jiù** to fill in the blanks.

   (*a*) Wǔ diǎn kāi huì, tā sì diǎn bàn ___ lái le.
   (*b*) Nǐ hái bù zhīdao ma? Wǒ zuótiān (*yesterday*) ___ zhīdao le.
   (*c*) Duìbuqǐ, Lǐ lǎoshī jīntiān bù néng lái. Tā míngtiān ___ lái.
   (*d*) Tā bù xiǎng míngtiān qù, tā xiǎng xiànzài ___ qù.
   (*e*) Yīnyuèhuì qī diǎn kāishǐ (*start*), tā qī diǎn yíkè ___ lái.

☑ *Xiǎo cèyàn*

How do you say:

   (*a*) It will take only five minutes to get there.
   (*b*) It will take (as long as) 50 minutes to get there.
   (*c*) In my family my father is the oldest.
   (*d*) The cinema is not far from my home.
   (*e*) Bananas cost 49p per pound.

8

ZĚNMEYÀNG?
What's it like?

In this unit you will learn:

- how to ask about sizes
- how to talk about clothes and shoes
- how to describe things
- how to express likes and dislikes
- how to express comparisons

Kāishǐ yǐqián

This unit will give you the necessary vocabulary and structures to ask people their opinions about things: **Nǐ kàn zěnmeyàng?** (*What's it like?*) and to make comparisons **Zhè ge méi yǒu nà ge hǎo** (*This one is not as good as that one*).

☑ *Shìshi*

Refer back to **Duìhuà 1** and **Duìhuà 3** in Unit 7 and answer the following questions:

1 Did the customer buy a pullover? Why?

2 How did the fruitseller justify his prices being higher than other people's? Give four reasons.

Zhǔyào cíhuì

bù zěnmeyàng	not so good
dàxiǎo	size
fēicháng	extremely
gèng	even more
guò	to pass or spend (*of time*)
hái kěyǐ	just so so
héshì	suitable
jiàqī	holiday, vacation
juéde	to feel, think
kuài	fast
màn	slow
měi	every
měi tiān	every day
mō(mo)	to feel, touch
nǎli nǎli	not really (*response to a compliment*)
nánkàn	ugly
píanyì	cheap
xià yǔ	to rain
xīn	new
xīn mǎi de	newly bought
xué(xí)	to learn, study
yánsè	colour
Yìdàlì	Italy
yǐhòu	later, in future
yǐqián	before
Yīngwén	English language
yǒu yìdiǎn(r)	a little
yòu ... yòu ...	both ... and ...
zǎo jiù	ages ago, for ages
zěnme le?	what is/was the matter?
zěnmeyàng?	how is it? how about it?
zhāng	*measure word for flat objects*
zhìliàng	quality
zhǐ yào	only need/cost
zhǔyì	idea
zúqiú	football

❋ *Xuéxí jìqiǎo*

Here's another set of pairs:
  j and **q**

zh and **ch**
sh and **r**

Go back to the Pronunciation Guide again and read the notes there.

The **j** in Chinese is the same as our own. Say *jeans*, in the same way as you would say 'cheese' to the camera, a few times and observe your mouth in a mirror. You will notice that the corners of your mouth are drawn back as far as they can go.

Q bears no resemblance to our **q**. It is pronounced *in exactly the same way as* **j** but you put air behind it to make the **q**. You have already done some practice on **q** in Unit 1 ➡️🅿️ 17, but as it is so different from **q** in English it is worth looking at again.

For **zh**, **ch**, **sh** and **r** you must curl your tongue back in a loose sausage-roll. They are all pronounced with the tongue in this position. **Zh** and **ch** are identical sounds except the **ch** is said with air behind it.

R is the one to watch. Listen to the cassette carefully and try to reproduce the sounds you hear as closely as possible. Recording your own voice and then comparing it with the original would be extremely helpful at this stage.

 ———————— **Duìhuà** ————————

 *Duìhuà 1*

Sùlán is showing her newly bought pullover to her boyfriend Colin. She is very pleased with it as the price was reduced. But what does Colin think of it?

Sùlán	Zhè shì wǒ xīn mǎi de máoyī. Nǐ kàn zěnmeyàng?
Colin	Búcuò, búcuò.
Sùlán	Dàxiǎo héshì ma?
Colin	En, yǒu diǎnr dà.
Sùlán	Yánsè hǎokàn ma?
Colin	En, bù nánkàn.
Sùlán	Nǐ mōmo. . . . Nǐ juéde zhìliàng zěnmeyàng?
Colin	En, hái kěyǐ. Duōshao qián?

Dà jiǎn jià
Big Reductions

Sùlán Bù guì, zhǐ yào jiǔshíjiǔ kuài.
Colin Shénme?! Jiǔshíjiǔ kuài wǒ kěyǐ mǎi sān zhāng zúqiú piào!

Duìhuà 2

Mr Li and Mrs Law are just back from holiday. How were their respective holidays?

Mrs Law Jiàqī guò-de hǎo ma?
Mr Lǐ Fēicháng hǎo, jiù shi dōngxi bù piányi.
Mrs Law Wǒ zǎo jiù zhīdao le.
Mr Lǐ Wǒ yǐqián juéde Yīngguo de dōngxi guì, xiànzài cái zhīdao Fǎguó de dōngxi gèng guì.
Mrs Law Yìdàlì de dōngxi yě hěn guì shì bu shi?
Mr Lǐ Yìdàlì de dōngxi yě bù bǐ Fǎguó de piányi. Nǐ de jiàqī guò-de zěnmeyàng?
Mrs Law Bù zěnmeyàng.
Mr Lǐ Zěnme le?
Mrs Law Měi tiān dōu xià yǔ.

Duìhuà 3

Martin is learning Chinese. He has met a Chinese girl who is studying English. What is their plan?

Bǎojié Nǐde Zhōngwén shuō-de zhēn hǎo.
Martin Nǎli, nǎli. Wǒde Zhōngwén méi yǒu nǐde Yīngwén hǎo.
Bǎojié Bù. Nǐde Zhōngwén bǐ wǒde Yīngwén hǎo deduō.
Martin Yǐhòu wǒ bāng nǐ xué Yīngwén, nǐ bāng wǒ xué Zhōngwén, zěnmeyàng?
Bǎojié Hǎo zhǔyi. Kěshì wǒ xué-de bú kuài.
Martin Méi guānxi, wǒ xué-de yě hěn màn.

—————— Jiěshì ——————

1 A bit . . . ?

To say something is *a little/bit* . . . use:
    adjective + **(yì)diǎnr**

hǎo (yì)diǎnr	*a bit better*
dà (yì)diǎnr	*a little older/bigger*

(See also ➡️🄿 88 where adjective + **yìdiānr** is used in comparisons.)

When you wish to convey a negative feeling even if it is only subjective on your part then **yǒu (yì)diǎnr** is put in front of the adjective:

Yǒu (yì)diǎnr guì.	*It's a bit on the expensive side.*
Yǒu (yì)diǎnr dà.	*It's a little on the big side.*

In all these examples you can miss out the **yì** to sound more colloquial.

2 How well do you speak Chinese?

When you are describing how the action of a verb is carried out, such as *quickly, slowly, well* you use **de** after the verb and *then* the word for *quick, slow, good,* and so on.

You do *not* have to change them into adverbs as in English – quick-quickly, good-well.

Nǐde Zhōngwén shuō-**de** **zěnmeyàng?**	*What's your Chinese like?*
Wǒde Zhōngwén shuō-**de bù** **hǎo.**	*I don't speak Chinese well.*
Wǒ xué-**de bú kuài.**	*I don't learn fast.*

This **de** is different from the **de** you met in Units 3 and 5 but they are written the same in pinyin and both are toneless. They are represented by two entirely different Chinese characters however.

● When sentences of this kind have an object you can either repeat the verb after the object adding **de** to the second verb:

Wǒ xué Zhōngwén **xué-de** hěn màn.	
subject verb object	*I'm learning Chinese very slowly.*
Tā kàn shū **kàn-de** hěn duō.	*He reads a lot.*

● Or you can miss out the first verb and have the object coming straight after the subject followed by the verb with **de**:

Nǐ Rìyǔ shuō-de zěnmeyàng?   *What's your Japanese like?*
  object
Wǒ Rìyǔ shuō-de bù hǎo.   *My Japanese is not very good.*

3   What's it like?

Zěnmeyàng (*What's it like? How?*) is a useful question word in Chinese. As you saw in Unit 2, ➡️📕 29 with **shéi** (*who*) and **shénme** (*what*), question words appear in the same position as the word or words which replace them in the answer:

Nǐ kàn **zěnmeyàng?**	*What do you think?*
Nǐ mōmo. Nǐ juéde	*Feel it. What do you think of the*
zhìliàng **zěnmeyàng?**	*quality?*
Jiàqī guò-de **zěnmeyàng?**	*How was your holiday?*
(Guò-de) bù **zěnmeyàng.**	*Not very good/not up to much.*

Note the neat expression **bù zěnmeyàng** (*not up to much*) in response to a question containing the question word **zěnmeyàng**.

4   Even more!

To say *even more expensive* in Chinese you only have to put the little word **gèng** in front of **guì**:

gèng guì	*even more expensive*
gèng piányì	*even cheaper, still cheaper*
gèng kuài	*even quicker, even more quickly*

Tā bǐ wǒ xué de **gèng** màn.	*He learns even more slowly than I do.*

You will sometimes find **hái** (*still*) used instead of **gèng**, but the meaning remains exactly the same:

Nǐ bǐ tā xiě de **hái** hǎo.	*You write even better than she does.*

5   Even more on comparisons!

You have already met **bǐ** in Unit 6, ➡️📕 73 and in Unit 7, ➡️📕 87–88. If you wish to say that something (A) is not up to a certain standard as represented by another person, living thing or object (B) use:

— **99** —

A **méi yǒu** B *adjective*/verb

Wǒde Zhōngwén (A) **méi yǒu** nǐde Yīngwén (B) **hǎo**.	*My Chinese is not as good as your English.*
Nǐde qìchē **méi yǒu** wǒde (qìchē) **kuài**.	*Your car is not as fast as mine.*

You will sometimes find **nàme** or **zhème** (*so*) in front of the adjective:

Zhè jiàn máoyī de dàxiǎo **méi yǒu** nà jiàn (máoyī de dàxiǎo) **nàme héshì**.	*This sweater doesn't fit as well as that one.*

This construction can also be used in the positive form by omitting **méi**, but it is not nearly so common as the negative form:

Wǒ jiějie **yǒu** nǐ gēge **gāo**.	*My elder sister is as tall as your elder brother.*

6 Each and every!

Měi (*each / every*) is often reinforced by putting **dōu** (*both / all*) before the verb:

Měi tiān **dōu** xià yǔ.	*It rains/rained every day.*
Tā **měi** nián **dōu** qù Zhōngguó.	*He goes to China every year.*

In the example above, it is clear that **dōu** has to refer back to **měi nián** rather than to **tā** which is singular.

Tiān and **nián** don't need a measure word between **měi** and themselves but other nouns do:

měi **ge** jiàqī	*every holiday*
měi **jiàn** máoyī	*every sweater*

Note that the measure word between **měi** and **rén** is optional.

Xuéxí jìqiǎo

Don't worry about making mistakes

The important thing is to keep talking. People quickly lose interest in talking to you if you look at them blankly and don't respond. Say something. Use gestures to help you out and don't worry about the mistakes. Don't be too ambitious in the initial stages – use vocabulary you know even if it means you have to keep the conversation simple. If all else fails, use a word in English (the foreign language most likely to be known by Chinese speakers), clearly pronounced, to keep things moving.

The Chinese are normally so delighted that someone has made the effort to learn their language that they are very patient and make enormous allowances for your accent and poor tones (or lack of them!), and are always very complimentary about your efforts.

Chéngjī
Achievements

Quēdiǎn
Shortcomings

Cuòwu
mistakes

Cultural tip

- Following on from the above, even if your Chinese is very poor you will usually be told how good it is! The correct response to such compliments is either **Guòjiǎng, guòjiǎng** (*you praise me too much*), or **Nǎli, nǎli** *lit. where, where?* (meaning that you don't see it the way they do!). Self-deprecation is definitely a Chinese art – you are invited to somebody's house and the table is groaning with delicious food and you are told that it is only **biànfàn** (*simple/convenience food*). The cook asks you to forgive his/her poor cooking when you can see that the opposite is the case. Examples such as these are endless and come under the general heading of **kèqi huà** (*polite talk*). You will find more examples of **kèqi huà** later on in the book. Why not start making a list of them for your own interest? Note people's self-deprecatory remarks and other people's responses to them.

- Never give Chinese friends white flowers. White is the colour for mourning in China. Be circumspect with red too – it's the colour associated with weddings (the bride's dress is traditionally red though with Western influence this is also changing). At Chinese New Year presents of money are given in little red envelopes (**hóng bāo**), and couplets expressing good luck and good fortune for the coming year are written on red paper and pasted on people's doors.

 ──────────── **Liànxí** ────────────

1 Match up the opposites:

(*a*) yǐqián		(*i*)	nánkàn
(*b*) dà		(*ii*)	màn
(*c*) guì		(*iii*)	róngyì
(*d*) hǎokàn		(*iv*)	piányi
(*e*) kuài		(*v*)	yǐhòu
(*f*) zǎo		(*vi*)	xiǎo
(*g*) nán		(*vii*)	wǎn

Items of clothing

Item	Measure word	
chènyī	(jiàn)	shirt
xié	(shuāng)	shoes (*a pair of*)
kùzi	(tiáo)	trousers
jiākè	(jiàn)	jacket
dàyī	(jiàn)	overcoat
xīfú	(tào)	suit (*Western*)
yǔyī	(jiàn)	raincoat
nèikù	(tiáo)	underpants
shuìyī	(jiàn)	nightdress, pyjamas

2 Refer to the tables of colour (Unit 7, ➡️📖 80) and items of clothing above. How would you ask for the following things in Chinese? (Note the measure words.)

Example: *a green jacket* yí jiàn lǜ jiākè

(*a*) a white shirt
(*b*) a yellow overcoat
(*c*) a blue suit

(*d*) a green skirt
(*e*) a pair of black shoes
(*f*) a pair of red trousers

3 Listen to the cassette and answer the following questions. If you don't have the cassette, read the passage below and then answer the questions.

(*a*) Xiǎo Cài jīntiān chuān (*wear*) shénme?
(*b*) Xiǎo Zhào jīntiān chuān shénme?
(*c*) Lǎo Fāng jīntiān chuān shénme?

Materials

bù	cotton/cloth
-bùxié	cloth shoes
pí	leather
-píxié	artificial leather
sīchóu	silk
rénzào gé	leather shoes

Xiǎo Cài jīntiān chuān yí jiàn bái chènyī, yì tiáo lán qúnzi. Xiǎo Cài hěn xǐhuan chuān píxié. Jīntiān tā chuān yì shuāng hóng píxié.

Xiǎo Zhào jīntiān chuān yí jiàn lán de sīchóu chènyī, yì tiáo hēi kùzi. Xiǎo Zhào zuì bù xǐhuan chuān píxié. Tā jīntiān chuān yì shuāng lǜ bùxié.

Lǎo Fāng jīntiān chuān yí tào hēi xīfú, yí jiàn bái chènyī, yì shuāng hēi píxié. Xīngqīyī dào xīngqīwǔ tā dōu chuān xīfú hé píxié.

4 Describe what the following people wear with the information provided:

> *Example*: Xiǎo Wáng/ white shirt/ black trousers/ yellow shoes.
> *Answer*: Xiǎo Wáng chuān yí jiàn bái chènshān, yì tiáo hēi kùzi, yì shuāng huáng píxié.

(*a*) Lǎo Mǎ/ black leather shoes/ blue shirt.
(*b*) Xiǎo Qián/ red shirt/ black trousers/ cloth shoes.
(*c*) Liú xiānsheng/ grey (**huī**) suit/ yellow shirt/ brown (**zōng**) leather shoes.

5 How well do they do the following things? Answer each of the following questions using the information given in brackets.

> *Example*: Xiǎo Zhū Fǎyǔ shuō-de zěnmeyàng? (*not at all well*)
>
> *Answer*: Tā Fǎyǔ shuō-de bù zěnmeyàng.

(a) Lǐ xiānsheng Déwén (*German*) shuō-de zěnmeyàng? (*very well*)

(b) Zhāng tàitai jiàqī guò-de hǎo bu hǎo? (*not very well*)

(c) Cháo xiǎojie Yīngwén xué-de kuài bu kuài? (*extremely quickly*)

(d) Mǎlì yòng kuàizi (*chopsticks*) yòng-de zěnmeyàng? (*not at all well*)

(e) Hēnglì shuō Rìyǔ (*Japanese*) shuō-de hěn qīngchu (*clearly*) ma? (*very clearly*)

6 Look carefully at the pictures of Zhāng Tóng and Mǎ Fēng below and the sentences comparing their height, age and weight. Then make up similar sentences comparing their cars, fridges (**bīngxiāng**) and handwriting (**zì**) using **méi yǒu . . .** and the adjectives given in brackets.

Zhāng Tóng's car (dà, guì)   Mǎ Fēng's car

> *Example*: Mǎ Fēng de chē **méi yǒu** Zhāng Tóng de chē **dà**.
> Zhāng Tóng de chē **méi yǒu** Mǎ Fēng de chē **guì**.

Zhāng Tóng's fridge   Mǎ Fēng's fridge

(a) bīngxiāng (*fridge*) (dà, guì)

Zhāng Tóng

Mǎ Fēng

(b)   (gāo, dà, zhòng)

5 July 1997

Dear Jack,
Weather here sunny and
warm. Having a great
holiday. See you soon!
    Zhang Tong

8/C.97

Hello Susan
  Raining again today. Why
did I have to come to
Scotland for my holidays?
Miss you —
          MaFeng

(c)   zì (*handwriting*) (qīngchu *clear*)

☑ Xiǎo cèyàn

What do you say?

(a) Say to someone that she speaks English very well.
(b) Say that something, e.g. a shirt, is a bit small.
(c) Ask someone how her holiday was.
(d) Say that England (**Yīnggélán**) is bigger than Ireland (**Ài'ěrlán**).
(e) Say that Germany is not as big as France.

Bù gōngpíng *Unfair*

9

QÙ . . . ZĚNME ZŎU?
How do I get to . . . ?

In this unit you will learn:

- how to ask for and understand directions
- how to use public transport
- how to ask people if they have ever done something
- how to express how long something happens for

Kāishǐ yǐqián

You will be able to say all sorts of things about where you are going, where you are coming from and by what means of transport, by the time you have worked your way through this unit. You will also be able to say which order you are going to do things in and whether you have ever done them before.

☑ Shìshi

1 Refer back to **Duìhuà 1** in Unit 8 and answer the following questions in Chinese:

    (*a*) How much was the pullover?
    (*b*) What could Colin have bought for the money instead?

2 (*a*) Somebody asks you whether French goods are more expensive than British ones. What do you reply?
    (*b*) The same person compliments you on your spoken Chinese. What is your response?

Zhǔyào cíhuì

Àomén	Macao
biān	side
-xībiānr	west side
chēzhàn	bus/train stop or station
chuán	ship, boat
cóng	from
dǎsuàn	to plan
dìfang	place
duìmiàn	opposite
dù jià	to take a holiday
-guo	have ever (*verb suffix*)
hái	still
háishi	would be better
huàn (chē)	to change (*bus*)
jià	holiday
jiù	*emphatic*
x lù (chē)	the number x bus
mǎlù	road
méi shénme	it's nothing, don't mention it
nàr	there
qián	front, ahead
tiān	day
Tiāntán	Temple of Heaven
tīngshuō	I heard, I am told
tuìxiū	to retire
wǎng	in the direction of
wǎng nán kāi de chē	southbound bus
xià chē	to get off the bus
Xiānggǎng	Hong Kong
xiànmu	to envy
xíng	OK
yǐhòu	after
yòng	to need, to use
zěnme	how
zhōumo	weekend
cóng A dào B	from A to B
. . . jiù dào le.	It takes only . . . to get there.
Qù X zěnme zǒu?	How do (I) get to X?
xiān . . . zài . . .	first. . . then. . .

Xuéxí jìqiǎo

1   **z** is pronounced like the **-ds** in *adds* or the **z** in *zoo*.

2   **c** is not at all like the **c** in English so be very careful with it. It is pronounced like the **-ts** in **its**. It is useful to practise it

together with **z** and to say them one after the other so that you can hear the difference clearly. Remember the top of your sheet of A4 (see Unit 6, ➡️ 68) should be blown away from you when you say **c** but not when you say **z**.

Duìhuà

📼 *Duìhuà 1*

Xiǎo Féng and Lǎo Qiáo are talking about taking their holidays. Where is Xiǎo Féng going and how will she get to those places? What about Lǎo Qiáo? How long is his holiday?

Qiáo Tīngshuō nǐ kuài yào qù dù jià le.
Féng Duì. Wǒ yǒu sān ge xīngqī de jià, cóng liùyuè èrshíqī hào dào qīyuè shíbā hào.
Qiáo Nǐ dǎsuàn qù nǎr?
Féng Xiānggǎng hé Àomén. Zhè liǎng ge dìfang wǒ dōu méi qù-guo.
Qiáo Nǐ zěnme qù?
Féng Wǒ xiān zuò fēijī dào Xiānggǎng, zài nàr zhù wǔ tiān. Zài cóng Xiānggǎng zuò chuán dào Àomén.
Qiáo Wǒ zhēn xiànmu nǐ.
Féng Nǐ shénme shíhou dù jià?
Qiáo Wǒ? O, shí'èryuè.
Féng Duō cháng shíjiān?
Qiáo Bù zhīdao.
Féng Zěnme huì bù zhīdao?
Qiáo Jīnnián shí'èryuè wǒ jiù yào tuìxiū le.
Féng Wǒ zhēn xiànmu nǐ.

As China is situated in the East, the most important cardinal point is east rather than north. In the West we say *north, south, east, west* but the Chinese start with **dōng** (*east*) and say **dōng、nán** (*south*), **xī、** (*west*), **běi** (*north*).

South-west in Chinese is **xīnán** (west, south), *north-east* is **dōng běi** (*lit.* east, north) and so on.

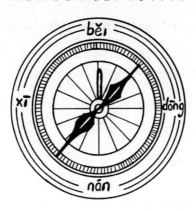

🔲 *Duìhuà 2*

Ann is touring in Beijing. Today she is going to visit Tiantan. Can you follow the directions given to her by a passer-by?

公共汽车站 🚌

Gōnggòng Qìchēzhàn *Bus stop*

Ann　　　　Qǐng wèn, qù Tiāntán zěnme zǒu?

Passer-by　Tiāntán zài xīnán biānr. Zuò chē sì zhàn jiù dào le.

Ann　　　　Zuò jǐ lù chē?

Passer-by　Nǐ xiān cóng zhèr wǎng dōng zǒu, zài zuò wǎng nán kāi de chē, shíwǔ lù、èrshísān lù dōu xíng. Chēzhàn zài yínháng duìmiànr.

Ann　　　　Yòng huàn chē ma?

Passer-by　Bú yòng. Xià chē yǐhòu wǎng qián zǒu yìdiǎnr. Tiāntán jiù zài mǎlù xībianr.

Ann　　　　Xièxie nín.

Passer-by　Méi shénme.

— Cultural tip —

When giving you directions, the Chinese (especially in the north) usually use the points of the compass rather than left and right. So it's good to know where north and south are when you ask somebody the way!

Duìhuà 3

James is suggesting something adventurous to his friend, Huáng Zìlì. What is his suggestion and does Huáng accept it?

James Nǐ qù-guo Tiānjīn ma?

Huáng Méi qù-guo.

James Xià ge zhōumo zánmen yìqǐ qù ba.

Huáng Hǎo'a. Nǐ dǎsuàn zěnme qù? Zuò qìchē háishi zuò huǒchē?

James Zánmen qí chē qù zēnmeyàng?

Huáng Shénme? Nǐ fā fēng le! Qí chē qù Tiānjīn yào liǎng、sān tiān, yòu lèi yòu wēixiǎn.

James Wǒ bú pà lèi, yě xǐhuan màoxiǎn!

Huáng Fǎnzheng wǒ bù gēn nǐ yìqǐ qù. Wǒ zài jiā kàn diànshì, yòu shūfu yòu ānquán.

ānquán	safe
diànshì	TV
fā fēng	mad
fǎnzheng	no way, in any case
gēn	with
jiā	home
lèi	tired, tiring
màoxiǎn	adventurous, to take the risk
pà	afraid
qí	to ride (*bicycle, motorbike, horse*)
qìchē	vehicle, bus, car
shūfu	comfortable
wēixiǎn	dangerous
xià ge	next
yào . . .	it takes . . .
yìqǐ	together
yòu . . . yòu . . .	both . . . and . . .
zìxíngchē	bicycle

Jiěshì

1 About to?

To say something is about to happen or is going to happen soon use:

yào (*want, will*) + verb . . . **le**

Nǐ **yào** qù dù jià **le**.	*You're going on holiday soon.*
Wǒ **yào** qù Xiānggǎng **le**.	*I'm about to leave for Hong Kong.*

Kuài (*quick*) or **jiù** (*then*) can also be put in front of **yào** to make the imminence of the action even clearer:

Jīnnián shí'èr yuè wǒ **jiù** **yào** tuìxiū **le**.	*I'll be retiring in December.*
Tā **kuài** yào kàn diànshì **le**.	*He's about to watch TV.*

2 From . . . to . . .

Simply use **cóng** (*from*) and **dào** (*to*).

cóng Xiānggǎng **dào** Àomén	*from Hong Kong to Macao*
cóng Běijīng **dào** Tiānjīn	*from Beijing to Tianjin*

And from one time to another:

cóng sānyuè shíbā hào **dào** sìyuè jiǔ hào	*from 18 March to 9 April*

There are only two small points to remember.

● The word-order cannot be reversed in Chinese. You cannot say *I am going to* (**dào**) *China from* (**cóng**) *Japan*. So **cóng** must always precede **dào**.

● In the sentence, *I am going to* (**dào**) *Macao from* (**cóng**) *Hong Kong by* (**zuò**) *boat*, 'from Hong Kong' must come first followed by the means of transport 'by boat' and then 'to Macao' last:

Wǒ **cóng** Xiānggǎng **zuò** chuán **dào** Àomén.

The Chinese are very logical – you cannot get to Macao unless you 'sit on the boat' **zuò chuán** first so that should come before 'to Macao' **dào Àomén**.

3 Have you ever ... ?

If you put the little word **guo** after the verb it will emphasise a past experience:

Wǒ qù-**guo** Yìdàlì.   *I've been to Italy* (at sometime or other).

Tā chī-**guo** Yìndù fàn.   *He has eaten Indian food* (at sometime in the past).

You make the negative by putting **méi yǒu** in front of the verb:

Wǒ **méi** (yǒu) qù-**guo** Zhōngguó.   *I have never been to China.*

You make the question by putting **ma** or **méi you** at the end of the statement:

Nǐ qù-**guo** Tiānjīn **ma**?   *Have you (ever) been to Tianjin?*
Nǐ zuò-**guo** fēijī **méi you**?   *Have you (ever) travelled by plane?*
Hái **méi yǒu** (qù-guo).   *Not yet.*
Méi zuò-guo.   *No, never.*

Note the two possible ways of answering a question with – **guo**.

4 First ... then ...

By using **xiān** (*first*) + verb followed by **zài** (*then*) + verb you show that the two actions are linked:

Wǒ **xiān** zuò fēijī dào Xiānggǎng, **zài** zuò huǒchē qù Běijīng.   *First I'll go Hong Kong by plane then I'll go by train to Beijing.*

Nǐ **xiān** cóng zhèr wǎng dōng zǒu, **zài** zuò wǎng nán kāi de chē.   *You walk eastwards from here first. Then you get on a bus going south* (*lit.* then sit towards south drive on bus).

The **xiān** + verb and the **zài** + verb may occur in two separate sentences but the idea of sequence of actions is still there:

(Wǒ) **xiān** zuò fēijī dào Xiānggǎng ... **Zài** cóng Xiānggǎng zuò chuán dào Àomén.   *First I'll go to Hong Kong by plane ... Then from Hong Kong I'll go to Macao by boat.*

By the way, this **zài** is written like the **zài** in **zàijiàn** not as in **zài** (*at, in*).

5 How long?

As you saw in Unit 1, time-words like *today, Wednesday, 6 o'clock* come before the verb in Chinese. However when you want to say how long you do the action of the verb the time-word comes after the verb:

Wǒ zài nàr zhù **wǔ tiān**.	*I'll stay there* five days.
Tā zài zhèr gōngzuò le **liǎng nián**.	*She worked here for* two years.

The **le** after the verb shows that the action of the verb has been completed.

6 Huì

You met **huì** (*can*) in Unit 6 ➡️ 74 with the meaning *to know how to do something* (having learnt to do it). Its other meaning is *to be likely to* or *to be possible*:

Tā xiàwǔ **huì** lái.	*He'll (is likely to) come in the afternoon.*
Zěnme **huì** bù zhīdao?	*How could (you) not know? (lit. how possible not know?)*

7 Both . . . and . . .

To express *both . . . and . . .* you put **yòu** in front of the two adjectives or verbs:

yòu lèi **yòu** wēixiǎn	*both tiring and dangerous*
yòu shūfu **yòu** ānquán	*both comfortable and safe*
yòu hǎo **yòu** bú guì	*both good and inexpensive*

8 R or not?

You will find **r** added to some words in this unit in order for you to get used to seeing and reading it. It is used a great deal by people in the north of China especially around Beijing. You certainly don't have to use it but it is important to know that it exists. It is to be found on the ends of words such as:

(yì) diǎn	(yì) diǎnr	*a little bit*
yì wǎn	yì wǎnr	*one bowl*
tiān	tiānr	*day*
duìmiàn	duìmiànr	*opposite*
biān	biānr	*side*
xībian	xībianr	*west side*
wán (verb)	wánr	*to enjoy oneself*

❊ *Xuéxí jìqiǎo*

Learn from your mistakes and keep trying

1 Everyone makes mistakes when learning a language. If you didn't make mistakes you wouldn't have to learn it! Small children also make mistakes when learning their own language so accept that this is perfectly normal and natural.

2 Some mistakes affect the meaning of what you say more than others. For instance, it is important not to confuse **mǎi** (3rd tone) (*to buy*) with **mài** (4th tone) (*to sell*) for obvious reasons. But surprisingly enough, poor tones don't seem to affect the ability of most Chinese people to understand what you are saying. There is also a wide variety of pronunciation across the whole of China because it is so vast.

So concentrate on getting your message across rather than on not making any mistakes. Learning to speak a foreign language is one case where quantity (as long as it is comprehensible) is better than quality! That is the way you will learn.

Nevertheless when a standard speaker of Chinese corrects your Chinese make a mental note of it and at the first opportunity write it down, learn it and try to use it.

3 It is good to deliberately try out new constructions and vocabulary. Practise them beforehand so that you won't be too hesitant the first time you try something. If it doesn't work as well as you'd hoped, look at them again and have another go. It's like learning to ride a bicycle. When you fall off you have to get on again straight away so that you don't lose confidence.

Cultural tip

It is still very difficult to buy return tickets in China especially for trains and long-distance buses. Normally you have to think when you are going to leave a place as soon as you have arrived in it and organise your return (or ongoing) ticket accordingly. China's large population makes queuing inevitable unless you book your ticket through an agency (hotel, China Travel Service and so on) which requires plenty of notice and a commission charge.

 Liànxí

1 Answer the following *Have you ever . . . ?* questions:
   Example: Nǐ qù-guo Zhōngguó ma? **Qù-guo** or **Méi qù-guo.**

   (*a*) Nǐ qù-guo Rìběn ma?   [ever been to Japan?]
   (*b*) Nǐ zuò-guo fēijī ma?   [ever travelled by plane?]
   (*c*) Nǐ kàn-guo Déguó   [ever seen German films?]
        diànyǐng ma?
   (*d*) Nǐ chī-guo Zhōngguó   [ever had Chinese food?]
        fàn ma?
   (*e*) Nǐ hē-guo Měiguó   [ever drunk American wine?]
        pútáojiǔ ma?

 2 Listen to the cassette (or read the following passage) and draw the way to the cinema (**diànyǐngyuàn**) on the plan below. Which letter represents the cinema?

Xiān wǎng nán zǒu. Dào Dōnghǎi Lù zuò wǎng dōng kāi de chē. Zuò liǎng zhàn. Diànyǐngyuàn jiù zài Dōnghǎi Lù de nánbiānr, shāngdiàn de duìmiànr.

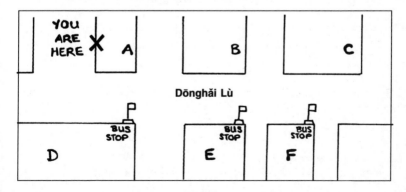

3 You are now in the cinema. You have just seen a film. Can you say in Chinese how you get back to the hotel you are staying in (A)?

4 Read the directions below which tell you where various places are situated. Then go back to the sketch and identify the buildings represented by the letters (B), (C), (D) and (E).

    (*a*) **Zhōngguó Yínháng** zài diànyǐngyuàn de xībianr.

    (*b*) **Shāngdiàn** zài diànyǐngyuàn de duìmiàn.

    (*c*) **Dōnghǎi Gōngyuán** zài Zhōngguó Yínháng de xībian.

    (*d*) **Xuéxiào** (*school*) zài Zhōngguó Yínháng de běibian, Fàndiàn de dōngbianr.

5 Answer the following questions using **(cóng) . . . dào . . . .** If you don't know, say **Wǒ bù zhīdao.** (But you could find out.)
    Example: When is Mr Wang's next holiday?
               (Cóng) wǔyuè sānshí hào **dào** liùyuè bā hào.

    (*a*) When is **your** next holiday?

    (*b*) What are the opening hours of **your** local (or school) library during the weekdays and weekends?

    (*c*) Which days of the week do **you** work? (e.g. from Monday to Friday)

    (*d*) What are **your** working hours during the week?

6 How do you get there?
Choose an appropriate means of transport from the list below to make complete sentences in Chinese according to the information given in (a)–(e). Take care with the word-order!

zuò gōnggòng qìchē	by bus
zuò huǒchē	by train
zuò dìtiě	by underground
zuò fēijī	by plane
zuò chuán	by ship
qí (zìxíng)chē	to cycle
kāi chē	to drive
zǒu lù	to walk

    Example: to go to work (qù shàng bān)
               Wǒ **qí zìxíngchē** qù shàng bān.

    (*a*) to go to work   [qù shàng bān]

    (*b*) to go to school   [qù xuéxiào]

(c) to do shopping   [qù mǎi dōngxi]
(d) to go to see a film (at your   [qù kàn diànyǐng]
      local cinema)
(e) to go to X train station   [qù X huǒchē zhàn]

7 In the box below you will find some useful words to describe
   things. Which pair would you use to describe the following
   things? Try to use **yòu . . . yòu . . . .**
   Example: Zuò fēijī **yòu** guì **yòu** bù shūfu.
              Zuò fēijī **yòu** kuài **yòu** shūfu.

guì	expensive	**bú guì**	not expensive
piányi	cheap	**bù piányi**	not cheap
fāngbiàn	convenient	**máfan**	troublesome
kuài	fast	**màn**	slow
wēixiǎn	dangerous	**ānquán**	safe

(a) Cóng Rìběn zuò chuán dào Zhōngguó
(b) Zài Lúndūn/Bālí (*Paris*) qí zìxíngchē
(c) Zuò gōnggòng qìchē qù shàng bān
(d) Cóng Yīngguó zuò fēijī dào Měiguó
(e) Kāi chē qù mǎi dōngxi

8 Listen to the cassette and answer the following questions about
   Mr White's holiday.

   See first if you can answer the questions in Chinese. If you find
   them too difficult, read the questions in English below and
   answer them either in English or in Chinese.

   If you haven't got a cassette, read the passage after the questions and then answer the questions. If you need to refer to it,
   the script is in the *Key to the exercises*.

(a) Bái xiānsheng dǎsuàn qù shénme dìfang?
(b) Tā zài Bālí zhù jǐ tiān?
(c) Tā gēn shéi yìqǐ qù Yìdàlì? Tāmen zěnme qù Yìdàlì?
(d) Bái xiānsheng dǎsuàn zài Yìdàlì zhù jǐ tiān?
(e) Tā zěnme huí Yīngguó?
(f) Tā péngyou zěnme huí Fǎguó?

(a) *Where did Mr White plan to go?*
(b) *How long does he plan to stay in Paris?*
(c) *Who will he go to Italy with? How will they travel to Italy?*
(d) *How long does Mr White plan to stay in Italy?*

(e) *How will he get back to the UK?*
(f) *How will his friend get back to France?*

Bái xiānsheng de jiàqī

Bái xiānsheng yào qù dù jià le. Tā yào qù liǎng ge dìfang. Tā xiān cóng Lúndūn zuò huǒchē dào Bālí. Tā dǎsuàn zài Bālí zhù sì tiān. Ránhòu tā gēn tāde Fǎguó péngyou kāi chē qù Yìdàlì. Tāmen dǎsuàn zài Yìdàlì zhù yí ge xīngqī. Zuìhòu tā cóng Yìdàlì zuò fēijī huí Lúndūn. Tāde péngyou kāi chē huí Fǎguó.

 ## Xiǎo cèyàn

(a) Ask how to get to the Bank of China (**Zhōngguó Yínháng**).
(b) Tell the Chinese who has asked you the way to take the number 10 bus.
(c) Then tell her that it will be five stops (before she gets there).
(d) Say that your friend has never been to China.
(e) Say it's going to rain soon.

Jìnzhǐ xī yān

10

NÍN XIǍNG CHĪ SHÉNME?
What would you like to eat?

In this unit you will learn:

- how to order a meal and drinks
- how to pay the bill
- how to say you have given up something (such as smoking)
- more about verb endings

Kāishǐ yǐqián

By the end of this unit you will be able to get yourself various things to eat and drink and even to question the bill! There's lots of very useful vocabulary so take your time.

✅ Shìshi

1 You need to tell a Chinese friend your itinerary once you have left the UK so she can book your hotel in Beijing and arrange your programme.

    (a) Tell her that you are going by air to Hong Kong first and staying there two days.

    (b) Then you are going from Hong Kong to Shanghai by train.

    (c) You plan to travel by air to Beijing on the morning of 10th August.

2 The same friend asks if you have ever been to Shanghai before. What does she say to you?

Zhǔyào cíhuì

àiren	husband/wife (*used in the People's Republic*)
bēi	a cup of
bié	don't
bīngqílín	ice-cream
cài	dish
càidān	menu
Chángchéng	the Great Wall
chī	to eat
chī-wán/chī-bǎo/chī-hǎo le	to have finished eating/be full/satisfied
chī sù	to be vegetarian (*lit.* eat non-meat food)
chōu (yān)	to smoke (*a cigarette*)
dòufu	beancurd
duì	to, for
duō	more; many
gēn wǒ lái	follow me
hǎochī	delicious, tasty
hē	to drink
jiè (yān)	to give up (smoking)
jié zhàng	to ask for the bill
júzizhī	orange juice
là (de)	hot, spicy (food)
lái	I'll have (*colloquial*)
jiǔ lái le	here comes the wine
mápó dòufu	spicy beancurd/tofu
pàng	fat
pútáojiǔ	wine
qīngcài	vegetables
ràng	to let, allow
rè	hot
ròu	meat
shǎo	less; few
shēntǐ	health
shōu	to accept, to receive
tāng	soup
-suānlà tāng	hot and sour soup
tiānqi	weather
xiànjīn	cash
xìnyòng kǎ	credit card
yú	fish
yùdìng	to book (*a room*)
zhī	(*measure word for cigarettes*)
zhǐ	only
zhīpiào	cheque / check
Nǐmen chī/hē diǎnr shénme?	What would you like to eat/drink?

❋ Xuéxí jìqiǎo

1 Practise the difference between **-uo** and **-ou** as in **duō** (*much/ many*) and **dōu** (*both/all*).

2 Practise the difference between **-an** and **-ang** as in **fàn** (*food*) and **fàng** (*to put*) and between **-en**, **-eng** as in **fēn** (*minute/ smallest unit of Chinese currency*) and **fēng** (*wind*).

3 Now go back and revise all the vowels with a nasal sound in the Pronunciation Guide, ➡️ 9. Listen to the cassette if you have it.

Hold your nose gently as you practise these sounds. You should be able to feel the vibration in it when you say **-ang**, **-eng**, **-iang**, **-ing**, **-iong**, **-ong** and **-uang**. This is particularly obvious when you say the sound in the 1st tone and hang on to it.

Duìhuà

Sìchuān Cāntīng
Sichuan Restaurant

📼 Duìhuà 1

Mr Brown and his friend Yúqiáo are going to have a Chinese meal. What drinks and food have they ordered?

Waitress Nǐmen yùdìng le ma?
Brown Yùdìng le. Wǒ jiào John Brown.
Waitress Wǒ kànyikàn. . . . Mr Brown, qī diǎn bàn, liǎng ge rén.
Brown Duì, duì.
Waitress Hǎo, qǐng gēn wǒ lái.

Waitress Zhè shì càidān. Nǐmen xiān hē diǎnr shénme?
Yúqiáo Wǒ yào yì bēi júzizhī.
Brown Nǐmen yǒu shénme pútáojiǔ?
Waitress Wǒmen yǒu Chángchéng bái pútáojiǔ hé Zhōngguó hóng pútáojiǔ.
Brown Lái yì bēi bái pútáojiǔ ba.

Waitress	Jiǔ lái le. Nǐmen yào shénme cài?
Yúqiáo	Wǒ bù chī ròu.
Brown	Nǐ chī bu chī yú?
Yúqiáo	Bù chī. Wǒ zhǐ yào qīngcài hé dòufu.
Brown	Shénme? Nǐ xiànzài chī sù le.
Yúqiáo	Shì'a. Wǒ yǐjīng hěn pàng le.
Waitress	Nǐmen xǐhuan chī là de ma?
Yùqiáo	Xǐhuan. Kěshì bié tài là le.
Waitress	Lái yí ge mápó dòufu ba.
Brown	Hǎo'a. Xiān lái liǎng ge suānlà tāng.
Yúqiáo	Jīntiān tiānqi yǐjīng hěn rè le. Wǒmen yīnggāi shǎo chī là de.
Waitress	Méi guānxi. Chī-wán fàn yǐhòu, nǐmen duō chī diǎnr bīngqílín. Wǒmen de bīngqílín fēicháng hǎochī.

Cultural tip

The custom when eating Chinese food is that all the dishes are put in the middle of the table and shared. The host helps her/his guest to the best titbits. Too bad if you don't share his/her taste! The soup is always eaten last in China except for some areas in the south.

Duìhuà 2

Mr Brown and Yúqiáo are chatting over the meal. Listen to or read their conversation and find out why Yúqiáo has given up smoking and Mr Brown hasn't.

Brown	Chōu zhī yān ba.
Yúqiáo	Wǒ bù chōu yān le.
Brown	Wèishénme?
Yúqiáo	Wǒ àiren bú ràng wǒ chōu le. Tā shuō chōu yān duì wǒde shēntǐ bù hǎo, duì tāde shēntǐ yě bù hǎo.
Brown	Wǒ yě bù xiǎng chōu le. Kěshì wǒ yǒu yí ge péngyou, jiè yān yǐqián bú pàng, jiè yān yǐhòu jiù pàng le. Wǒ pà pàng.
Yúqiáo	Wǒ yě pà pàng, kěshì jīntiān de cài tài hǎochī le.
Brown	Nǐ chī-bǎo le ma?
Yúqiáo	Chī-bǎo le.
Brown	Wǒmen jié zhàng ba. Fúwùyuán, qǐng jié zhàng.
Waitress	Nǐmen chī-hǎo le ma?

Yúqiáo   Chī-hǎo le, xièxie.
Brown   Nǐmen shōu bu shōu xìnyòng kǎ hé zhīpiào?
Waitress   Duìbuqǐ, wǒmen zhǐ shōu xiànjīn.

Duìhuà 3

Ann and Xiǎo Fāng have arrived at the street market (see **Duìhuà 3**, Unit 7). What are they going to do next? Are they going to get a bargain this time?

Ann   Wǒ è le. Wǒmen **suíbiàn** chī diǎnr ba.
Fāng   Nàr yǒu ge xiǎo **tānzi**. Tāmen de **chǎomiàn** hǎochī-**jíle**.
(At the food stall)
Ann   *(whispering)* Wǒ kàn zhèr bú tài **gānjìng**.
Fāng   Méi guānxi, tāmen huì gěi wǒmen **wèishēng kuàizi**.
Fāng   Qǐng lái liǎng **wǎnr** chǎomiàn、liǎng **tīng kěkǒukělè**.

* * *

Waiter   Qǐng xiān **fù qián**. Liǎng wǎnr chǎomiàn shí'èr kuài, liǎng tīng kěkǒukělè shísì kuài, **yígòng** èrshíliù kuài.
Fāng   Shénme? Nǐ **suàn-cuò** le ba. **Shàng cì** chǎomiàn wǔ kuài yì wǎnr.
Waiter   Méi suàn-cuò. Shàng cì shì shàng cì, xiànzài yì wǎnr liù kuài le.

è	hungry
chǎomiàn	fried noodles
fù qián	to pay (*money*)
gānjìng	clean
-jíle	(*suffix*) extremely
kěkǒukělè	cocacola
kuàizi	chopsticks
shàng cì	last time
suàn-cuò le	to have calculated wrongly
suíbiàn	casually
tānzi	stall
tīng	*measure word for cans (of drink)*
wǎn(r)	bowl
wèishēng	hygiene, hygienic
yígòng	altogether

Cultural tip

When eating from street stalls or fast-food outlets make sure you ask for **wèishēng kuàizi** (*hygienic*, i.e. disposable, *chopsticks*) which should, of course, come wrapped. You have to break them apart which shows you that they are still unused. Or carry your own with you, plus tissues to wipe your bowl or plate.

 ——————————— **Jiěshì** ———————————

1 Already & le

Remember using **le** in Unit 4 to show that something has happened or has already taken place? When **yǐjīng** (*already*) appears in front of a verb it reinforces this idea of something having happened so you will find **le** at the end of such sentences:

Wǒ **yǐjīng** hěn pàng **le**.	*I'm already very fat.*
Jīntiān **yǐjīng** hěn rè **le**.	*It's already very hot today.*

2 More before the verb!

To say *eat more*, put the little word **duō** (*much/many*) in front of the verb *to eat*:

duō chī   *eat more*

This works with all full verbs – i.e. verbs that cannot also act as adjectives such as **hǎo** (*good*), **pàng** (*fat*) and so on.

duō hē	*drink more*
duō yào	*want more*
duō gěi	*give more*

You do exactly the same thing if you want to say *eat less*, *drink less*, and so on but you put **shǎo** (*less/few*) in front of the verb instead of **duō**:

shǎo chī	*eat less*
shǎo hē	*drink less*
shǎo yào	*want less*
shǎo gěi	*give less*

3 Not any more!

To say that you don't do something any more use:

bù verb (+ object) **le**

Wǒ **bù** chōu yān **le**.

I don't smoke any more/ I've given up smoking.

Wǒ tàitai **bù** ràng wǒ chōu **le**.

My wife doesn't let me smoke any more.

Tā **bù** hē jiǔ **le**.

She's given up drinking.

Tāmen **bù** niánqīng **le**.

They're no longer young.

If the verb is **yǒu** (*to have*) you have to use **méi** instead of **bù**:

You   Nǐ yǒu **mei** yǒu hóng chènshān? (*Do you have a red shirt?*)

Shop assistant **Méi** yǒu **le**, mài-wán le. *We're out of stock. They're sold out.* (*lit.* not have any more, sell finish le).

4 Smoking is not good for your health!

As you know, **duì** means *right, correct*. In certain contexts it also means *to* or *for*. Learn the following useful phrases:

A **duì** shēntǐ (bù) hǎo.   *A is (not) good* **for** *the health/body.*

Y **duì** X (bù) hǎo.   *Y is (not) good* **to** *X.*

Thus **Chōu yān duì wǒde shēntǐ bù hǎo** means *Smoking is not good for my health*.

5 . . . After!

In English you say **after** *I've been to the restaurant* but in Chinese you say *I've been to the restaurant* **after** – the reverse of the English word order:

Jiè yān **yǐhòu**   *After giving up smoking*

Chī fàn **yǐhòu**   *After eating*

The same happens with **yǐqián** (*before*) and **de shíhou** (*when*). (You will meet **de shíhou** later in Units 12–21):

Jiè yān **yǐqián**   *Before giving up smoking*

Fù qián **yǐqián**   *Before paying*

Jié zhàng **de shíhou**   *When working out the bill*

6 To eat your fill

To say that you *have eaten your fill* in Chinese you put **bǎo** (*full*) after the verb **chī** (*to eat*):

Wǒ chī-**bǎo** le.   *I'm full (lit. I eat full le).*

The **le** after the verb shows completed action. (See Unit 9, ➡️🅿️ 113).

Other little words, or endings, which appear after the verb in this way have other meanings:

Nǐmen chī-**hǎo** le ma?	*Have you finished eating* (to your satisfaction)?
Chī-**hǎo** le.	*Yes, we have* (finished eating to our satisfaction).
Nǐ suàn-**cuò** le ba.	*You must have got it wrong* (*lit.* you calculate wrong le, haven't you).
Méi suàn-**cuò**.	*No, I haven't* (*lit.* not have calculate wrong).
Nǐmen hē-**wán** le ma?	*Have you finished your drinks* (*lit.* you drink finish le ma)?
Wǒmen hē-**wán** le.	Yes, we have (*lit.* we drink finish le).
Nǐ kàn-**jiàn** tā le ma?	*Did you see him* (*lit.* you look perceive him le ma)?
Wǒ méi kàn-**jiàn** ta.	*I didn't see him* (*lit.* I not have look perceive him).

If you put **bù** between the verb and **one** of these endings as in the examples below you have the meaning of **cannot + verb + ending**:

Wǒ kàn-**bu**-jiàn.	*I can't see.*
Tā tīng-**bu**-dǒng.	*She can't understand.*
	(*lit.* she listen cannot understand).
Wǒmen hē-**bu**-wán.	*We can't finish* (our drinks).

If on the other hand you put **de** (yes, **de** again!) between the verb and one of these endings you have the meaning of **can + verb + ending**:

Wǒ kàn-**de**-jiàn.	*I can see.*
Tāmen tīng-**de**-dǒng.	*They can understand.*
	(*lit.* they listen can understand.)
Wǒmen hē-**de**-wán.	*We can drink up.*

This is the same **de** as the one used in Unit 8, ➡️🅿️ 98.

7 Tins, bowls and bottles

You should be familiar with measure words by now but did you spot
the ones for *bottle, bowl* and *tin* in this Unit?

yì **píng** Fǎguó jiǔ   *a bottle of French wine*
liǎng **wǎn(r)** chǎomiàn   *two bowls of fried noodles*
liǎng **tīng** kěkǒukělè   *two tins of Coke*

8 Don't . . . !

To tell somebody not to do something, all you have to do is put the
word **bié** (*don't*) in front of what you don't want them to do:

Bié shuō huà.   *Don't speak.*
Bié zǒu.   *Don't go.*

Adding **le** at the end of such sentences helps to soften the idea of
giving an order or command.

✳ *Xuéxí jìqiǎo*

Do you feel comfortable with the grammar?

Having now got to the half-way mark in the book it is probably a
good idea to see how well you're doing with grammar and how to
revise and consolidate what you know.

1   Units 1 to 10 contain all the grammar you will need to know to
    study Units 12 to 21 so it is important that you feel comfortable
    with it before proceeding. Go back to the **Liànxí** of Units 1 to
    10 and pick out one or two exercises from each unit and do
    them again. If you find any particular exercise difficult, revise
    the relevant **Jiěshì** carefully and try the exercise again.

2   By the time you have completed **1** you should be feeling more
    confident. When you go on to study Units 12 to 21 look at the
    structures in the **Duìhuà** and fit them into the pattens you have
    already learnt. You might like to jot these down so that you
    have a list of examples under each structure. You will find this
    helps the consolidation process.

Liànxí

1   Listen to the dialogue and tick on the menu what Mr Jones has
    ordered for his meal. You will need to know the word for *beer*
    which is **píjiǔ** in Chinese.

Fúwùyuán	Nín xiǎng chī diǎnr shénme?
Jones	Wǒ xǐhuan chī là de.
Fúwùyuán	Wǒmen yǒu yúxiāng ròusī hé mápó dòufu.
Jones	Wǒ yào yí ge yúxiāng ròusī ba.
Fúwùyuán	Nín yào tāng ma?
Jones	Nǐmen yǒu shénme tāng?
Fúwùyuán	Suānlà tāng hé zhàcài tāng.
Jones	Lái yí ge suānlà tāng ba.
Fúwùyuán	Yào jiǔ ma?
Jones	Yào yì píng píjiǔ.
Fúwùyuán	Wǔxīng píjiǔ háishi Qīngdǎo píjiǔ?
Jones	Lái yì píng Wǔxīng píjiǔ.
Fúwùyuán	Hǎo de.

càidān
mápó dòufu
yúxiāng ròusī
....
....
suānlà tāng
zhàcài tāng
....
....
Wǔxīng píjiǔ
Qīngdǎo píjiǔ

2 How many? Put the correct number and measure word under each of the items in the pictures below. You may not be able to use all of these measure words: **píng, gè, bēi, zhāng, wǎn, jiàn, tīng, zhī.**

Example: yì **běn** shū (*a book*)

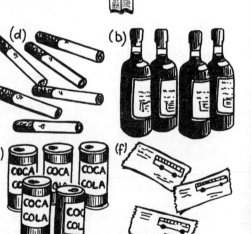

(a) (d) (b)

(e) (c) (f)

3 Have things changed?
If something has changed, you use **. . . le**.
If it has not changed, you say **méi yǒu**, or **gēn yǐqián yíyàng**
(*the same as before*).

    Example: Dōngxi guì **le** ma?
              Guì **le** (yìdiǎnr).
              Méi yǒu or **Gēn yǐqián yíyàng.**

(*a*) Dōngxi guì le ma?   (compared with five years ago)
(*b*) Nǐ pàng le ma?   (compared with five years ago)
(*c*) Tiānqi lěng le ma?   (compared with a month ago)
(*d*) Nǐ zhǎng (*to grow*)   (compared with five years ago)
      gāo le ma?

4 The following dialogue is between you and a waitress. Complete
your part.

(*a*) **You**   (*Waiter! The bill please.*)
      Fúwùyuán Nǐmen chī-hǎo le ma?
(*b*) **You**   (*Yes. Thank you.*)
      Fúwùyuán Yígòng sānbǎi kuài.
(*c*) **You**   (*I think you've got it wrong.*)
      Fúwùyuán Wǒ zài kànkan (*let me look at it again*). Duìbuqǐ.
                 Wǒ suàn-cuò le.
(*d*) **You**   (*That's all right.*)

5 Which is correct, **méi** or **bù**, in the following sentences?

(*a*) Tā yǐqián chōu yān, xiànzài **méi/bù** chōu yān le.
(*b*) Wǒ liùyuè qù dù jià le, xiànzài **méi/bù** yǒu jià le.
(*c*) Yǐqián wǒ yǒu yì tiáo gǒu (*dog*), xiànzài **méi/bù** yǒu le.
(*d*) Tiānqi tài rè le, wǒ **méi/bù** chī là de le.

☑ *Dà cèyàn* (Big test)

1 On the cassette, you will hear different years being said.
    Example: yī-jiǔ-jiǔ-qī nián 1997
Repeat each one and write them down.

2 You have learned two ways of asking *yes* or *no questions*. Can
you try to turn the following statements into questions using
both ways?

Example: Statement – Jīntiān tiānqi hěn hǎo.
              Question 1 – Jīntiān tiānqi hǎo ma?
              Question 2 – Jīntiān tiānqi hǎo bu hǎo?

(*a*) Tāmen shì jiěmèi.
(*b*) Tāde chǎomiàn zhēn hǎochī.
(*c*) Míngtiān tā tàitai qù mǎi dōngxi.
(*d*) Nǐ bú rènshi tā.
(*e*) Xiǎo Lǐ yǒu yì tiáo hóng kùzi.

3   Which of the following statements talk about habitual things
    one does or does not do (call these X), and which state things
    one has done at some point or has never done (call these Y)?

(*a*) Xiǎo Fāng chōu-guo yān.
(*b*) Tā měi tiān chōu yān.
(*c*) Tā méi chī-guo Yìdàlì fàn.
(*d*) Tā bù xǐhuan chī Yìdàlì fàn.

4   Pair up the question words in Chinese with their English equiva-
    lents.

(*a*) shéi		(*i*)	*where*
(*b*) nǎr		(*ii*)	*what*
(*c*) shénme		(*iii*)	*which*
(*d*) zěnme		(*iv*)	*how many*
(*e*) nǎ		(*v*)	*who*
(*f*) jǐ		(*vi*)	*how*

5   Can you answer the following questions about Jane?

(*a*) Tā qù-guo Zhōngguó
      ma?

(*b*) Tā 1985 qù nǎr le?
(*c*) Tā huì shuō Déyǔ ma?
(*d*) Tā qù-guo Fǎguó ma?
(*e*) Tā xiànzài hái chōu yān
      ma?
(*f*) Tā chī-guo Yuènán fàn
      ma?
(*g*) Tā míngnián qù nǎr?

JANE

• *went to USA in 1985*
• *studied German for one
  year in 1990*
• *visited France in 1992*
• *had Vietnamese food for
  the first time in 1993*
• *stopped smoking in 1994*
• *will visit China and Japan
  next year for the first time*

(tíng)
No stopping

Jìnzhǐ tíng chē
No parking (*lit.* forbid stop vehicle)

Good luck with the rest of the book!

11

WǑMEN KÀNKAN HÀNZÌ BA!
Let's look at Chinese characters!

In this unit you will be introduced to the Chinese writing system and learn:

● the structure of Chinese characters
● the rules of writing
● how to write the numbers 1–99
● how to write the days of the week and the date
● how to write the time

─────────── **Kāishǐ yǐqián** ───────────

You will remember from the introduction that this unit is largely independent of the rest of the book, so if you have decided not to get involved with the Chinese script you can miss it out. Alternatively, you can choose to come back to it later when you have finished the other units. Even if you don't do any of the exercises in this unit it would be good if you could still read it, so that at least you have some idea what the Chinese script is all about. This will help your understanding of the Chinese language as a whole and hence of the people who speak it.

The Chinese Writing System

Chinese characters are the symbols used to write the Chinese language. Written Chinese does not use a phonetic alphabet. This means that you cannot guess how a character is pronounced just by looking at it. The Chinese script is very, very old. Its earliest written records date back over 3,500 years. These are the markings on oracle bones (tortoise shells and animal bones) on which the priests used to scratch their questions to the gods. The earliest characters were pictures representing easily recognisable objects, such as the sun, the moon, fire, water, a mountain, a tree, and so on.

火 fire　水 water　山 mountain　雨 rain

Such characters were known as *pictographs*. Some of them are still in use even today.

The next step was for *pictographs* to be combined to form new characters known as *ideographs* because they express an idea:

日 *sun* + 月 *moon*　= 明 *bright*

女 *woman* + 子 *child* = 好 *good*

日 *sun* + 木 *tree*　= 東 *east* (the sun coming up behind a tree)

人 *person* + 木 *tree*　= 休 *to rest* (a person leaning up against a tree)

So far so good! Unfortunately only a limited number of ideas could be expressed in this way so then characters were created which contained a *meaning* element (often known as the *radical*) and a *phonetic* element which was to help with the pronunciation of the character. Of course, pronunciation has changed over the centuries, so that now this phonetic element is only of limited help. Let's look at a few of these *radical-phonetic* or compound characters. You can see how such characters came into being and what they look like today.

fēn *divide; separate* **fěn** *powder*

Both the characters above are pronounced the same, although they have different tones. This is quite normal. The next pair have the same pronunciation and the same tone, but this is unusual.

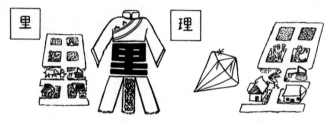

lǐ *village; mile; inside* **lǐ** *polish; reason; principle*

At the opposite end of the spectrum we have the following three characters, which have a common phonetic element 母 **mu**, but are pronounced quite differently. This is the worst scenario!

mǔ *mother* měi *every* hǎi *sea*

The basic rules for writing Chinese characters

As you can imagine, there are some basic rules for writing Chinese characters which you need to master. This is important if you are to remember them, and so the brain needs to operate a kind of orderly filing system. To do this, it needs help. Chinese characters should always be written the same way, so that they become fixed in your imaginary filing system. Most characters are made up of two or more basic structural parts called 'character components', although of course some character components such as 日 **rì** (*sun*) can stand by themselves, as we have mentioned earlier. Although the total number of characters is quite large, the number of character components is limited. These components are written with a number of basic strokes, which are illustrated below:

Stroke	Name	
`	diǎn	*dot*
─	héng	*horizontal*
│	shù	*vertical*
﹨	piě	*left-falling*
╲	nà	*right-falling*
╱	tí	*rising*
﹄ﺍﻝﻝ	gōu	*hook*
﹁﹄	zhé	*turning*

These strokes are basically straight lines and were traditionally written in ink with a hair brush. The main directions are from top to bottom and from left to right. The arrows on the basic strokes below show how the characters are written by indicating the direction each stroke takes:

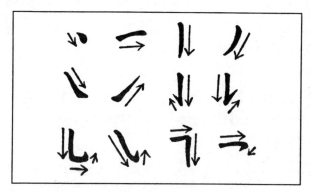

The rules of stroke order in writing Chinese characters and character components are as follows:

Example	Stroke	Order				Rule
十	一				十	First horizontal, then vertical
人	丿				人	First left-falling, then right-falling
三	一	二			三	From top to bottom
州	丶	丿	丬	州 州	州	From left to right
月	丿	刀	月		月	First outside, then inside
四	丨	冂	冈	四	四	Finish inside, then close
小	亅	小			小	Middle, then the two sides

Numbers 1–10

Now let's try writing the numbers 1 to 10. We have shown the direction and sequence of each stroke to help you. It is helpful to think of each character, however simple or complex, as occupying a square of the same size.

Numbers 11–99

11 is	10 + 1	=	十一
12 is	10 + 2	=	十二
20 is	2 × 10	=	二十
30 is	3 × 10	=	三十
65 is	6 × 10 + 5	=	六十五
99 is	9 × 10 + 9	=	九十九

Liànxí

1 What numbers do the following characters represent?

(a) 二   (f) 二十四
(b) 六   (g) 八十三
(c) 十   (h) 六十九
(d) 五   (i) 五十七
(e) 十一   (j) 三十六

2 Write out the following numbers in Chinese characters:
(a) 3 (b) 8 (c) 10 (d) 15 (e) 42 (f) 98 (g) 67

(The answers to all the **Liànxí** are in the *Key to the exercises* at the back of the book.)

Days of the week

All you need to know to write the characters for the days of the week are the two characters **xīng** (*star*) and **qī** (*period*) which, when combined together, form the word for *week*; plus the numbers 1 to 6 and the characters for *sun* (**rì**) or *day* (**tiān**). **Xīng** is made up of the radical 日 **rì** (*sun*) and 生 **shēng** (*to give birth*):

Qī is made up of the phonetic element 其 **qī** and the radical 月 **yuè** (*moon*).

You have already met 日 **rì** (*sun*).

Tiān (*day*) is also a nice easy character:

tiān

It is actually made up of one horizontal stroke plus the character 大 **dà** (*big*).

Revise the days of the week (see ➡ P. 57) and then do the following exercise:

✔ —————————— **Liànxí** ——————————

3 Which day of the week . . .

  (*a*) do people go to church? 星期 ☐

  (*b*) comes after Tuesday? 星期 ☐

  (*c*) are many football matches played in the UK? 星期 ☐

  (*d*) comes before Friday? 星期 ☐

4 Now fill in the missing characters for the days of the week given below:

  (*a*) Sunday 星期 ☐ or 星期 ☐

  (*b*) Tuesday 星 ☐ 二

  (*c*) Friday 星 ☐ 五

  (*d*) Thursday ☐ 期四

  (*e*) Saturday ☐ 期六

How to write the date

For this you need to revise your numbers (1–31) and the characters for *moon* or *month* (**yuè** 月). Having done that, check up on how to say the date in Chinese (see ▶️🅿️ 61). In formal *written* Chinese **rì** 日 is used instead of **hào** 号. Thus, 21 February is:

二月二十一日   èryuè èrshíyī **rì**

✌️ ——————————— **Liànxí** ———————————

5   Can you recognise the following dates?
    (a) 十一月三日
    (b) 六月十八日
    (c) 七月十一日
    (d) 十月十四日
    (e) 八月二十九日

6   Can you write out the following dates in Chinese characters?
    (a) Christmas Day (25 December)

    (b) International Women's Day (8 March) (see cartoon at the end of this unit)

    (c) Your birthday! (you might not fill all the squares in)

    (d) Your father's birthday

    (e) Your mother's birthday

How to write the years

This is dead easy! Revise what you learnt on ➡️ 61.

1945 is 一九四五 **nián** (*year*)

Nián is written:

年 | ノ | ⸜ | ⸜ | ⸜ | 仁 | 年

 ——————————— **Liànxí** ———————————

7 Write down the years represented by the Chinese characters in the boxes next to each one:

e.g. 一九一四年 ___1914___

(a) 一九一八年 _____

(b) 一九三七年 _____

(c) 一九四九年 _____

(d) 一八八五年 _____

(e) 一六四二年 _____

How to write the time

For this you will need to learn to write the character for *minute* **fēn** 分 and the characters for *o'clock* **diǎn** (**zhōng**). Before you do this, revise how to tell the time on ➡️ 59–60. Now let's look at the two characters **diǎn** and **zhōng**.

点
diǎn

is made up of the radical for fire **huǒ** ⺗ (also written 火) and the phonetic element 占 **zhàn**. Whoops! This one has moved a long way from its original pronunciation. **Diǎn** is written as follows:

丨 | 卜 | 上 | 占 | 占 | 点 | 点 | 点 | 点   **diǎn**

钟
zhōng

is made up of the radical for *metal* **jīn** 钅 (also written 金) and the phonetic element 中 **zhōng**. Whew! This character is pronounced **zhōng** too! **Zhōng** is written as follows:

| 丿 | 𠂉 | 𠂉 | 𠂉 | 钅 | 钅 | 钌 | 钌 | 钟 | **zhōng** |

So   **3.20** is 三点二十分

   5.00 is 五点钟

You will also need to know the characters for *quarter* **kè**, for *half* **bàn**, and for *minus* or *to lack* **chà**.

刻
kè

is made up of the radical for *knife* **dāo** 刂 (also written 刀) and the phonetic element 亥 **hái**: **Kè** is written as follows:

| 丶 | 二 | 亠 | 𠂇 | 亥 | 亥 | 刻 | 刻 | **kè** |

半
bàn

is made up of the vertical line radical 丨 and the phonetic element 八 **bā** (often written 丷 as here), plus two horizontal lines. **Bàn** is written as follows:

| 丶 | 丷 | 丷 | 半 | 半 | **bàn** |

差
chà

is made up of the radical for *sheep* **yáng** 羊 (slanted here) and the phonetic element 工 **gōng**. No help here for pronunciation, unfortunately. **Chà** is written as follows:

| 丶 | 丷 | 丷 | 丷 | 兰 | 羊 | 差 | 差 | 差 | **chà** |

Liànxí

8 What time is it?
  (*a*) 九点一刻 9.15 (*d*) 差十分四点
  (*b*) 十二点二十五分 (*e*) 八点差一刻
  (*c*) 六点半

Can you write out the following times in Chinese characters? (One square represents one Chinese character, but there are alternatives.)

(*a*) 6.20

(*b*) 11.45

(*c*) 10.10

(*d*) 4.48

(*e*) 7.30

Congratulations! If you have got this far you obviously have an aptitude for writing and recognising Chinese characters. You will be able to build on your knowledge in the second half of the book. Hopefully some of the signs in the first half of the book will also make a bit more sense to you.

The different style of writing Chinese characters is an art form known as calligraphy, which is highly valued by the Chinese. You have just had a little taste of it!

International Women's Day (8th March) and the day after...

12

ZÀI LǙGUǍN
At the hotel

In this unit you will learn:

- how to check into a hotel
- how to say if something is wrong
- how to make requests
- how to make complaints

fàndiàn *hotel*

Kāishǐ yǐqián fùxí (Revise before you start)

The numbers in brackets refer to the unit in which the item first appears.

- use of possessive **de** (3)
- measure words (4)(7)
- making comparisons (6)(7)
- room numbers (3)
- new situation **le** (5)
- verb endings (10)
- helping verbs (6)
- How long (9)
- When ... (10)
- **tài ... le** (7)
- not any more (10)
- to do something for somebody (6)
- to be in the middle of doing something (6)

长城饭店	和平宾馆	东风旅馆
CHÁNGCHÉNG FÀNDIÀN	**HÉPÍNG BĪNGUǍN**	**DŌNGFĒNG LǙGUǍN**

In Chinese, there are several words for something that has just one word in English. Read the following passage and find out what those words are and what they mean. Furthermore, if you go to China as a foreigner can you stay in just any hotel so long as you can afford it?

——— Xuǎnzé Lǚguǎn ———

Hotel zhèi gè cí de Zhōngwén kěyǐ shì **bīnguǎn**、 **fàndiàn**、 **lǚguǎn** hé **lǚdiàn**. Fàndiàn hé bīnguǎn yìbān hěn dà, lǚguǎn hé lǚdiàn yìbān bú dà. **Guǎn** hé **diàn** dōu shì 'house' de yìsi. **Bīn** de yìsi shì 'guest', **lǚ** de yìsi shì 'travel'. **Fàn** shì 'food' de yìsi.

Zài Zhōngguó hěn duō lǚguǎn hé lǚdiàn bú ràng wàiguó-rén zhù. Wèishénme? Yǒu gèzhǒng gèyàng de yuányīn. Yǐqián hěn duō dà fàndiàn、 dà bīnguǎn bú ràng Zhōngguó-rén zhù, xiànzài ràng le. Dà fàndiàn、 bīnguǎn de tiáojiàn bǐ lǚguǎn、 lǚdiàn de tiáojiàn hǎo duōle. Dāngrán tāmen yě bǐ lǚguǎn、 lǚdiàn guì duōle.

cí	word
fàn	food; meal
gèzhǒng gèyàng de	all kinds of
lǚguǎn	hotel
tiáojiàn	condition
wèishénme?	why?
xuǎnzé	to choose
yìbān	usually
yuányīn	reason
zì	(Chinese) character

✅ Liànxí 1

Read the opening passage twice. Then answer the following questions in Chinese. You may need to read the passage a few more times to answer all the questions.

(a) What are some of the Chinese words for *hotel*?
(b) What do they mean?
(c) Can foreigners stay in any hotel in China?
(d) Does the passage tell you why this is the case?
(e) What is the position for Chinese people themselves?

 ——————— **Zhǔyào cíhuì** ———————

ānjìng	quiet
Bāo zǎocān ma?	Is breakfast included?
-zǎocān/zǎofàn	breakfast
biǎo	form
biéde	other
bǐjiào	relatively
búguò	but, however
cèsuǒ	toilet
chǎo	noisy
cì	time, occasion
dǎ diànhuà	to telephone
dānrén/shuāngrén fángjiān	single/double room
... de shíhou	when
diànshì	television
fúwù	service
fúwùtái	reception (*lit.* service platform)
gàosù	to tell
hái yǒu	another thing (*lit.* still have)
huán	to return something to
hùzhào	passport
jiān	(*measure word for rooms*)
jīnglǐ	manager
línyù	shower
měiyuán	US dollar
néng	to be able to, can
rúguǒ	if
shénme shíhou	when, what time?
shuǐ	water
tián	to fill in (*a form*)
wǎnfàn	dinner, supper
xiǎng yào	would like
xiǎoshí	hour
xǐzǎojiān	bathroom
xiū	to repair
yàoshi	key
yídìng	certainly, definitely

yǒu wèntí	to have problems
zhǎo	to ask for, to want to see
zhèngzài	at this moment
zǒu	to leave

Duìhuà

Duìhuà 1

Frank is checking into a hotel. Listen to or read the dialogue between Frank and the **fúwùyuán** (*attendant*), and then do **Liànxí 2**.

Fúwùyuán Nín hǎo!
Frank Nǐ hǎo! Wǒ xiǎng yào yì jiān dānrén fángjiān.
Fúwùyuán Nín yùdìng le ma?
Frank Méi yǒu.
Fúwùyuán Nín yào zhù jǐ tiān?
Frank Sān、 sì tiān. Wǒ míngtiān gàosù nǐ wǒ shénme shíhou zǒu, kěyǐ ma?
Fúwùyuán Kěyǐ.
Frank Yì tiān duōshao qián?
Fúwùyuán Dānrén fángjiān měi tiān wǔshí měiyuán.
Frank Bāo zǎocān ma?
Fúwùyuán Dāngrán bāo.
Frank Yǒu xǐzǎojiān ma?
Fúwùyuán Yǒu. Búguò zhǐ yǒu línyù hé cèsuǒ.
Frank Hǎo ba.
Fúwùyuán Qǐng xiān tián **yíxiàr** zhèi zhāng biǎo. . . . Qǐng gěi wǒ nínde hùzhào. Nín zǒu de shíhòu huán gěi nín.
Frank Zhè shì wǒde hùzhào.
Fúwùyuán Nínde fángjiān shì èr-líng-yāo, zài èr lóu. Zhè shì yàoshi.
Frank Xièxie.
Fúwùyuán Rúguǒ nín yǒu wèntí, qǐng gěi fúwùtái dǎ diànhuà.
Frank Bú huì yǒu wèntí ba.

Yíxià(r) placed after the verb softens the meaning; it is often used after instructions or advice as in the example above.

✓ Liànxí 2

Are these statements about **Duìhuà 1 duì** or **bú duì**?

	duì/bú duì?
(*a*) The price does not include breakfast.	☐ ☐
(*b*) The guest can take a bath in his room.	☐ ☐
(*c*) The hotel keeps the guest's passport during his stay.	☐ ☐
(*d*) The guest's room is on the first floor.	☐ ☐
(*e*) The guest is asked to ring reception if he has any problems.	☐ ☐

Fúwùtái

服务台

Reception

Duìhuà 2

Frank is ringing reception from his hotel room to make some complaints. What are his complaints and how are they resolved?

Fúwùyuán Nín hǎo. Fúwùtái.

Frank Wǒ shì zhù èr-líng-yāo fángjiān de Frank Goodway. Wǒde fángjiān tài chǎo le. Néng bu néng huàn yì jiān ānjìng yìdiǎnr de?

Fúwùyuán Duìbuqǐ, méi yǒu biéde dānrén fángjiān le. Zhǐ yǒu shuāngrén fángjiān.

Frank Shuāngrén fángjiān yì wǎnshang duōshao qián?

Fúwùyuán **Bǐ** dānrén fángjiān **guì èrshí měiyuán**.

Frank Tài guì le.

Fúwùyuán Rúguǒ míngtiān wǒmen yǒu biéde dānrén fángjiān, yídìng gěi nín huàn.

Frank Hǎo ba. Ò, hái yǒu, wǒde línyù zěnme méi yǒu rè shuǐ?

Fúwùyuán Duìbuqǐ, xiànzài zhèngzài xiū. Wǔ ge xiǎoshí yǐhòu jiù yǒu le.

Frank Wǔ ge xiǎoshí yǐhòu? Bù xíng. Wǒ yào zhǎo nǐmende jīnglǐ.

You know how to say A is much more expensive than B:

A bǐ B guì deduō/duōle.

If you want to say exactly by how much A is more expensive than B you use:

A bǐ B **guì** + (*by how much*)

Shuāngrén fángjiān **bǐ** dānrén   *A double room is $20 US*
fángjiān **guì** èrshí měiyuán.   *more expensive than a single.*

✔ Liànxí 3

You are staying in a hotel in China. The following dialogue is between you and the hotel *receptionist* (**fúwùyuán**). You are ringing to complain:

Fúwùyuán Nín hǎo. Fúwùtái.
(*a*) **You**   (*Say your name and that you are in room 301 and your room is too small. Ask if it is possible to change to a bigger one.*)
Fúwùyuán Duìbuqǐ, méi yǒu biéde dānrén fángjiān le. Zhǐ yǒu shuāngrén fángjiān.
(*b*) **You**   (*Ask how much a double room costs.*)
Fúwùyuán Bǐ dānrén fángjiān guì èrshí měiyuán.
(*c*) **You**   (*Say that's too much. Another thing. Ask why there is no television in your room.*)
Fúwùyuán Duìbuqǐ, diànshì xiànzài zhèngzài xiū. Liǎng ge bàn xiǎoshí yǐhòu jiù xiū-hǎo le.
(*d*) **You**   (*Say the football match will be starting in half an hour!*) (*Use* after half an hour)

Zhǔyào cíhuì

cāntīng	restaurant, canteen
chī de	something to eat
hē de	something to drink
huǒtuǐ	ham
jiā	to add
jīròu	chicken (*meat*)
jiàoxǐng	to (*call to*) wake up
kāfēi	coffee
máfan	(*to*) trouble

nǎi	milk
nǎilào	cheese
niúròu	beef
qǐ	to get up
sānmíngzhì	sandwich
shénme yàng de?	what kind?
sòng lái	to send over (*to the speaker*)
sòng qù	to send over (*away from the speaker*)
táng	sugar
wǎn'ān	good night
xiànzài	now
yìhuǐ(r)	a short while
yǐnliào	drink(s)

Duìhuà 3

Frank gets back to his hotel very late and finds the bar (jiǔbā) closed. Read the dialogue and find out.

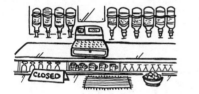 

Jiǔbā

Fúwùyuán Nín hǎo. Fúwùtái.

Frank Wǒ shì èr-líng-yāo fángjiān de Frank Goodway. Néng bu néng máfan nǐmen gěi wǒ sòng **lái** yìdiǎnr chī de? Wǒ è le.

Fúwùyuán Duìbuqǐ, cāntīng xiànzài guān mén le. Wǒmen zhǐ yǒu sānmíngzhì hé yǐnliào.

Frank Kěyǐ. Nǐmen yǒu shénme yàng de sānmíngzhì?

Fúwùyuán Wǒmen yǒu nǎilào de、huǒtuǐ de、jīròu de hé niúròu de.

Frank Wǒ yào yí ge nǎilào de、yí gè niúròu de、hé yì bēi kāfēi.

Fúwùyuán Hǎo de. Kāfēi yào jiā nǎi, jiā táng ma?

Frank Yào jiā nǎi, bù jiā táng.

Fúwùyuán Xíng. Wǒmen yìhuǐr jiù sòng **qù**.

Frank Hái yǒu. Míngtiān zǎoshàng wǒ yào qǐ-de hěn zǎo. Nǐmen néng bu néng dǎ diànhuà jiàoxǐng wǒ?

Fúwùyuán Kěyǐ. Jǐ diǎn?

Frank   Qī diǎn bàn.
Fúwùyuán Méi wèntí.
Frank   Xièxie nǐ. Wǎn'ān.
Fúwùyuán Wǎn'ān.

The Chinese language is much more specific about the direction in which things are said or done by the speaker than English. This means that you will often find the little words **qù** (*go*) or **lái** (*come*) at the end of a sentence: **qù** indicates *away* from the speaker and **lái** indicates *towards* the speaker:

Néng bu néng máfan nǐmen gěi wǒ sòng **lái** yìdiǎnr chī de?	*Could I trouble you to send me up something to eat?*
Wǒmen yìhuǐr jiù sòng **qù**.	*We'll send it up as soon as we can* (*lit.* in a moment).

Cultural tip

Qǐng wù dǎrǎo!   *Do not disturb!*

All hotel rooms in China are equipped with thermos flasks containing hot water for you to make tea. These are emptied and refilled every morning often quite early so if you don't want to be disturbed at say 7a.m. remember to put the 'Don't disturb' notice on your door. When you leave your room you can put the thermos flask(s) outside your door so that they can be refilled before your return.

Liànxí 4

Make the following requests in Chinese using the pattern: **Néng bu néng gěi wǒ . . . ?**. If you want to be more polite, you can say **néng bu néng máfan nǐ(men) gěi wǒ . . . ?**. The measure word for each object is written in brackets after it.

(*a*) Can you send me up something to eat?
something to drink?
a cup of tea, with milk but no sugar?
two sandwiches, one cheese, and one ham?

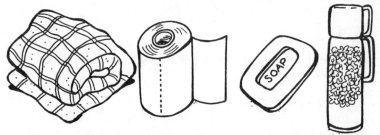

tǎnzi (tiáo)   wèishēngzhǐ (juǎn)   xiāngzào (kuài)   nuǎnshuǐpíng (gè)

(*b*) Can you give me a wake-up call?
give me a phone call?
buy me a bottle (**píng**) of wine?
give me another blanket/roll of toilet paper?
give me a bigger piece of soap?
give me a thermos flask (of hot water)?

Liànxí 5

Listen to the cassette and fill in the following blanks. You need to know the words **fúwù** (*service*) and **lǐmào** (*to be polite/courteous*). If you haven't got a cassette, read the dialogue which comes after this exercise and then fill in the blanks.

(*a*) Frank now stays at _____ Hotel.
(*b*) The conditions in the hotel are _____ .
(*c*) The service there is _____ .
(*d*) The staff are _____ .
(*e*) He has changed his hotel _____ .

Lìli   Nǐ xiànzài zhù zài nǎr?
Frank   Dōngfāng Bīnguǎn.
Lìli   Tiáojiàn zěnmeyàng?
Frank   Tiáojiàn búcuò, kěshì fúwù bù zěnmeyàng.
Lìli   Fúwù zěnme bù hǎo?
Frank   Fúwùyuán bú tài lǐmào.
Lìli   Wèishénme bú huàn yí ge dìfang?
Frank   Wǒ yǐjing huàn le liǎng **cì**. Zhè shì dì sān **cì** le.

Cì (*time(s)*) is like **tiān** (*day*) and **nián** (*year*) in that it acts as both a measure word and a noun. *Once* is **yí cì**, *twice* is **liǎng cì** (note that it is **liǎng** and not **èr**), *three times* is **sān cì**, and so on. To say the first time, the second time, and so on all you have to do is put the little word **dì** in front. Note, however, that the second time is **dì èr cì** and not **dì liǎng cì**.

✓ Liànxí 6

The receptionist at a hotel is asking you a few questions. How would you respond?

Fúwùyuán Nǐ yùdìng le ma?
(*a*) **You**   (*No. I hope* (**xīwàng**) *you've still got rooms.*)
Fúwùyuán Wǒmen hái yǒu jǐ jiān. Nǐ yào shénme fángjiān?
(*b*) **You**   (*A double room and a single room.*)
Fúwùyuán Nǐmen dǎsuàn zhù jǐ tiān?
(*c*) **You**   (*Three or four days. We'll tell you tomorrow when we'll be leaving. Is that OK?*)
Fúwùyuán Xíng. Jīntiān wǎnshang zài bīnguǎn chī wǎnfàn ma?
(*d*) **You**   (*No thank you, we've already eaten.*)

✓ *Xiǎo cèyàn*

You are checking into a hotel. Ask the following questions in Chinese.

(*a*) Is breakfast included?
(*b*) When is lunch (**wǔfàn**)?
(*c*) Is there a television in the room?
(*d*) Have you got a bigger single room?
(*e*) How much is it per night?

13

HUŎCHĒ、PIÀO HÉ CHŪZŪCHĒ

Trains, tickets and taxis

In this unit you will learn:

- how to ask for and understand information about trains
- how to understand train announcements
- how to buy train tickets
- many useful time expressions

Kāishǐ yǐqián fùxí

● yāo (*one*)	(3)	● duō + verb	(10)
● numbers over 100	(7)	● how long	(9)
● measure words	(4)(7)	● first . . . then . . .	(9)
● use of de	(3)(5)	● use of háishi	(6)
● making comparisons	(6)(7)	● use of ba	(3)
● tài . . . le	(7)	● when . . .	(10)
● Noun + on	(5)		

——— Trains in China ———

In China all trains are numbered. For example, train number 21 is called **èrshíyī cì**. Train number 161 is either **yāo-liù-yāo cì** or **yìbǎi liùshíyī cì**. The route of these numbered trains is fixed. **Èrshíyī cì** goes from Beijing to Shanghai, and **èrshíjiǔ cì** is the train from Beijing to Huangzhou. In general the smaller the number of the train the faster it is.

There are three types of train: special express (**tèkuài**), express (**zhíkuài** or **kuàichē**) and normal (**pǔtōng kèchē**). The general word for train in Chinese is **huǒchē** for which the literal translation is *fire vehicle*.

In China they don't have first-class tickets (**tóuděng piào**) and second-class tickets (**èrděng piào**). But they do have four types of tickets: **ruǎnwò, ruǎnzuò, yìngwò** and **yìngzuò. Ruǎnwò** is really a first-class sleeper. **Ruǎnzuò** is just first-class. **Yìngwò** is second class sleeper and **yìngzuò** is second-class. As you may have noticed, these Chinese words involve different combinations of four characters: **ruǎn** meaning *soft*, **yìng** (*hard*), **wò** (*lying down*), and **zuò** (*seat*).

Note that train numbers use the word **cì** ➡️ 145 (Unit 12) after the number:

> train number 21 = **21 cì** (**èrshíyī cì**)
> train number 161 = **161 ci** (**yìbǎi liùshíyī cì; yāo-liù-yāo cì**)

Train numbers of three digits can either be broken down into single digits or said as one number. **Yāo** is used instead of **yī** to avoid any confusion (see Unit 3, ➡️ 39).

When train announcements are made, the sequence is different from the one you are used to in English. The order is normally **kāi wǎng** (*drive towards*) + destination + number (of train). The time is not usually mentioned. Do note that your ticket is only valid for a particular time.

Kāi wǎng tiāntán

🍀 Liànxí 1

What is the Chinese for these phrases:

(*a*) 'soft' sleeper
(*b*) 'hard' seat
(*c*) 'soft' seat
(*d*) 'hard' sleeper
(*e*) first class
(*f*) second class

What is the English for these Chinese words:

(*g*) kèchē
(*h*) tèkuài
(*i*) huǒchē
(*j*) kuàichē
(*k*) zhíkuài

Zhǔyào cíhuì

cì	(*number of trains*)
dàgài	approximately
děi	to need, must
děng	to wait
hòutiān	the day after tomorrow
kāi	to drive
míngbai	to understand (*colloquial*)
něi zhǒng?	which kind?
rénmínbì	Chinese currency
shàng	to board (*vehicle*)
shuì	to sleep
suǒyǐ	so, therefore
ya	(*end particle indicating surprise*)
Yōnghé Gōng	the Lama Temple
yǒu shénme	in what ways . . . ? (*lit.* has what)
Yǒu shénme bù yíyàng?	In what ways are they different?
zhǎo (qián)	to give change
èrděng	second-class (*ticket*)
ruǎnwò	'soft' sleeper
ruǎnzuò	'soft' seat
tèkuài	special express
tóuděng	first-class (*ticket*)
yìngwò	'hard' sleeper
yìngzuò	'hard' seat
zhíkuài	express (*train*)

Duìhuà

Duìhuà 1

Frank is buying a train ticket from Běijīng to Shànghǎi. Listen to, or read, the dialogue and find out which trains go to Shànghǎi.

Frank   Wǒ xiǎng mǎi yì zhāng qù Shànghǎi de huǒchē piào.
Assistant Něi tiān de?
Frank   Hòutiān de.
Assistant Yào něi cì chē de?
Frank   Wǒ bù míngbai nǐde yìsi.
Assistant Qù Shànghǎi de huǒchē yǒu shísān cì、 èrshíyī cì hé
                     yāo-liù-yāo cì.
Frank   Tāmen yǒu shénme bù yíyàng?
Assistant Shísān cì hé èrshíyī cì shì tèkuài, yìbǎi liùshíyī cì shì
                     zhíkuài.
Frank   Shénme shì tèkuài hé zhíkuài?
Assistant Tèkuài jiù shì fēicháng kuài de yìsi. Shísān cì tèkuài bǐ
                     yāo-liù-yāo cì zhíkuài **kuài sì、 wǔ ge xiǎoshí**.
Frank   Shì bu shì tèkuài de piào yě bǐ zhíkuài de piào guì?
Assistant Nà dāngrán le.

Note that if you want to say that train no. 13 is four hours quicker
than train no. 161 you say:

> 13 cì bǐ 161 cì **kuài** (*quick*) + *by how much*
> 13 cì bǐ 161 cì **kuài sì ge xiǎoshí**

There is another example using **màn** *slow* in **Dùihuà** 2. Look out
for it!

This is the same pattern as you used in (Unit 12)➡️📖 148, only here
you are talking about a difference in time rather than money.

Shì bu shì can also be put at the beginning or in the middle of a
sentence as well as at the end (see Unit 3). It conveys the idea that
the speaker is confident that what he says is correct but wishes to
soften the tone. You might have noticed that there is no tone on the
second **shi** when it occurs at the end of a sentence.

✅ Liànxí 2

Please answer the following questions based on the opening passage and **Duìhuà 1**.

(*a*) Which trains go to Shanghai?
(*b*) Which train is faster, **zhíkuài** or **tèkuài**?
(*c*) Is it cheaper to buy a ticket for a **tèkuài** than a **zhíkuài** train?
(*d*) What are the two ways of saying train number 351 in Chinese?
(*e*) Is train number 243 faster than train number 43?

火车站

Huǒchēzhàn Train station

候车室

Hòuchēshì Waiting room

Duìhuà 2

Ann is now at the Beijing Railway Station ticket office. What type of ticket does she want to buy and what ticket does she end in buying?

Ann   Qǐng wèn, hái yǒu shíbā hào èrshíyī cì de piào ma?

Assistant Yǒu. Nín yào něi zhǒng piào?

Ann   Wǒ yào sān zhāng yìngwò.

Assistant Duìbuqǐ. Yìngwo zhǐ yǒu yì zhāng le. Wǒmen hái yǒu ruǎnwò hé yìngzuò.

Ann   Ruǎnwò bǐ yìngwò guì duōshao?

Assistant Yìbǎi bāshí kuài.

Ann   Nàme shíbā hào yāo-liù-yāo cì hái yǒu yìngwò ma?

Assistant Yǒu.

Ann   Tài hǎo le! Wǒ mǎi sān zhāng shíbā hào yāo-liù-yāo cì de yìngwò piào.

Assistant Yāo-liù-yāo cì bǐ èrshíyī cì màn sì ge xiǎoshí.

Ann   Méi guānxi. Wǒmen kěyǐ zài huǒchē shàng duō shuì sì ge xiǎoshí.

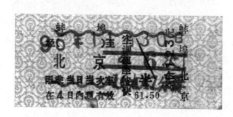

— 157 —

Some useful time expressions

qiánnián	the year before last
qùnián	last year
jīnnián	this year
míngnián	next year
hòunián	the year after next

shàng shàng ge yuè	the month before last
shàng (ge) yuè	last month
zhè/zhèi (ge) yuè	this month
xià (ge) yuè	next month
xià xià ge yuè	the month after next

shàng shàng ge xīngqī	the week before last
shàng (ge) xīngqī	last week
zhè/zhèi (ge) xīngqī	this week
xià (ge) xīngqī	next week
xià xià ge xīngqī	the week after next

qiántiān	the day before yesterday
zuótiān	yesterday
jīntiān	today
míngtiān	tomorrow
hòutiān	the day after tomorrow

☑ **Liànxí 3**

In **Duìhuà 2** there are two useful structures, or patterns, for buying tickets.

(i) **Qǐng wèn, hái yǒu X ma?** *Have you still got X?*
(ii) **Wǒmen mǎi** (X) **zhāng** *We would like to have X*
   (*time*) **de** (*type/event*) **piào.** *number of y tickets for Z*
   (where Y is the type of ticket and Z is the time).

Now here's some practice: You want to know if the following kinds of tickets are still available.

Example: tickets for next Tuesday's football match
You ask: **Qǐng wèn, hái yǒu xià ge xīngqī'èr de zúqiú piào ma?**

(*a*) tickets for tonight's film
(*b*) tickets for the flight (use **fēijī**) on October 4th
(*c*) tickets for train number 153
(*d*) tickets for trains going to Tianjin

If the answer to your above questions is *yes*, you can simply say **Wǒ yào x zhāng**.

If, however, you know the tickets you want to buy are available, you would use pattern (ii).

> *Example*: Two film tickets for 2 o'clock Sunday afternoon.
> You say: **Wǒ mǎi liǎng zhāng xīngqī'èr xiàwǔ liǎng diǎn de diànyǐng piào.**

(*e*) 3 tickets for tonight's film
(*f*) 4 tickets for the flight on October 4th
(*g*) 5 tickets for train number 153
(*h*) 6 tickets for trains going to Tianjin

✔ Liànxí 4

Can you tell your Chinese friends something about British trains in Chinese?

(*a*) There are two types of tickets: first class and second class.
(*b*) First-class tickets are more expensive than second-class tickets.
(*c*) Trains in Britain are both fast and comfortable.

If you are from **Fǎguó**, **Měiguó**, **Déguó**, **Yìdàlì** or other countries, say something similar to the above sentences in Chinese.

▦ Duìhuà 3

Chūzūqìchēzhàn *Taxi station*

The following dialogue is between a taxi driver (**sījī**) and his customer (**chéngkè**). Before you read the dialogue, listen to the recording first and answer the following two questions:

1 How many places did the man plan to visit?
2 How much did the taxi-driver charge him in the end?

Now read the **Duìhuà** and see if you answered the questions correctly.

Sījī   Nín qù nǎr?
Chéngkè Wǒ xiǎng xiān qù Yōnghé Gōng, zài qù Tiāntán.
Sījī   Qǐng shàng chē ba.
Chéngkè Nǐ néng bu néng xiān gàosù wǒ qù zhè liǎng ge dìfang dàgài děi duōshao qián?
Sījī   Qù Yōnghé Gōng sìshíwǔ kuài, zài qù Tiāntán yě shì sìshíwǔ kuài.
Chéngkè Shì rénmínbì háishì měiyuán?
Sījī   Rénmínbì.
Chéngkè Hǎo ba.
         (*getting off at Tiāntán Park*)
Chéngkè Xièxie nǐ. Zhè shì yìbǎi kuài. Bié zhǎo (qián) le.
Sījī   Duìbuqǐ. Yígòng yìbǎi jiǔshí kuài.
Chéngkè Zěnme shì yìbǎi jiǔshí kuài?
Sījī   Nǐ qù Yōnghé Gōng de shíhou, wǒ děng le nǐ liǎng ge xiǎoshí. Děng yí ge xiǎoshí wǔshí kuài. Suǒyǐ yígòng yìbǎi jiǔshí kuài.
Chéngkè Nǐ zěnme méi xiān gàosù wǒ?
Sījī   Nǐ méi wèn ya.

Line 4 in **Dùihuà 3** is a long sentence. **Bié zháojí** (*don't worry*)! Try the following two exercises and you'll be able to say it fluently.

☑ **Liànxí 5**

The first exercise is called 'back chaining'. You practise long sentences like these by reading them phrase by phrase (the whole gradually increasing in length), starting with the end of the sentence first.

yìngwò piào
yāo-liù-yāo cì de yìngwò piào
shíbā hào yāo-liù-yāo cì de yìngwò piào
Wǒ mǎi sān zhāng shíbā hào yāo-liù-yāo cì de yìngwò piào
I'll buy three second-class sleepers for train number 161 on the 18th.
(*lit.* I buy three measure word eighteen number one six one time hard sleeper ticket.)

duōshao qián?

dàgài děi duōshao qián?

qù zhè liǎng ge dìfang dàgài děi duōshao qián?

xiān gàosu wǒ qù zhè liǎng ge dìfang dàgài děi duōshao qián?

Nǐ néng bu néng xiān gàosu wǒ qù zhè liǎng ge dìfang dàgài děi
duōshao qián?

Can you first tell me roughly how much it costs to go to these two places?

(*lit.* you can not can first tell me go these two places roughly need how much money?)

☑ Liànxí 6

The long sentence you have just practised has two parts.

The main part is:

Nǐ néng bu néng gàosu wǒ 'x'.   *Can you tell me 'x'?*

The second part can be an independent question such as *how old is he?* or *where does she live?*. In the dialogue the independent question is **qù zhè liǎng ge dìfang yào duōshao qián**? (*how much does it cost to get to these two places?*).

Now request the following information starting with **nǐ néng bu néng gàosu wǒ**:

Example: How old is he?

You ask: Nǐ néng bu néng gàosu wǒ tā duō dà le?

First try these independent questions and then combine each one with the main sentence.

(*a*) Where does she live?

(*b*) What is your telephone number?

(*c*) How old is his daughter?

(*d*) How long do they intend staying there?

☑ Liànxí 7

Put each group of phrases into the correct order to make complete questions in Chinese.

Example: How much, by train, go to Nanjing?

You ask: Zuò huǒchē qù Nánjīng děi duōshao qián?

(*a*) How much/ to go to Xī'ān/ by train?
(*b*) To fly/ how long/ from London to Shànghǎi?
(*c*) To go to Hépíng Hotel/ by taxi/ how much?
(*d*) By ship (chuán)/ how long/ to go from Japan to China?

☑ Xiǎo cèyàn

Can you match the Chinese words on the left with their English equivalents on the right? There will be one word in the left-hand column that you'll not recognise. Which one is it? What must it mean? (Notice that all the Chinese words have the character **chē** in them.)

(*a*) zìxíngchē
(*b*) huǒchē
(*c*) chūzūchē
(*d*) gōnggòng qìchē
(*e*) kuàichē
(*f*) chángtú qìchē
(*g*) pǔtōng kèchē

(*i*) coach
(*ii*) express (train)
(*iii*) bicycle
(*iv*) train
(*v*) taxi
(*vi*) normal (passenger) train
(*vii*) bus

Chūzūqìchē

14

YÚLÈ HUÓDÒNG
Free time and entertainment

In this unit you will learn:

- how to say what you like doing in your free time
- how to ask somebody what they would like to do
- about sports and hobbies
- about making arrangements
- about summer and winter, indoor and outdoor activities

Kāishǐ yǐqián fùxí

- use of **de** after verb   (8)
- **zuì** (*most*)   (7)
- **gèng** (*even more*)   (8)
- use of **háishi**   (6)
- both . . . and . . .   (9)

- to be in the middle
  of doing something   (6)
- making comparisons   (6)(7)
- A is the same as B   (6)

A park in Chinese is actually a public garden. Do you remember Frank in Unit 6? If you go to China, try to get up early at least one morning, say at 6 o'clock, and go to a local park. You too will be fascinated by what some of the Chinese do there. The following passage tells us a little bit more about what people do in a park.

Qù gōngyuán

Hěn duō Zhōngguó-rén qǐ-de hěn zǎo. Tāmen rènwéi zǎo shuì zǎo qǐ duì shēntǐ hǎo. Zǎoshàng tāmen zuò shénme? Bù shǎo rén qù gōngyuán.

Zài gōngyuán lǐ, tāmen dǎ tàijíquán、zuò qìgōng、chàng gē、tiào wǔ, děngděng. Yǒu de lǎo rén zài gōngyuán sànbù、xià qí、dǎ pái、chàng jīngjù.

Hěn duō gōngyuán dōu yǒu hú. Zài běifāng xiàtiān kěyǐ zài hú lǐ yóuyǒng, dōngtiān kěyǐ zài hú shàng huá bīng.

Zhǔyào cíhuì

běifāng	the north
chàng (gē)	to sing (song)
chàng jīngjù	to sing Peking opera
dǎ pái	to play cards
děngděng	etc.
dōngtiān	winter
gōngyuán	park
hú	lake
huá bīng	to skate

lǎo	old
– lǎo rén	old person/people
qǐ	to get up
rènwéi	to think, to believe
sàn bù	to stroll
shǎo	few, less
– bù shǎo	quite a lot
tiào wǔ	to dance
xià qí	to play chess
xiàtiān	summer
yóuyǒng	to swim
zài (hú) lǐ/shàng	in/on (the lake)
zǎo	early
– zǎo shuì	early to rise
– zǎo qǐ	early to bed

 Liànxí 1

When you have the opportunity, ask a Chinese person these questions:

(*a*) Do the Chinese get up very early?
(*b*) Where do you go in the morning?
(*c*) What do old people do in the park?
(*d*) Do you swim in the lake?

Cultural tip

There is a huge difference between the type of Chinese which is spoken and the type of Chinese which is written. Spoken Chinese is normally much more informal than written Chinese. Sometimes a different word is used in written Chinese to convey the same meaning as a simpler word in the spoken language. There is a good example of this in the passage above where **rènwéi** (*to be of the opinion that*) is used instead of **xiǎng** (*to think*).

This need not concern you very much on a practical level because you are concentrating on spoken Chinese. Unless, of course, you plan to get to grips with the Chinese writing system at some stage and therefore read material in Chinese characters. Why not go on to *Teach Yourself Chinese* once you've finished this book?

Zhǔyào cíhuì

bàn	to handle
chǎng	(*measure word for a show*)
dànyuànrúcǐ	I hope so
dào	to arrive
děng	to wait
fāngbiàn	convenient
gèng duō de	more (*of something*)
hǎo jiǔ bú jiàn	long time no see
hòu bàn (chǎng)	second half (*of a show*)
huódòng	activity
jiémù	programme, performance
jīhuì	opportunity
jīngcǎi	wonderful (*display, show*)
juédìng	to decide
liànxí	to practise, exercise
lóushàng	upstairs
lǚxíng	to travel; travel
lǚxíngtuán	tourist group
niánqīng	young
pái	row (of seats)
X pái Y hào	number Y in row X
qiānzhèng	visa
qiūtiān	autumn
Shì'a.	You're right.
Shì nǐ ya!	It's you!
shòu	thin
shūfu	comfortable
tán	to talk, chat
tán liàn'ài	to be in love, go steady (*lit.* talk love)
tǐng	quite, fairly
wèizi	seat
yǎn	to act
yǎnyuán	actor, actress
yúlè	entertainment
yùndòng	sports, take exercises
zhǎo	to look for
zhěngtiān	all day
zìjǐ	oneself
zìrán	natural
zìyóu	freedom
zuìjìn	recent, recently

Nǐ xǐhuan shénme yùndòng? *What's your favourite sport/game?*

dǎ	play	**(tī) zúqiú**	(*play*) football
− **pīngpāngqiú**	pingpong	**qí mǎ**	horse riding
− **lánqiú**	basketball	**huá xuě**	skiing
− **yǔmáoqiú**	badminton	**(dǎ) Tàijíjiàn**	(*do*) Tai Chi sword
− **qūgùnqiú**	hockey		
− **wǎngqiú**	tennis		

🔲 *Duìhuà 1*

Edward and Xiǎo Fù are talking about their favourite sports. Listen to the cassette first and make a note of what sports they each like before you read the dialogue.

Edward Nǐ xǐhuan shénme yùndòng?
Xiǎo Fù Wǒ zuì xǐhuan **wǎngqiú** (i) hé **yóuyǒng** (ii).
Edward Wǒ yě xǐhuan **wǎngqiú** (i), kěshì gèng xǐhuan **zúqiú** (iv).
Xiǎo Fù Nǐ xǐhuan **tī** (iii) **zúqiú** (iv) háishì kàn **zúqiú** (iv)?
Edward Dōu xǐhuan.
Xiǎo Fù Wǒ zhǐ xǐhuan kàn, bù xǐhuan **tī** (iii).

✔️ Liànxí 2

Use the groups of words below to substitute for the sports in **Duìhuà 1**. (*a*) under column (i) substitutes for (i) in the dialogue ie **pīngpāngqiú** substitutes for **wǎngqiú**, (*a*) under column (ii) substitutes for (ii) in the dialogue and so on. Do the same with (b) to (e). Each time you have completed one row of substitution read out the dialogue using the new words.

	(*i*)	(*ii*)	(*iii*)	(*iv*)
(*a*)	pīngpāngqiú	huá bīng	dǎ	lánqiú
(*b*)	lánqiú	xià qí	dǎ	yǔmáoqiú
(*c*)	yǔmáoqiú	qí mǎ	dǎ	qūgùnqiú
(*d*)	qūgùnqiú	huá xuě	dǎ	tàijíquán
(*e*)	tàijíquán	tàijíjiàn	dǎ	pái

✔️ Liànxí 3

What do you like and dislike?

You are given three activities each time. Use (i) on the next page to show an ascending order of preference. Use (ii) to rank your dislikes. We have given you sample answers in the *Key to the exercises*.

(*i*) Wǒ xǐhuan A, gèng xǐhuan B, zuì xǐhuan C.
(*ii*) Wǒ bù xǐhuan A, gèng bù xǐhuan B, zuì bù xǐhuan C.

Example: diànyǐng, jīngjù, yīnyuèhuì
  (*i*) Wǒ xǐhuan kàn jīngjù, gèng xǐhuan kàn diànyǐng, zuì xǐhuan tīng yīnyuèhuì.
  (*ii*) Wǒ bù xǐhuan tīng yīnyuèhuì, gèng bù xǐhuan kàn diànyǐng, zuì bù xǐhuan kàn jīngjù.

(*a*) zuò fēijī, zuò chuán, zuò huǒchē
(*b*) qí zìxíngchē, qí mǎ (*horse*), qí mótuōchē (*motorbike*)
(*c*) zuò gōnggòng qìchē (*bus*), zuò dìtiě (*underground*), zuò chūzūchē
(*d*) kàn jīngjù, kàn diànshì, kàn diànyǐng
(*e*) tīng gǔdiǎn (*classical*) yīnyuè, tīng xiàndài (*modern*) yīnyuè, tīng liúxíng (*pop*) yīnyuè

Duìhuà 2

Yáo Mínglì is asking Ann about her forthcoming holiday. Why has Ann not yet made up her mind?

Mínglì Tīngshuō jīnnián qiūtiān nǐ yào qù Zhōngguó lǚxíng.
Ann Duì. Kěshì wǒ hái méi juédìng zěnme qù.
Mínglì Zěnme qù? Dāngrán zuò fēijī qù. Zuò huǒchē yòu màn yòu bù shūfu.
Ann Wǒ bú shì nèi ge yìsi. Wǒ hái méi juédìng gēn lǚxíngtuán qù háishì zìjǐ qù.
Mínglì Shì'a. Gēn lǚxíngtuán qù hěn fāngbiàn, kěshì yòu guì yòu bù zìyóu.
Ann Zìjǐ qù yòu piányi yòu zìyóu, kěshì zhēn bù fāngbiàn.
Mínglì Zěnme bù fāngbiàn?
Ann Wǒ yào zìjǐ qù bàn qiānzhèng、dìng fēijī piào、zhǎo lǚguǎn, děngděng.
Mínglì Kěshì zìjǐ qù kěyǐ yǒu gèng duō de jīhuì liànxí Zhōngwén.

Note that if you want to say that something still hasn't happened you put the word **hái** in front of **méi** (*yǒu*):

Kěshì wǒ **hái** méi juédìng   *But I haven't yet decided how*
zěnme qù.   *to go.*
Tā **hái** méi yǒu lái (ne).   *She still hasn't come.*

There is an optional **ne** at the end of such sentences.

✅ Liànxí 4

The following passage is based on **Duìhuà** 2. Fill in the blanks (use one word per blank) according to the information given in the dialogue.

Ann jīnnián _(a)_ dǎsuàn qù Zhōngguó _(b)_ . Kěshì tā _(c)_ _(d)_ juédìng gēn lǚxíngtuán qù _(e)_ zìjǐ qù. Gēn lǚxíngtuán qù _(f)_ guì _(g)_ bù zìyóu. Zìjǐ qù yòu _(h)_ yòu _(i)_ . Kěshì zìjǐ qù hěn _(j)_ fāngbiàn. Tā yào zìjǐ qù _(k)_ qiānzhèng, _(l)_ fēijī piào, _(m)_ lǚguǎn, děngděng.

📼 *Duìhuà 3*

Lǎo Qián and Xiǎo Zhào meet at the cinema entrance. Listen to, or read, the dialogue to find out what they have been doing lately.

Xiǎo Zhào Lǎo Qián, hǎo jiǔ bú jiàn.
Lǎo Qián Xiǎo Zhào, shì nǐ ya!
Xiǎo Zhào Nín xiànzài zài zuò shénme?

电影院

diànyǐngyuàn   cinema

Lǎo Qián Gēn yǐqián yíyàng. Měi tiān dǎda pái、 xiàxia qí、 dǎda tàijíquán, tǐng yǒu yìsi.
Xiǎo Zhào Nín bǐ yǐqián niánqīng duōle.
Lǎo Qián Nǎli, nǎli. Lǎo duōle. Xiǎo Zhào, nǐ zuìjìn zài zuò shénme?
Xiǎo Zhào Wǒ zhèngzài tán liàn'ài. Zhěngtiān mǎi dōngxi、 kàn diànyǐng、 tīng yīnyuèhuì. Zhēn méi yìsi.
Lǎo Qián Nǐ bǐ yǐqián shòu duōle.
Xiǎo Zhào Tán liàn'ài yòu lèi yòu bú zìyóu.
Lǎo Qián Nǐde nǚ péngyou ne?
Xiǎo Zhào Tā hái méi lái ne. Wǒ zài děng tā.

Tán lián'ài **Gāng jié hūn** **Sān nián yǐhòu**
To be in love. Just married. Three years later.

✔ Liànxí 5

You are having a conversation with a Chinese friend. You begin:

(a) **You** (*Greet Xiǎo Wáng and say you haven't seen him for ages.*)
Friend Nǐ hǎo, Xiǎo Mǎ. Shì nǐ ya!

(b) **You** (*Ask him what he is up to these days.*)
Friend Gēn yǐqián yíyàng. Hái zài xuéxiào (*school*) gōngzuò.

(c) **You** (*Ask if he is married.*)
Friend Hái méi yǒu. Wǒmen míngnián jié hūn.

(d) **You** (*Ask him who he is waiting for.*)
Friend Wǒ zài děng wǒ nǚ péngyou. Nǐ qù nǎr?

(e) **You** (*Tell him that you are going swimming.*)
Friend Hǎo, zánmen yǐhòu zài tán.

(f) **You** (*Say goodbye to him.*)
Friend Zàijiàn!

Duìhuà 4

Edward and Xiǎo Fù run into each other again during the interval of a show. Where are they sitting and what do they think of the performance tonight?

Edward Nǐ zuò nǎr?
Xiǎo Fù Wǔ pái sì hào.

Edward   Nǐ de wèizi zhēn hǎo.
Xiǎo Fù Nǐ zài nǎr?
Edward   Wǒ zài lóushàng shí pái
         sānshí hào.
Xiǎo Fù Nǐ juéde jīntiān de jiémù
         zěnmeyàng?
Edward   Nèige nǚ yǎnyuán chàng-de
         tǐng hǎo. Nán yǎnyuán
         chàng-de bù zěnmeyàng.
Xiǎo Fù Wǒ juéde tāmen chàng-de
         hái búcuò. Kěshì yǎn-de bú
         zìrán.
Edward   Tīngshuō hòu bàn chǎng hěn
         jīngcǎi.
Xiǎo Fù Dànyuànrúcǐ.

Lóushàng
Upstairs

Lóuxià
Downstairs

Note that there are still a few traces of the classical Chinese language in use today. Classical Chinese was monosyllabic but it often put four characters together to express a particular idea. Many of these four character phrases became set phrases and still appear in the language today. **Dànyuànrúcǐ** is an example of such a four character phrase. Other examples are:

wànshìrúyì   (*lit.* 10,000 things like wish) *your heart's desire*
yílùpíng'ān   (*lit.* all road peace) *bon voyage*
yílùshùnfēng   (*lit.* all road following wind) *bon voyage*

Such phrases are usually preceded by **zhù nǐ (men)** . . . (*wish you* . . .). This is sometimes omitted, especially in written Chinese.

——— Cultural tip ———

Seating in Chinese cinemas and theatres: as you can see in **Liànxí 6** below, all the even seat numbers are grouped together on one side and all the uneven ones on the other. Only seat numbers 1 and 2 are next to each other sequentially. This means that when you go into a Chinese cinema you need to check whether your seat numbers are even **shuānghào** or odd **dānhào**. If they are even you will need to follow the sign for 双号 seats and if odd the signs for 单号 seats. It is obviously important to understand the way the seating is organised if ever you are buying seats yourself.

✒ Liànxí 6

Three rows of seats are given in each section. Give the Chinese for the seat number ○ in each of the three sections A, B, C, below.

双号
Shuānghào

Example: Row 14, No. 19, upstairs
Lóushàng shísì pái shíjiǔ hào.

单号
Dānhào

A 1 30 28 26 24 ... ... 8 6 4 2 1 3 5 7 ... ... 21 23 ○ 27
    2 30 28 26 24 ... ... 8 6 4 2 1 3 ○ 7 ... ... 21 23 25 27
    3 30 28 ○ 24 ... ... 8 6 4 2 1 3 5 7 ... ... 21 23 25 27

B 24 30 28 26 ○ ... ... 8 6 4 2 1 3 5 7 ... ... 21 23 25 27
    25 30 28 26 24 ... ... 8 6 ○ 2 1 3 5 7 ... ... 21 23 25 27
    26 30 28 26 24 ... ... 8 6 4 2 1 3 5 7 ... ... 21 ○ 25 27

C [Lóushàng]
    11 30 28 26 24 ... ... 8 ○ 4 2 1 3 5 7 ... ... 21 23 25 27
    12 30 ○ 26 24 ... ... 8 6 4 2 1 3 5 7 ... ... 21 23 25 27
    13 30 28 26 24 ... ... 8 6 4 2 1 3 5 7 ... ... ○ 23 25 27

✒ Liànxí 7

Tell your Chinese guests where their seats are.

(a)	(b)	(c)	(d)
Row A No. 12	Row J No. 37	Row F No. 40 upstairs	Row K No. 2

✒ Liànxí 8

Your Chinese guests are planning a night out. Tell them in Chinese the options they have in their local area which are shown in the advertisements on the next page.

bāléi	ballet	**gējù**	opera
huàjù	play	**tiān'é**	swan

You also need to know the word **bàng**. This time it means *pound* in money. (see Exercise 2, Unit 7 where it means pound in weight.) You should not now be surprised to learn that the Chinese character for **bàng** (*pound*) in money is different from the character for **bàng** (*pound*) in weight. Here they are:

bàng

The right-hand side is exactly the same for both but a pound in money has metal or gold on the left-hand side and a pound in weight has stone or mineral.

bàng

Film: *Winter Time*
18.00, 20.00, 22.00
Saturday, 25th October
Tickets: £4.50

Play: *When we were young*
Time: 19.15
Saturday 25th October
Tickets: £6, £7.50

Ballet: *Swan Lake*
Time: 19.30
Sunday 26th October
Tickets: £8, £10, £12

Opera: *Carmen*
Time: 20.00
Sunday 26th October
Tickets: £15, £20, £25

✔ *Xiǎo cèyàn*

Yán Lóngfēng and his girlfriend Liú Língmǐn are discussing how they are going to spend the evening. Listen to, or read, the dialogue and answer the questions after it.

Yán Zánmen qù kàn diànyǐng ba.
Liú Yǒu shénme hǎo diànyǐng?
Yán Tīngshuō «**Wǒmen niánqīng de shíhou**» búcuò.
Liú Wǒ kàn-guo le. Méi yìsi.
Yán Nàme wǒmen qù tīng yīnyuèhuì ba.
Liú Yǒu shénme yīnyuèhuì?
Yán Nǐ xiǎng tīng Zhōngguó yīnyuè háishì Xīfāng yīnyuè?
Liú Dōu bù xiǎng tīng.
Yán Nàme nǐ xiǎng zuò shénme?
Liú Wǒ xiǎng qù tiào wǔ.

(*a*) What did Yán Lóngfēng first suggest that they did?
(*b*) Did Liú Língmǐn accept his suggestion? Why or why not?
(*c*) What types of concert did Yán Lóngfēng ask his girlfriend to choose from?
(*d*) Was Liú Língmǐn interested?
(*e*) What did Liú Língmǐn want to do?

15

ZÀI YÓUJÚ HÉ HUÀN QIÁN
At a post office and changing money

In this unit you will learn:

- how to buy stamps
- how to send (and collect) a parcel
- how to make a long distance call
- how to send a fax
- numbers above 1,000

Kāishǐ yǐqián fùxí

- from . . . to . . .   (9)
- measure words   (4) (7)
- money   (7)
- weights   (7)
- zuì (*most*)   (7)

- verb endings   (10)
- use of **háishi**   (6)
- use of **de**   (3) (5)
- **huì**   (9)
- foreign currency   (7)

The following passage tells you something about **Yóujú** (*post office*) in China. Are there things you can do in a Chinese **yóujú** that you don't normally do in a post office in Britain?

———— **Yóujú** ———— 邮局

post office

Zhōngguó de yóujú gēn Yīngguó de yóujú chàbuduō. Zài yóujú nǐ kěyǐ jì xìn、jì qián、jì bāoguǒ, yě kěyǐ mǎi yóupiào、xìnfēng hé míngxìnpiàn, hái kěyǐ cún

qiān、qǔ qián. Zài Yīngguó nǐ kěyǐ zài yóujú fù zhàng. Zhōngguó de yóujú mùqián hái méi yǒu zhèi zhǒng fúwù.

Zài Zhōngguó dǎ chángtú diànhuà hé guójì diànhuà bú tài fāngbiàn, yìbān yào qù dà yóujú dǎ. Zài dà yóujú hái kěyǐ dǎ diànbào hé fā chuánzhēn. Yóujú de kāi mén shíjiān gēn yínháng chàbuduō, cóng shàngwǔ bā diǎn bàn dào xiàwǔ liù diǎn. Xīngqīliù、xīngqītiān dōu kāi mén.

Shùnbiàn shuō yíxià, Zhōngguó de xìnxiāng shì lǜsè de, Yīngguó de xìnxiāng shì hóngsè de.

 ──────────── **Zhǔyào cíhuì** ────────────

bāoguǒ	parcel
chàbuduō	similar (*lit.* different not much)
X gēn Y chàbuduō	X is not much different to Y
chángtú	long distance
cún qián	to deposit money
diànbào	telegram
fā	to send
fā chuánzhēn	to send a fax
fù zhàng	to pay bills
guójì	international
jì	to post
míngxìnpiàn	postcard
mùqián	at present, currently
qǔ qián	to withdraw money
shùnbiàn shuō yíxià	by the way
yóujú	post office
yóupiào	stamp
xìn	letter
xìnfēng	envelope
xìnxiāng	letter box

 Liànxí 1

Now would you like to tell the Chinese something about postoffices in Britain?

(*a*) You can send letters and parcels in a post office.

(*b*) Post offices in Britain do not open on Saturday afternoons or Sundays.

(*c*) Letter boxes in Britain are red, not green.

(*d*) In Britain there is no need to go to a post office to make long-distance calls.

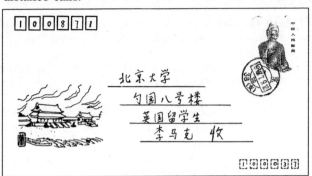

 —————————— **Zhǔyào cíhuì** ——————————

chá	to look up (*something*)
chāo zhòng le	to have exceeded the weight limit
chèng	scales
dǎ (diànhuà)	to make (*a telephone call*) (*lit.* hit telephone)
dào	to go to
dìqū	district
fā-wán le	to have sent (*a fax*) through
fàng	to put
fēng	(*measure word for letters*)
hǎiyùn	(*to post*) by sea
hángkōng	(*to post*) by air
hǎokàn	nice-looking
jì dào	to post to
jiǎo	corner
-yòushàngjiǎo	upper right-hand corner
lùxiàng(dài)	video (tape)
nèibiān	over there
shōujù	receipt
shū	book
tào	set (*stamps*)
tiē	to stick to
zhèixiē/nèixiē	these/those
yè	page
yòu	right (*the opposite of left*)
yuànyì	would like to, to be willing to
zhàn xiàn	(*line*) engaged
zhuǎn	to change to (*extension*)

▣ *Duìhuà 1*

Ann is now at a post office in China. At the end of the dialogue she will have done three things. What are they?

Ann   Qǐng wèn, zhèi fēng xìn jì dào Yīngguó, duōshao qián?
Assistant Qǐng fàng zài chèng shàng. . . . Chāo zhòng le. Sān kuài jiǔ.
Ann   Jǐ tiān néng dào?
Assistant Bù yídìng. Yìbān wǔ、 liù tiān. Zhè shì nínde yóupiào, qǐng tiē zài xìnfēng de yòushàngjiǎo.
Ann   Zhèi zhāng yóupiào zhēn hǎokàn. Wǒ néng mǎi yí tào ma?
Assistant Dāngrán kěyǐ. Yí tào liù kuài qī.
Ann   Wǒ hái xiǎng jì yí ge bāoguǒ.
Assistant Shì shénme dōngxi?
Ann   Dōu shì shū hé lùxiàngdài.
Assistant Yě qǐng fàng zài chèng shàng. . . . Liǎng gōngjīn. Nín jì hángkōng háishi hǎiyùn?
Ann   Hángkōng.

Cultural tips

As you have seen from the passage about post offices, postboxes in China are usually green.

Airmail stickers, envelopes and stamps often have no adhesive on them so go to China prepared! Of course you can always use the glue at the post office.

✓ Liànxí 2

You are now in a post office talking to the assistant. You begin:

(a) **You**   (*Ask how much it is to send this parcel to America.*)
    Assistant Shì shénme dōngxi?
(b) **You**   (*Say they are all books.*)
    Assistant Qǐng fàng zài chèng shàng. . . . Wǔshísān kuài.
(c) **You**   (*Ask how many days it takes (to get to America)?*)
    Assistant Bù yídìng. Yìbān sì、wǔ tiān.
(d) **You**   (*Say you would like to buy postcards and ask how much it is for a set.*)
    Assistant Zhèi tào dà de liù kuài. Nèi tào xiǎo de sì kuài wǔ.
(e) **You**   (*Say you'll have a set of the big ones, and two sets of the small ones.*)
    Assistant Bāoguǒ wǔshísān kuài, yí tào dà de míngxìnpiàn liù kuài, liǎng tào xiǎo de jiǔ kuài, yígòng liùshíbā kuài.
(f) **You**   (*Say here are 70 yuan.*)
    Assistant Zhǎo nín liǎng kuài.
(g) **You**   (*Say thank you and goodbye.*)
    Assistant Zàijiàn!

Duìhuà 2

Colin zài **shāngwù zhōngxīn** fā chuánzhēn. (*Colin is sending a fax at a business centre.*)

Colin   Xiǎojie, qǐng wèn, kěyǐ zài zhèr fā **(yí) ge** chuánzhēn ma?
Assistant Kěyǐ. Fā dào nǎr?
Colin   Déguó.
Assistant Yígòng jǐ yè?
Colin   Liǎng yè.
Assistant Hǎo de. Qǐng gěi wǒ chuánzhēn hàomǎ.
Colin   Zhè shì chuánzhēn hàomǎ.
Assistant Qǐng děngyiděng. . . . Fā-wán le. Zhè shì shōujù.
Colin   Duōshao qián?
Assistant Sìshí kuài. Qǐng dào nèibiān fù qián.
Colin   Xièxie nǐ.
Assistant Bú kèqi.

商务中心
Shāngwù Zhōngxīn
Business centre

Note that in spoken Chinese, when **yī** (*one*) occurs with a measure word the **yī** is often omitted.

☑ Liànxí 3

You will find it useful to be able to ask and understand the following questions and instructions in Chinese. Look carefully at the example given in each section and then have a go at translating the English sentences which follow it into Chinese.

(*a*) Asking for services:
    Example: Qǐng wèn, kěyǐ zài zhèr fā ge diànchuán ma?

    Can I make a phone call here?
    Can I send a parcel here?
    Can I send a telegram here?

(*b*) Asking for items:
    Example: Qǐng gěi wǒ chuānzhēn hào(mǎ).

    Can I have your telephone number?
    Can I have his fax number?
    Can I have your passport?
    Can I have their address (**dìzhǐ**)?

(*c*) Giving instructions/directions:
    Example: Qǐng dào nèibiān fù qián.

    Please change money over there.
    Please make the phone call outside (**wàibiān**).
    Qǐng dào hòubiān pái duì (*Please queue at the back*) is another useful instruction you may wish to learn.

▤ *Duìhuà 3*

Xiè Qúnyì is making a long-distance call.

Operator Nín hǎo. Nánfāng Dàxué.
Xiè   **Qǐng zhuǎn** sì-èr-qī fēnjī.
Operator Duìbuqǐ, sì-èr-qī zhàn xiàn. Nín yuànyì děngyiděng háishì yìhuǐr zài dǎ **lái**?

Xiè   Wǒ zhè shì chángtú. Nín néng bu néng jiào sì-èr-qī de
             Wáng Bǎopíng gěi wǒ dǎ ge diànhuà?

Operator Nínde hàomǎ shì duōshao?

Xiè   Dìqū hào shì líng-bā-yāo. Wǒde diànhuà shì èr-yāo-liù qī-
             qī-jiǔ-èr.

Operator Nín guì xìng?

Xiè   Wǒ jiào Xiè Qúnyì.

Operator Méi wèntí.

Xiè   Xièxie nín.

You learnt about straightforward telephone numbers in Unit 3,
➡️❷ 39. If, having got through to the main switchboard, you need to
ask for an extension number, such as 473, you say:

Qǐng zhuǎn sì-qī-sān (fēnjī).   *Extension 473 please.*
                                      (*lit.* invite transfer 4–7–3 branch
                                      machine)

Note the little word **lái** at the end of the operator's second speech
in **Duìhuà 2**:

Nǐ yuànyì děngyiděng háishi   *Do you wish to wait or phone*
  yìhuǐr zài dǎ **lái**?   *again in a little while?*
                                     (*lit.* you wish wait a little
                                     while again hit [the electric
                                     speech] come?)

This use of **lái** indicates direction towards the speaker (see also
Unit 12, ➡️❷ 150).

✔️ **Liànxí 4**

Read the dialogue and answer the following questions in English.

(*a*) Where is the caller phoning?
(*b*) Who is the caller wanting to speak to?
(*c*) Why couldn't the operator connect the caller to the extension
     he gave her?
(*d*) What seemed to be the mistake?

—— A Telephone Conversation ——

Operator	Nín hǎo, Hépíng Bīnguǎn.
Mark	Qǐng zhuǎn wǔ-bā-sì fēnjī.
Operator	Duìbuqǐ, wǒmen méi yǒu wǔ-bā-sì fēnjī.
Mark	Shénme? Méi yǒu wǔ-bā-sì fēnjī?!
Operator	Nín yào zhǎo shéi?
Mark	Wǒ zhǎo cóng Měiguó lái de Bái Huá xiānsheng.
Operator	Tā zhù něi ge fángjiān?
Mark	Duìbuqǐ, wǒ bu zhīdào.
Operator	Qǐng děngyiděng. Wǒ chá yíxià. A, Bái Huá xiānsheng. Tā zhù wǔ-sì-bā fángjiān. Tā de fēnjī yě shì wǔ-sì-bā.
Mark	Duìbuqǐ. Nàme qǐng gěi wǒ zhuǎn yíxià.

gōngyòng diànhuà

It is not difficult to change money in big cities, but it can be difficult in small cities and towns. The following passage tells us one of the reasons.

the Bank of China

—————— Huàn qián ——————

Wàiguó-rén zài Zhōngguó huàn qián mùqián zhǐ néng zài Zhōngguó Yínháng huàn, *duìhuànlǜ* dōu yíyàng. *Kěnéng jiānglái* huì bù yíyàng. Yǒude bīnguǎn hé shāngdiàn yě yǒu Zhōngguó

Yínháng de *yíngyèbù*, suǒyǐ yě kěyǐ zài nèixiē dìfang huàn qián. Yínháng de kāi mén shíjiān gēn pǔtōng de shāngdiàn chàbuduō, yìbān cóng shàngwǔ bā diǎn bàn dào xiàwǔ liù diǎn. Kěshì zài fàndiàn、 bīnguǎn lǐ de Zhōngguó Yínháng *yíngyèbù* kāi mén shíjiān bǐjiào *línghuó, kěnéng* huì kāi-dào hěn wǎn.

diǎn (yìdiǎn)	to count
duìhuànlǜ	exchange rate
jiānglái	in the future
kěnéng	possible, possibly
línghuó	flexible
yíngyèbù	branch (*of a bank*)
zhènghǎo	just right (*amount*)

Liànxí 5

Respond with **duì** or **bú duì** to the following statements about the passage above.

duì/ bú duì

(a) One can change money at branches of the Bank of China. ☐ ☐

(b) You can find a branch of the Bank of China in some big hotels. ☐ ☐

(c) The opening hours of the Bank of China are different from those of ordinary shops. ☐ ☐

(d) The opening hours of branches of the Bank of China in big hotels and department stores are the same as at branches in the high street. ☐ ☐

měiyuán	US dollar	fǎláng	French franc
yīngbàng	UK pound	mǎkè	German mark
rìyuán	Japanese yen	gǎngbì	HK dollar
lǐlā	Italian lira	rénmínbì	Chinese yuan

Numbers above 1,000

1,000	yìqiān	100,000	**shíwàn** (*ten wàns*)
10,000	yíwàn	480,000	sìshíbā wàn
20,000	èr/liǎng wàn	1,000,000	yìbǎi wàn
35,000	sānwàn wǔqiān		(*one hundred wàns*)

9 × 1000 = jiǔ**qiān**
but 10 × 1000 = yí**wàn**

There is no specific word for one million. It is *100 wàns*! Two million is therefore *200 wàns* and so on.

🔲 *Duìhuà 4*

The customer in the dialogue below wants to change some money. First he will have to fill out a **duìhuàndān** (*exchange memo*). Figures can be difficult to understand, so listen to the dialogue a few times and concentrate on the figures. What currency does the customer wish to exchange for *rénmínbì*? What is the exchange rate? How much does he want to change?

Customer Qǐng wèn, jīntiān měiyuán hé rénmínbì de duìhuànlǜ shì duōshao?
Teller Yī bǐ qī diǎnr jiǔ.
Customer Yì měiyuán huàn qī kuài jiǔ, duì ma?
Teller Duì.
Customer Wǒ xiǎng huàn liǎngbǎi měiyuán de rénmínbì.
Teller Qǐng xiān tián zhèi zhāng duìhuàndān.
Customer ... Tián-hǎo le. Zhè shì liǎngbǎi měiyuán.
Teller Qǐng děngyiděng. ... Zhè shì yìqiān wǔbǎi bāshí kuài. Qǐng diǎnyidiǎn.
Customer Zhènghǎo. Xièxie nǐ.
Teller Bú kèqi.

✅ Liànxí 6

How would you ask for the exchange rate of the following currency against **rénmínbì yuán**?

Example: lira
        (Jīntiān) lǐlā hé rénmínbì de duìhuànlǜ shì duōshǎo?

(*a*) £   (*d*) FFr
(*b*) US$ (*e*) Yen
(*c*) DM   (*f*) HK $

✅ Liànxí 7

Now ask again for the exchange rates in **Liànxí 6** and this time give the answer according to the table below. Try to use both expressions used in **Duìhuà 3** for talking about the rates. (Leave out this exercise if you don't like working with figures.)

Example: 10,000 lira
(*i*) Yíwàn (lǐlā) bǐ wǔshísān (kuài rénmínbì)
(*ii*) Yíwàn lǐlā huàn wǔshísān kuài rénmínbì.

Foreign currencies   *Rénmínbì RMB (yuán)*

(*a*)	US $	100.00	840.00
(*b*)	HK $	100.00	108.00
(*c*)	£	100.00	1320.00
(*d*)	FFr	100.00	165.00
(*e*)	DM	100.00	562.00
(*f*)	Yen	10,000.00	782.00

Liànxí 8

You want to change the following amount of currency into **RMB yuán**. What would you say?

Example: 75,000 lira
Wǒ xiàng huàn qīwàn wǔqiān lǐlā de rénmínbì.

(*a*)	£ 100	(*d*)	Fr 400
(*b*)	US$ 200	(*e*)	HK$ 500
(*c*)	DM 300	(*f*)	60,000 Yen

Xiǎo cèyàn

How do you ask or say:

(*a*) How much is it to post this postcard to Britain?
(*b*) I want to buy a set of stamps.
(*c*) What's the exchange rate between sterling and RMB today?
(*d*) I want to exchange £150 for RMB.
(*e*) My extension is 2115.

16

ZUÒ KÈ
Being a guest

In this unit you will learn:

- how to make a toast
- how to make appropriate remarks and responses during a meal

Kāishǐ yǐqián fùxí

- When ...   (10)
- cái   (7)
- measure words   (4)(7)
- polite talk   (4)(8)
- tài ... le   (7)
- use of háishi   (6)
- verb endings   (10)

- duō + verb   (10)
- use of de after verb   (8)
- yǐjīng (*already*) + le   (10)
- not any more   (10)
- gěi (*for*)   (6)
- verb + guo   (9)

No doubt you have eaten Chinese meals. But where? At a Chinese home or in a Chinese restaurant? Or both? Have you noticed some of the differences in the way Westerners and Chinese eat their meals? Now read the following passage which sums up some of the differences in simple Chinese.

Chī Zhōngguó fàn

Zhōngguó-rén chángcháng wèi kèrén zuò hěn duō cài. Tāmen xīwàng kèrén duō hē jiǔ, duō chī cài.

Zhōngguó-rén hé Xīfāng-rén chī fàn de xíguàn bù yíyàng. Dàbùfen Zhōngguó-rén yìbān xiān chī fàn, hòu hē tāng. Zài Xīfāng, rénmen yìbān xiān hē tāng, hòu chī fàn. Zhōngguó-rén chángcháng xiān hē jiǔ, chī liáng cài, ránhòu chī rè fàn、 rè cài, zuìhòu chī shuǐguǒ. Xīfāng-rén xiān chī tóupán, ránhòu chī zhèngcān, zuìhòu chī tiánshí huò shuǐguǒ. Zhōngguó-rén chī fàn yòng wǎn hé kuàizi; Xīfāng-rén chī fàn yòng pánzi hé dāochā.

Zhōngguó-rén zài jiā lǐ chī fàn hé zài fànguǎn chī fàn chàbuduō, dàjiā yìqǐ chī suǒyǒude cài. Xīfāng-rén zài fànguǎn zìjǐ chī zìjǐ de cài. Zài jiā chī fàn de shíhou, bùtóng de cài xiān fàng zài pán li, ránhòu cái chī.

 ———— **Zhǔyào cíhuì** ————

bùtóng de	different
chángcháng	often
dàbùfen	majority
dàjiā	everyone
dāochā (i.e. dāozi, chāzi)	knife (*and*) fork
hòu	later
huò(zhě)	or (*used in statements*)
liáng	cold, cool
rénmen	people (*in general*)
shuǐguǒ	fruit
suǒyǒude	all
tiánshí	dessert
tóupán	starter
wèi	for (*formal*)
Xīfāng	West
xíguàn	habit, customs
xīwàng	to hope; hope
zhèngcān	main course
zìjǐ chī zìjǐ de	to eat one's own
zuìhòu	last

We mentioned the enormous difference between spoken and written Chinese in Unit 14, **▶P** 165 and there are further examples of this in the passage above. **Wèi** is used instead of **gěi** in the first sentence, **hòu** is used instead of **ránhòu** in line 2 (**▶P** 186) and **huò** is used instead of **huòzhě** in line 6. Using one-syllable words instead of two, or using a more 'ancient' word (**wèi** instead of **gěi**) gives a more formal feel to the language.

Note that **dōu** (*all*) can only be used in front of a verb. So, for example, when you want to say all *people* you have to use another word for *all* which is **suǒyǒude**:

Tā xǐhuan **suǒyǒude** rén.	*She likes everybody* (*lit.* all people).
Dàjiā yìqǐ chī **suǒyǒude** cài.	*Everybody shares all the dishes* (*lit.* big family together eat all dish).

✔ Liànxí 1

Choose the most appropriate words from the ones given in brackets to fill the blanks in the sentences below. You will be able to use all the words given in (a) and (b) but you will have to make a choice in (c), (d) and (e).

(a) Zhōngguó-rén yìbān xiān_____, ránhòu _____, zuìhòu _____.
(hē tāng, chī rè fàn、rè cài, hē jiǔ)

(b) Xīfāng-rén yìbān xiān _____, ránhòu _____, zuìhòu _____.
(chī shuǐguǒ, hē tāng, chī zhèngcān)

(c) Zhōngguó-rén chī fàn yòng ___ hé ___.
(dāozi, kuàizi, chāzi, pánzi, wǎn)

(d) Xīfāng-rén chī fàn yòng ___ gēn ___.
(dāochā, kuàizi, pánzi, wǎn)

(e) ___ zài fànguǎnr chī fàn hé zài jiā lǐ chī fàn xíguàn yíyàng.
(Zhōngguó-rén; Xīfāng-rén)

Zhǔyào cíhuì

ài	to love, to like very much; love
báijiǔ	strong alcohol
chá	tea
chī-bu-xià le	to be unable to eat any more
chúfáng	kitchen
Gān bēi!	Cheers!

gān yī bēi	to have a drink
gěi	to give
hǎochī (de)	delicious (*food*), tasty
hé	box
hē-bu-xià le	to be unable to drink any more
hē-bu-liǎo	to be unable to drink
huānyíng	to welcome; welcome
huí qù	to go back
jiācháng biànfàn	simple home meal
kètīng	sitting room
– kètīng lǐ zuò ba	come and sit in the sitting room
mànzǒu	take care (*as in goodbye; lit.* walk slowly)
píjiǔ	beer
qiǎokèlì	chocolates
shìqing	matter, thing
shūshu	uncle
tián (de)	sweet
wàiguó	foreign country
wàiguó-rén	foreigner
xiàndàihuà (de)	modern
xiāng	fragrant
zuò kè	to be a guest
zuǒshǒu	left hand
gōngzuò shùnlì	*lit.* work smooth
Lùshàng xiǎoxīn.	Take care on the road. (*Have a safe journey*)
quánjiā xìngfú	*lit.* whole family happy
shēnghuó yúkuài	*lit.* life pleasant
wànshì rúyì	*lit.* ten thousand things as you wish
Gěi nǐ(men) tiān máfan le.	Sorry to have troubled you.
Nà jiù bù liú nǐ le.	I won't keep you then.
Nǐ tài kèqi le.	You are being too polite.
Wèi . . . gān bēi!	To . . . (*used as a toast*).
Wǒ chī/hē-bu-xià le.	I can't eat / drink any more.
Wǒ gāi huí qù le.	I must be off now.
Wǒ sòngsong nǐ.	I'll see you out.
Wǒ zìjǐ lái.	I'll help myself.

 —————————— **Duìhuà** ——————————

Duìhuà 1

Mr White, who is called Lǎo Bái by his Chinese friends, is invited to dinner at the Yuáns' home. Listen to, or read, the dialogue and note how Mr White presents his gifts to the family.

Mr Yuán	Lǎo Bái, huānyíng, huānyíng.
Lǎo Bái	Lǎo Yuán, nǐ hǎo. Wǒ zhīdao nǐ ài hē jiǔ. Zhè shì gěi nǐde jiǔ.
Mr Yuán	Fǎguó pútáojiǔ! Nǐ tài kèqi le.
Lǎo Bái	Zhèi hé qiǎokèlì shì gěi nǐmen nǚ'ér de.
Mr Yuán	Zhēn Zhēn, kuài xièxie Bái shūshu.
Zhēn Zhēn	Xièxie Bái shūshu.
Lǎo Bái	Bú yòng xiè. . . . Zhēn xiāng a! Yuán tàitai, zuò shénme hǎochī de ne?
Mrs Yuán	Méi shénme hǎochī de. Dōu shì jiācháng biànfàn.
Lǎo Bái	Nǐmen de chúfáng tǐng xiàndàihuà de.
Mrs Yuán	Kěxī tài xiǎo le.
Mr Yuán	Lǎo Bái, kètīng lǐ zuò ba.
Lǎo Bái	Hǎo, hǎo. Nǐmen de kètīng zhēn piàoliang.
Mr Yuán	Nǎli, nǎli. Lǎo Bái, nǐ xiǎng hē diǎnr shénme?
Lǎo Bái	Hē diǎnr chá ba.

Note the various examples of **kèqi huà** (*polite talk*) in the dialogue above and in **Duìhuà 3** which was referred to in Unit 8, ➡️📖 101.

Cultural tip

It is quite usual to take off your shoes when going into other people's houses or flats and your host will usually provide some **tuōxié** (*slip-ons*, *lit.* drag shoes) for you.

✔️ Liànxí 2

The two patterns below are often used when giving something to somebody. You will need a *measure word* (MW) in pattern (ii):

(*i*) Zhè shì gěi nǐ de X. *This is an X for you.*
(*ii*) Zhè MW X shì gěi nǐ de. *This MW X is for you.*

You have brought with you the following things as presents when invited to dinner with a Chinese family. How would you present them? Try to use both (i) and (ii) patterns.

Example: Zhè shì gěi nǐ de huà.
 Zhè fú huà shì gěi nǐ de.

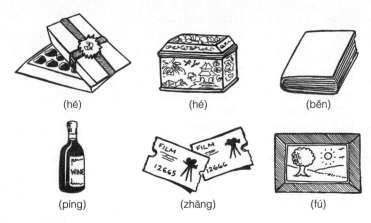

(hé)	(hé)	(běn)
(píng)	(zhāng)	(fú)

☑ Liànxí 3

Now use the presents and the patterns in **Liànxí 2**, but this time you've bought them for different people.

Example: my father, painting
  Zhè shì gěi wǒ bàba de huà.
  Zhè fú huà shì gěi wǒ bàba de.

(*a*) my elder sister, chocolates
(*b*) his wife, a tin of green tea
(*c*) her uncle, a book
(*d*) her boyfriend, a bottle of wine
(*e*) their company (**gōngsī**), a painting
(*f*) your (pl) friends, two film tickets

四海如家

Chinese proverb: **Sì Hǎi Rú Jiā**
(*lit*. four seas like home)

Duìhuà 2

The following dialogue is between Mr White and his Chinese hosts Mr and Mrs Yuán during a meal. Listen out for the **kèqi huà**.

Mr Yuán   Lǎo Bái, zánmen xiān hē yì bēi.
Lǎo Bái   Hǎo a.
Mr Yuán   Nǐ hē píjiǔ、 pútáojiǔ háishi lái diǎnr báijiǔ.
Lǎo Bái   Báijiǔ wǒ hē-bu-liǎo. Hē diǎnr pútáojiǔ ba.

Mr Yuán	Bái de háishi hóng de?
Lǎo Bái	Hóng de ba.
Mr Yuán	Zhèi zhǒng jiǔ bù tián. Wǒ zhīdao wàiguó-rén yìbān bù xǐhuān hē tián de jiǔ.
Lǎo Bái	Shì, wǒ bù xǐhuan hē tián de jiǔ.
Mr Yuán	Zánmen xiān gān yi bēi. Zhù nǐ gōngzuò shùnlì, shēnghuó yúkuài!
Lǎo Bái	Zhù nǐmen quánjiā xìngfú, wànshì rúyì!
Mr Yuán	Gān bēi!
Lǎo Bái	Gān bēi!
Mrs Yuán	Bié kèqi, duō chī diǎnr.
Lǎo Bái	Hǎo, hǎo, wǒ zìjǐ lái.

Lǎo Bái	Cài dōu fēicháng hǎochī.
Mr Yuán	Zài duō chī diǎnr.
Lǎo Bái	Wǒ yǐjīng chī-bǎo le.
Mrs Yuán	Nǐ chī-de tài shǎo le.
Lǎo Bái	Wǒ zhēnde chī-bu-xià le.
Mr Yuán	Nǐ tài kèqi le.
Lǎo Bái	Wǒ bú kèqi.

More examples of useful four-character phrases can be found in Unit 14, ➡️ 171).

Zhù nǐ(men) {	gōngzuò shùnlì!	*May your work go smoothly!*
	shēnghuó yúkuài!	*May your life be happy!*
	quánjiā xìngfú!	*May your whole family be blessed!*

─────────── **Cultural tip** ───────────

Gān bēi (*Drain your glass*) does not have to be taken literally, particularly in the case of 70 % proof *máotái* which is often used for toasts at banquets!

Liànxí 4

The following are some useful expressions which might come in handy when you are having dinner with a Chinese family. Do you know how to say them in Chinese?

(*a*) Cheers!

(*b*) I really can't eat any more.

(*c*) It smells nice.

(*d*) I'll help myself.

(*e*) Wishing you every happiness.

🔲 Duìhuà 3

Read the dialogue and note carefully the exchanges between the guest and his hosts.

Lǎo Bái	Wǒ kěyǐ yòng yíxià nǐmende cèsuǒ ma?
Mr Yuán	Zuǒshǒu dì èr jiān jiù shì.
Lǎo Bái	Oh, yǐjing jiǔ diǎn duō le. Wǒ gāi huí qù le.
Mr Yuán	Hái zǎo ne. Zài zuò yìhuǐr ba.
Lǎo Bái	Bú zuò le. Míngtiān zǎoshang wǒ hái yǒu shìqing.
Mr Yuán	Hǎo ba. Nà jiù bù liú nǐ le.
Lǎo Bái	Gěi nǐmen tiān máfan le.
Mrs Yuán	Méi shénme. Huānyíng nǐ zài lái.
Lǎo Bái	Yídìng, yídìng.
Mr Yuán	Wǒ sòngsong nǐ.
Lǎo Bái	Bú yòng le. Qǐng huí qù ba.
Mr Yuán	Màn zǒu.
Mrs Yuán	Lùshàng xiǎoxīn.
Lǎo Bái	Méi wèntí. Zàijiàn!
Mr & Mrs Yuán	Zàijiàn!

☑️ Liànxí 5

What do you say?

(a) What do you say when you think it's time to leave?
(b) How might your host respond if he/she doesn't want you to leave yet?
(c) How do you thank your host for all the trouble s/he has taken?
(d) What's your host's response to (c)?
(e) What do you say when your host suggests seeing you off?
(f) How do you tell somebody to take care driving or cycling?
(g) What's the common parting remark made by the host to his/her guest?

🔲 Duìhuà 4

The following is a dialogue between a Chinese managing director, his wife and his foreign counterpart of a joint venture. They are at a banquet. Listen to the cassette, and try to answer the following questions before you read the dialogue. Or read the dialogue and then answer the questions. This time the new words and expressions come after the dialogue, and we're given you the English translation of the questions.

Questions:
(a) Bái xiānsheng kuàizi yòng-de zěnmeyàng?
   (*Does Mr White use chopsticks very well?*)
(b) Tā shuō tā Zhōngguó fàn zuò-de hǎo bu hǎo?
   (*How well does he say he cooks?*)
(c) Tā chángcháng qù nǎr chī Zhōngguó fàn?
   (*Where does he often go for Chinese meals?*)
(d) Duìhuà lǐ shuō Baí xiānsheng chī-guo shénme?
   (i) yànwō tāng
   (ii) Máotáijiǔ
   (iii) fèngzhǎo
(e) *According to the dialogue what of the following has Mr White ever eaten/drunk?*
   (*i*) *birds' nest soup*
   (*ii*) *Máotái*
   (*iii*) *chicken feet*

Dǒngshìzhǎng	Bái xiānsheng, nín kuàizi yòng-de zhēn hǎo.
Mr White	Wǒ chángcháng chī Zhōngguó fàn.
Fūren	Nín zìjǐ zuò fàn ma?
Mr White	Wǒ zuò-de bù hǎo. Wǒ cháng qù Zhōngguóchéng de fànguǎnr chī fàn.
Dǒngshìzhǎng	Lái, xiān hē yì bēi. Zhè shì máotáijiǔ. Nín hē-guo ma?
Mr White	Hē-guo liǎng cì.
Dǒngshìzhǎng	Wèi wǒmen liǎng ge gōngsī de chénggōng hézuò gān bēi!
Mr White	Wèi Dǒngshìzhǎng hé Dǒngshìzhǎng fūren de jiànkāng gān bēi!
Fūren	Zhè shì yànwō tāng, fēicháng yǒu yíngyǎng.
Mr White	Wǒ tīngshuō-guo, kěshì méi hē-guo.
Dǒngshìzhǎng	Zhè shì fèngzhǎo, bù zhīdao nín chī-guo ma?
Mr White	Kàn-jian-guo, hái méi chī-guo.
Fūren	Zhènghǎo, qǐng chángchang ba.
Fūren	Duō chī diǎnr cài.
Dǒngshìzhǎng	Zài hē yì bēi.
Mr White	Wǒ chī-bu-xià le, yě hē-bu-xià le.
Dǒngshìzhǎng	Zài hē zuìhòu yì bēi. Wèi Zhōng-Yīng liǎng guó rénmín de yǒuyì gān bēi!
Mr White	Gān bēi! Xīwàng nǐmen yǒu jīhuì qù Yīngguó fǎngwèn.

Zhǔyào cíhuì

cháng (chang)	to taste
cháng	often
chénggōng	successful
dǒngshìzhǎng	managing director
fǎngwèn	visit (*formal*)
fèngzhǎo	chicken feet
fūren	wife (*formal*), madam
gōngsī	company
hézuò	cooperation, cooperate
jiànkāng	health, healthy
jīhuì	opportunity
kàn-jian	to see
máotái	maotai (*a very strong Chinese spirit*)
yànwō	birds' nest
yǒu yíngyǎng	nutritious
zhènghǎo	just right
Zhōngguóchéng	Chinatown
Zhōng-Yīng liǎng guó rénmín de yǒuyì	The friendship between the Chinese and British peoples
– liǎng guó	two countries
– rénmín	the people (*of a country*)
– yǒuyì	friendship
zuò (fàn)	to cook

Liànxí 6

Look at the Chinese words in the left-hand column and pair each of them with one in the right-hand column.

(*a*) fǎngwèn

(*b*) hézuò

(*c*) jīhuì

(*d*) fūren

(*e*) gōngsī

(*f*) chénggōng

(*i*) cooperate, cooperation

(*ii*) madam

(*iii*) to visit, visit (*formal*)

(*iv*) success, successful

(*v*) opportunity

(*vi*) company

Liànxí 7

The words in **Liànxí 6** are some of the words you might need in formal business encounters.

Now cover up the Chinese in the exercise above and just look at the English. Can you remember how to say them in Chinese?

You met **zhè/zhèi** (*this*) and **nà/nèi** (*that*) in Unit 2. They are normally followed by a measure word (see Unit 7). By putting the collective measure word **xiē** after **zhè/zhèi** and **nà/nèi** you have **zhèxiē/zhèixiē** (*these*) and **nàxiē/nèixiē** (*those*):

zhèxiē (shū)	*these (books)*
nàxiē (cài)	*those (dishes)*

Polite forms of address

The formal way of addressing a married woman in Chinese is **fūren** and not **tàitai**. Chinese speakers often translate **fūren** as *madam*:

Chén **fūren** *Madam Chen*

When writing in English, a Chinese speaker may well address his or her letter to Madam Jones which seems rather strange to most English speakers. **Fūren** can also be put after titles which carry a certain status such as manager or headmaster and can refer to female postholders' or male postholders' *wives*:

Dǒngshìzhǎng **fūren**	*Madam Manager* (used in Mr White's toast)
Xiàozhǎng **fūren**	*Madam Headmaster*

☑ Xiǎo cèyàn

When you hear these toasts, do you know what they mean?

(*a*) Zhù nǐ shēntǐ jiànkāng!
(*b*) Zhù nǐ shēnghuó yúkuài!
(*c*) Zhù nǐ wànshì rúyì!
(*d*) Zhù nǐ gōngzuò shùnlì!
(*e*) Zhù nǐ chénggōng!
(*f*) Wèi wǒmen de yǒuyì gān bēi!
(*g*) Wèi wǒmen de hézuò gān bēi!

17

KÀN YĪSHĒNG
Seeing a doctor

In this unit you will:

- learn how to describe symptoms to the doctor or the pharmacist
- understand the instructions on the medicine bottle
- learn about acupuncture, Chinese herbal medicine, **tàijíquán** and **qìgōng**

Kāishǐ yǐqián fùxí

● measure words	(4)(7)	● verb + **guo**	(9)
● both ... and ...	(9)	● use of **ba**	(3)
● **yǒu yìdiǎnr** (*a bit*)	(8)	● on + noun	(5)
● sentences ending in **le**	(4)	● When ...	(10)
● verb + **le**	(9)	● **bié** (*don't*)	(10)
● **shì bu shi**	(3)	● **gěi** (*for*)	(6)
● use of **háishi**	(6)		

The Chinese medical system is not the same as in Britain. The following passage tells us a little bit about some of the differences.

———— Zhōngguó de *Yīliáo* ————

Zài Zhōngguó, hěn duō *dānwèi* yǒu zìjǐ de *yīwùsuǒ*. Xiǎo de yīwùsuǒ zhǐ yǒu yí gè *yīshēng*, dà de kěyǐ yǒu *jǐ* ge yīshēng hé *hùshi*. Rúguǒ nǐ yǒu *bìng*, nǐ kěyǐ qù dānwèi de yīwùsuǒ, yě kěyǐ *zhíjiē* qù *yīyuàn*.

Zhōngguó de yīyuàn yìbān *fēnchéng* bùtóng de *kē*. *Yǒude* yīyuàn shì *zhuānkē* yīyuàn, zhǐ *kàn* yì、liǎng *zhǒng bìng*. Dà de yīyuàn yìbān yòu yǒu *Zhōngyī*, yòu yǒu *Xīyī*. Nǐ kěyǐ kàn Zhōngyī, yě kěyǐ kàn Xīyī.

bìng	illness
bìngrén	patient
dānwèi	work unit
fēnchéng	to divide/to be divided into
hùshi	nurse
jǐ	several, a few
kàn bìng	to see a doctor (*to have the illness looked at*)
kē	department (*in a hospital*)
Xīyī	Western medical (*doctor*); Western medicine
yīliáo	medical care
yīshēng	doctor
yīwùsuǒ	clinic (*attached to a work unit*)
yīyuàn	hospital
yǒude	some
zhíjiē	direct(*ly*)
zhǒng	kind, sort (*measure word*)
Zhōngyī	Chinese medical (*doctor*); Chinese medicine
zhuānkē	specialised; speciality . . .

Liànxí 1

According to the above passage, are the following statements **duì** or **bú duì**?

	duì/bú duì
(*a*) Yǒude dānwèi méi yǒu yīwùsuǒ.	☐ ☐
(*b*) Zài dà de yīyuàn, Zhōngyī、Xīyī dōu yǒu.	☐ ☐
(*c*) Yǒude yīwùsuǒ méi yǒu hùshi.	☐ ☐
(*d*) Bìngrén bù kěyǐ zhíjiē qù yīyuàn.	☐ ☐

Zhǔyào cíhuì

bú xiè	not at all
cānjiā	to attend
chī (yào)	to take (*medicine*)
dùzi	stomach, tummy

-lā dùzi	to have diarrhoea
fàn hòu	after meals
fàn qián	before meals
fúyòng fāngfǎ	instructions (*for taking medicine*)
gǎnmào	to have a cold
Hànzì	Chinese characters
kāfēi	coffee
kāishuǐ	boiled water
késou	cough
kǔ	bitter
lì	pill
ná	to take, fetch
piàn(r)	tablets
píngzi	bottle
téng	painful; pain
tóuténg	headache
wán(r)	(*Chinese medicine*) ball
wēn	warm
Xīyào	Western medicine
yànhuì	banquet
yào	medicine
yàofāng	prescription
yàofáng	pharmacy
yìxiē	some
yǒu shíhou	sometimes
yǒu xiào	effective
zhā	to pierce, to put in a needle, to do acupuncture
zhēnjiū	acupuncture
zhěnsuǒ	clinic (*open to the general public*)
zhèyàng	like this, in this way
Zhōngyào	Chinese medicine
Wǒ bù shūfu.	I don't feel well.
Wǒ . . . téng.	My . . . hurts.
Wǒde tiān a!	Good heavens!

 ──────────── **Duìhuà** ────────────

Duìhuà 1

Mr White is not feeling at all well. He decides to go to the company's clinic. Listen to the dialogue and try to find out what's wrong with him. What does he think has caused the problem, and what does the doctor think the cause is? What medicine does the doctor prescribe?

Yīshēng Nǐ nǎr bù shūfu?
Bái Wǒ dùzi bù shūfu.
Yīshēng Lā dùzi ma?
Bái Yǒu yìdiǎnr.
Yīshēng Nǐ zuótiān chī shénme le?
Bái Wǒ cānjiā le yí ge yànhuì, chī le fèngzhǎo, hē le yànwō tāng.
Yīshēng Nèixiē dōu shì hǎo dōngxi, duì nǐ shēntǐ hǎo.
Bái Wǒ kěnéng chī-de tài duō le.
Yīshēng Nǐ hē le hěn duō jiǔ, shì bu shi?
Bái Bù duō, zhǐ hē le bā bēi.
Yīshēng Wǒ míngbai le. Wǒ gěi nǐ yìxiē yào. Nǐ yuànyì shìshi Zhōngyào ma?
Bái Wǒ méi chī-guo Zhōngyào. Tīngshuō Zhōngyào hěn kǔ, shì ma?
Yīshēng Yǒude kǔ, yǒude bù kǔ. Wǒ gěi nǐ de yào bù kǔ.
Bái Nà wǒ shìshi ba.
Yīshēng Zhè shì yàofāng. Qǐng dào yàofáng qù ná yào.
Bái Yīshēng, xièxie nín.
Yīshēng Bú yòng xiè.

首都医院 | **急诊室**
Shǒudū Yīyuàn | **Jízhěnshì**
Capital Hospital | *Emergency Room*

Liànxí 2

You have a cold, (which is a common illness in China as well) and you're seeing a Chinese doctor. Complete the following dialogue.

    Yīshēng Nǐ zěnme le?
(a) **You** (*Tell her that you have a headache.*)
    Yīshēng Hái yǒu nǎr bù shūfu?
(b) **You** (*Say you cough a bit.*)
    Yīshēng Wǒ xiǎng nǐ yǒu yìdiǎnr gǎnmào.
(c) **You** (*Say you also feel it's a cold.*)
    Yīshēng Wǒ gěi nǐ diǎnr yào. Nǐ chī Zhōngyào ma?
(d) **You** (*Say you've never taken it before and ask the doctor if Chinese medicine is effective.*)
    Yīshēng Yídìng yǒu xiào.
(e) **You** (*Say it's OK and you will give it a try.*)

Duìhuà 2

At the pharmacy.

药房

Yàofáng *Pharmacy*

Pharmacist	Zhè shì nínde yào.
Mr White	Zěnme chī ya?
Pharmacist	Píngzi shàng yǒu fúyòng fāngfǎ.
Mr White	Duìbuqǐ, wǒ hái bú rènshi Hànzì.
Pharmacist	O. Duìbuqǐ. Wǒ gàosù nǐ. Yì tiān chī sān cì, yí cì chī èrshí lì.
Mr White	Shénme? Yì tiān chī liùshí lì?!
Pharmacist	Duì.
Mr White	Wǒde tiān a!
Pharmacist	Chī yào de shíhou bú yào hē kāfēi、 chá hé jiǔ. Yīnggāi hē wēn kāishuǐ.
Mr White	Wèishénme?
Pharmacist	Chī yào dōu yīnggāi zhèyàng.
Mr White	Wǒde yào fàn qián chī háishì fàn hòu chī?
Pharmacist	Dōu kéyǐ.
Mr White	Xièxie nín.
Pharmacist	Bú xiè.

You have seen that '**time when**' expressions such as *Tuesday, 9 o'clock*, come before the verb (Unit 1, ➡️📖 20) and that '**time during which**' expressions such as how long you do something for come after the verb (Unit 9, ➡️📖 113).

Time *within* which something happens comes *before* the verb:

Wǒ **yì tiān** chī liǎng cì.	*I eat twice (in)* ***a day***.
Yì tiān yào chī liùshí lì.	*(You) have to take (lit.* eat*) 60 pills (in)* ***a day***.

Fàn qián is a more formal way of saying **chī fàn yǐqián** (*before a meal, lit.* eat cooked rice before) and **fàn hòu** of saying **chī fàn yǐhòu** (*after a meal – lit.* eat cooked rice after). Note that (**yǐ**)**qián** and (**yǐ**)**hòu** go after the noun in Chinese, the reverse of the English word order.

Instructions for taking Chinese medicine are given in the reverse of the way they are usually given in English-speaking countries. The normal word order in Chinese is:

fàn qián/hòu	*meal before/after*
yì tiān	*per day*
jǐ cì	*how many times*
yí cì chī/hē lì/piàn/wán(r)	*every time eat/drink pills/tablets/balls*

Chinese medicine sometimes comes in the form of small balls which you have to chew. This is not all unpleasant (they are often flavoured with liquorice), but this form of medicine is not so commonly found in Chinese herbal medicine shops in the West catering for Westerners. The Chinese seem to believe that Westerners prefer to take pills!

Liànxí 3

Read the instructions about taking the following medicines. Indicate whether each medicine is to be taken before or after meals and fill in the gaps (two per line).

服用方法

Fúyòng fángfǎ
Instructions for taking (the) medicine

(*a*) before/after meal; ＿＿ times a day; take ＿＿ every time
(*b*) before/after meal; ＿＿ times a day; take ＿＿ every time
(*c*) before/after meal; ＿＿ times a day; take ＿＿ every time
(*d*) before/after meal; ＿＿ times a day; take ＿＿ every time

---

1 Zhèi zhǒng Zhōngyào fàn qián chī, yì tiān liǎng cì, yí cì yì wánr.

2 Zhèi ge yào fàn hòu chī, yì tiān chī sì cì, yí cì chī sān piànr.

3 Nèi ge yào bú yào fàn qián chī. Fàn hòu yí ge xiǎoshí zài chī. Yì tiān chī sān cì, yí cì hē yì sháo (*tablespoon*).

4 Zhè ge yào zǎoshang chī yí cì, wǎnshang chī yí cì. Yí cì chī liǎng、sān piàn.

Duìhuà 3

The following dialogue is between a Westerner visiting a Chinese clinic and a Chinese doctor working at the clinic. Before reading the dialogue, listen to the cassette and try **Liànxí 4** first. You can then check your answers when you read it.

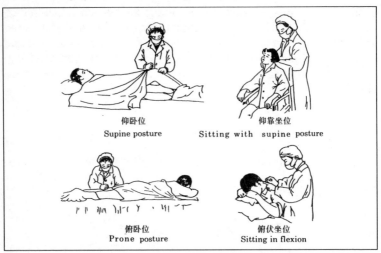

仰卧位
Supine posture

仰靠坐位
Sitting with supine posture

俯卧位
Prone posture

俯伏坐位
Sitting in flexion

Visitor Nǐmen zhěnsuǒ bīngrén duō ma?

Doctor Bù shǎo.

Visitor Nǐmen dōu kàn shénme bìng?

Doctor Gèzhǒng gèyàng de bìng. Nǐ kàn, zhèi ge bìngrén chángcháng tóu téng. Tā kàn-guo Xīyī, chī-guo Xīyào, kěshì hái bù hǎo. Wǒmen gěi tā zhā le zhēnjiū, xiànzài tā hāo duōle.

Visitor Zhēnde? Wǒ yě yǒu shíhou tóu téng. Tā zhā le jǐ cì le?

Doctor Sì cì le.

Visitor Zhēnjiū shì bu shì hěn téng?

Doctor Zhēnjiū shì bù shūfu, kěshì chángcháng hěn yǒu xiào.

Visitor Zhēnde ma?

Doctor Nǐ yǒu shénme bìng? Wǒ kěyǐ gěi nǐ zhā.

Visitor Bú yòng、bú yòng, wǒ méi bìng. Wǒde shēntǐ hěn hǎo. Xièxie nín.

☑ Liànxí 4

Select the correct answer to complete the statements which are based on **Duìhuà 3**.

(a) There are ___ patients visiting the clinic. (*a lot, quite a few, few*)

(b) The clinic treats ___ illnesses. (*all sorts of, some, one or two kinds of*)

(c) The patient being treated in the clinic often has ___. (*diarrhoea, headaches, stomach ache*)

(d) The visitor declined the offer of acupuncture because he ___. (*was scared, had no illness, had not the time*)

When two **le**'s occur in the same sentence as in the Visitor's 3rd line in **Duìhuà 3**, one after the verb and one at the end of the sentence, they convey the idea that the action of the verb is still going on:

Tā zài Lúndūn zhù **le** sān nián **le**.   *He's been living in London for three years (and still is).*

(Nǐ gěi tā) zhā **le** jǐ cì (zhēnjiū) **le**?   *How many times have you given her acupuncture (so far)?*

By putting **shì** in front of a verb or adjective you emphasise it:

Zhēnjiū **shì** bu shūfu.   *Acupuncture is uncomfortable.*

Xiě Hànzì **shì** hěn nán.   *Writing Chinese characters is difficult.*

Cultural tip

To the Chinese way of thinking, each individual (and on a much larger scale the universe) is made up of **yīn** (*the female or passive/negative principle*) and **yáng** (*the male or active/positive principle*). To enjoy good health your **yīn** and **yáng** must be in balance. Chinese medicine seeks to redress any imbalance that exists.

Liànxí 5

When a part of your body aches, you say **Wǒ(de) ___ téng**.

If you feel uncomfortable somewhere, you may say **Wǒ(de) ___ bù shūfu**.

If you don't know the Chinese word for the part of body you want to refer to, you can simply point at the place and say **Wǒ zhèr** (*here*) **téng**, or **Wǒ zhèr bù shūfu**.

Now practise these two patterns using the different parts of the body in turn (the Chinese for them is given in the drawing). You are answering the doctor's question **Nǐ nǎr bù shūfu?**. So for the head you would say:

Wǒ tóu téng, *or*
Wǒ tóu bù shūfu.

——— Cultural tip ———

Acupuncture is an ancient Chinese method of treating disease. It is based on the theory that the human body has a whole series of meridians up and down it through which your **qì** (sometimes written **ch'i** in the West) (*vital energy*) flows.

Having made his/her diagnosis, the acupuncturist inserts fine needles at various points (which all have different names) in your meridians to clear any blockages to your **qì**.

Some conditions seem to respond particularly well to acupuncture – rheumatoid-arthritis, gynaecological problems and the after-effects of strokes to mention just a few.

Why not be brave and try acupuncture treatment yourself if you suffer from a long-standing condition that has not improved with conventional methods? But be sure you go to a reputable acupuncturist who is accredited or better still ask your GP or enquire at your local health shop to see if they can recommend someone.

Liànxí 6

Find the Chinese equivalents in Section B to match the English sentences in Section A. Then say the Chinese sentences in the same order as the English sentences and you'll see a short passage about **qìgōng** in Chinese.

Section A:

(a) There are all kinds of qigong.
(b) Many people believe that qigong can cure all sorts of illness.
(c) Qigong is very popular nowadays in China.
(d) It's good for your health to do qigong very often.
(e) Both Tai Chi and qigong are slow forms of exercise.
(f) Some forms (of qigong) are not difficult (to practise); some are not easy.

Section B:

(i)   Xiànzài zài Zhōngguó, zuò qìgōng hěn liúxíng.
(ii) Yǒude qìgōng bù nán, yǒude hěn bù róngyì.
(iii) Chángcháng zuò qìgōng duì shēntǐ hǎo.
(iv) Qìgōng yǒu gèzhǒng gèyàng de.
(v)   Hěn duō rén rènwéi qìgōng kěyǐ zhì gèzhǒng gèyàng de bìng.
(vi) Qìgōng gēn tàijíquán dōu shì hěn màn de yùndòng.

Xiǎo cèyàn

(a) You see your Chinese friend looking unwell. Ask what's wrong with him (*lit.* where he is not comfortable).
(b) Say you want to try acupuncture.
(c) Say you think you have a cold.
(d) Tell the doctor that you have never taken Chinese medicine.
(e) Tell the doctor that you sometimes have a headache.

18

DUÌFU WÈNTÍ
Coping with problems

In this unit you will learn:

- how to ask for help
- some key expressions to describe your problems
- to practise some expressions required in an emergency
- the basic Highway Code in China

Kāishǐ yǐqián fùxí

- **gēn . . . yíyàng**   (6)
- **zuì** (*most*)   (7)
- noun + **on**   (5)
- **yòu . . . yòu**   (9)
- helping verbs   (6)
- measure words   (4) (7)
- use of **háishi**   (6)

- how long   (9)
- reduplicated verbs   (6)
- **méi yǒu** (*not to have*) (2)
- **gěi** (*for*)   (6)
- verb endings   (10)
- **yǒu (yì)diǎnr**   (8)
- sentences ending in **le**   (4)

What do you know about the transport in China? A lot of bikes? That's right. But read the passage below and find out something more about it.

—— Zhōngguó de *Jiāotōng* ——

Zài Zhōngguó, kāi chē hé qí zìxíngchē dōu *zǒu lù de yòubiān*. Zhè gēn zài Měiguó hé *Ōuzhōu dàlù* yíyàng, gēn zài Yīngguó bù yíyàng.

Zhōngguó shì *shìjiè shàng* zìxíngchē zuì duō de *guójiā*. Zài dà *chéngshì* yǒu hěn duō *zìxíngchē dào*. Xiànzài zài Zhōngguó *zū* qìchē hái hěn nán, kěshì zū zìxíngchē bǐjiào fāngbiàn. Qí zìxíngchē yòu piányì yòu yǒu yìsi.

Zài Zhōngguó yǒu *dìtiě* de chéngshì hěn shǎo. Bù shǎo chéngshì yǒu *diànchē*.

Yīnwei Zhōngguó-rén tài duō, suǒyǐ *lù shàng zǒngshì* hěn jǐ. *Gōnggòng qìchē* yě fēicháng jǐ. Dāngrán nǐ kěyǐ zuò chūzūchē. Chūzūchē bù jǐ, kěshì bù piányì.

Yàoshì nǐ cóng yí gè chéngshì qù *lìng yí gè* chéngshì, nǐ kěyǐ zuò fēijī, huǒchē, yě kěyǐ zuò *chángtú qìchē*. Chángtú qìchē yǒu shíhou bú tài shūfu.

chángtú qìchē	coach (*lit.* long distance vehicle)
chéngshì	city
diànchē	tram (*lit.* electric vehicle)
dìtiě	underground
duìfu	to cope with
gōnggòng qìchē	bus (*lit.* public together steam vehicle)
guójiā	country
jiāotōng	transport, traffic
lìng yí gè	another
lù shàng	on the road
Ōuzhōu dàlù	Continental Europe
shìjiè (shàng)	(*in the*) world
yīnwei	because
yàoshi	if
yòubiān	right side
-zǒu lù de yòubiān	to drive/cycle on the right
zìxíngchē dào	bicycle lane
zǒngshì	always
zū	to hire, rent
zuǒ	left (*opposite of right*)

 Liànxí 1

How do you say the following in Chinese about traffic in the West?

At first sight the sentences may seem to be difficult. But if you model them on the sentences in the passage above you should find them quite manageable.

(*a*) In Britain driving and cycling are on the left-hand side of the road.
(*b*) This is the same as in Japan and Ireland but not the same as on the Continent.
(*c*) America is the country that has the most cars in the world.
(*d*) In the West it's not difficult to hire a car.

Placewords such as **lǐ** (*inside*) can also have a longer form so you will sometimes see **lǐmiàn(r)** (*lit*. in surface) or **lǐbiān(r)** (*lit*. in side) instead of just **lǐ**. There is no difference in meaning however. This also applies to words like **shàng** (*on* or *on top of*), **xià** (*underneath*) and **wài** (*outside*).

Note that **shìjiè shàng** does not mean *on top of the world* but *in the world*. **Lǐ** is only used when you can actually get inside something, such as a shop, or when referring to money *in* a purse.

 ———————— **Zhǔyào cíhuì** ————————

bāo	bag
– **qiánbāo**	purse/wallet
bié rén	other/another person
chēdài	tyre
– **bǔ chēdài**	to mend a tyre
chéng lǐ	in the city, in urban areas
cuò	fault, mistake
dàshǐguǎn	embassy
dēng	lights
diū	to lose
duō yuǎn?	how far?
– **hái yǒu duō yuǎn?**	How far is it still to . . . ?
èrbā de	28 inch (*bike*)
èrliù de	26 inch (*bike*)
gāoxìng	happy
guǎi	to turn
hǎoxiàng	to seem
hòulái	later
huài	broken, not working; bad
jǐngchá	policeman
jǐn(yi)jǐn	to tighten
liàng	(*measure word for vehicles including bicycles*)
líng	(*for brakes*) to work well
mǎshàng	at once
nánchē	bike for men

nǚchē	bike for women
shéide?	whose?
shēnfènzhèng	identity card
shīfu	*title used when addressing a skilled worker* (*lit.* master)
shǒu	hand
shuài le yì jiāo	to have had a fall
tōngzhī	to inform
xiāoxi	news, information
yī . . . jiù	no sooner . . . than . . . , as soon as
yòng-bù-zháo	not necessary
zěnme huí shì?	what's the matter?
zhá	brakes
zhàoxiàngjī	camera
zhuàng	to collide
zhuàng-huài (le)	damage(d) (*lit.* collide broken)
Zhēn dǎoméi!	How unfortunate! Bad luck!

Duìhuà

Duìhuà 1

When visiting a Chinese city, it is worth hiring a bicycle to explore the local area. It's economical too! This is what Ann and her friend are trying to do when they visit Nanjing. Listen to, or read, the dialogue and find out what kind of bicycle is available and how much they cost.

Ann	Wǒ xiǎng zū liǎng liàng zìxíngchē.
Shopkeeper	Yǒu shēnfènzhèng ma?
Ann	Yǒu. Zhè shì wǒde hùzhào.
Shopkeeper	Hǎo. Nín zū něi zhǒng chē? Èrliù de háishì èrbā de? Nánchē háishì nǚchē?
Ann	Wǒ yào yí liàng èrliù de nǚchē. Wǒde péngyǒu yào yí liàng èrbā de nánchē.
Shopkeeper	Nǐmen zū jǐ tiān?
Ann	Yì tiān.
Shopkeeper	Nèi liǎng liàng búcuò. Nǐmen shìshi ba.
Ann	Yǒu mei yǒu hóngsè de?
Shopkeeper	Duìbuqǐ, jīntiān méi yǒu.
	Ann and her friend try the bikes.
Ann	Zhèi liàng chē de zhá hǎoxiàng bú tài líng.

Shopkeeper	Shì ma? Wǒ gěi nín jǐnyijǐn.
Ann	Zhèi xiē chē zěnme dōu méi yǒu dēng?
Shopkeeper	Zài chéng lǐ yòng-bù-zháo dēng.
Ann	Hǎo ba. Wǒ zū zhèi liǎng liàng. Duōshao qián?
Shopkeeper	Zhèi liàng èrbā de yì tiān bā kuài. Nèi liàng èrliù de yì tiān qī kuài. Yígòng shíwǔ kuài.
Ann	Gěi nín èrshí kuài.
Shopkeeper	Zhǎo nín wǔ kuài.

Note that **èrliù** is short for **èrshíliù (cùn)** (*26 inches*).
Èrbā is short for **èrshíbā (cùn)** (*28 inches*).

Cultural tip

Bicycle parking lots abound in Chinese cities. For a very modest charge you can leave your bicycle there. It will be much safer.

Cúnchēchù

Bicycles in China are not required by law to have lights. It is worth bearing this in mind as a cyclist or a motorist: as a cyclist it means you are difficult to be seen, as a motorist it means you have to be extra alert when driving in the dark.

 Liànxí 2

Now you are visiting Taiwan and you want to hire a car. Complete the **Duìhuà** below. **Duìhuà 1** should help you.

(a) **You** (*Say you would like to hire a car.*)
  Clerk Nín yǒu jiàzhào (*driving licence*) ma?
(b) **You** (*Say yes and yours is a British one.*)
  Clerk Nín yào něi zhǒng chē?
(c) **You** (*Say you'd like to have a small one.*)
  Clerk Zhèi liàng kěyǐ ma?
(d) **You** (*Say it's fine.*)
  Clerk Nín zū jǐ tiān?
(e) **You** (*Say two days.*)
  Clerk Qǐng dào nèibiān fù qián.

(*f*) **You**   (*Ask if they take credit cards?*)
Clerk Shōu.

Duìhuà 2

Unfortunately Ann has got a flat tyre on her bike. She sees a bike repair man by the side of the road and walks over for help.

Ann   Shīfu, wǒde chēdài huài le, nín néng bāng wǒ xiūxiu ma?
Shīfu Méi wèntí.
Ann   Děi duō cháng shíjiān?
Shīfu Yìhuǐr jiù xíng.
Ann   Shīfu, chōu zhī yān ba.
Shīfu Hǎo、hǎo. Xièxie、xièxie.
Ann   Shīfu, qù Xiāngshān hái yǒu duō yuǎn?
Shīfu Wǎng běi qí èrshí fēnzhòng, zài wǎng xī guǎi jiù dào le.

*   *   *

Shīfu Xiū-hǎo le.
Ann   Zhēn kuài. Xièxie nín. Zhèi liàng chē de zhá bú tài líng, nín néng kànkan ma?
Shīfu Kěyǐ. Wǒ gěi nín jǐnjin. . . . Xíng le.
Ann   Xièxie nín. Yígòng duōshao qián?
Shīfu Bǔ chēdài liǎng kuài wǔ. Jǐn zhá jiù bù shōu nǐ qián le.
Ann   Xièxie shīfu. Nín zài lái zhī yān ba.

雪中送碳

Chinese proverb: **xuě zhōng sòng tàn**
Send charcoal in snowy weather – provide timely help.

Liànxí 3

In **Duìhuà 2**, you saw several noun phrases consisting of a verb and an object, such as: **bǔ chēdài**, **jǐn zhá**, and **qù Xiāngshān**.

These phrases can be used at the beginning of a sentence as a kind of topic – the opposite of the word order in English. You can see this clearly from the example:

Kāi chē shàng bān děi yào   *How long does it take **to drive**
duō cháng shíjiān?   **to work**?*

Now try the same thing with the sentences below when you put them into Chinese.

(*a*) It takes an hour *to drive to work*.
(*b*) How much does it cost *to have the tyre mended*?
(*c*) How do I *get to the Fragrant Hills by bus*?
(*d*) It costs 30 yuan *to hire a bike*.

📰 Duìhuà 3

Ānyīn notices that her friend Ben is looking rather unhappy. Listen to, or read, the **Duìhuà** and find out what happened to Ben.

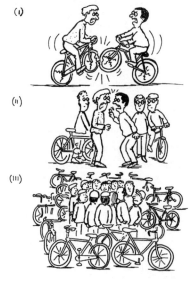

Ānyīn	Nǐ hǎoxiàng yǒu diǎnr bù gāoxìng. (i)
Ben	Méi shénme.
Ānyīn	Nǐde shǒu zěnme le?
Ben	O, wǒ shuāi le yì jiāo.
Ānyīn	Zěnme huí shì?
Ben	Zhēn dǎoméi! Wǒ gēn bié rén zhuàng chē le. (ii)
Ānyīn	Shì shéide cuò?
Ben	Wǒ shuō shì tāde cuò, tā shuō shì wǒde cuò.
Ānyīn	Chē zhuàng-huài le ma? (iii)
Ben	Zhuàng-huài le.
Ānyīn	Nǐmen zhǎo jǐngchá le ma?
Ben	Zhǎo le. Jǐngchá shuō wǒmen dōu yǒu cuò.
Ānyīn	Hòulái ne?
Ben	Hòulái, wǒmen dōu qù xiū zìjǐ de chē le.

———— Cultural tip ————

In China you can turn right at a red light (*hóng dēng*) so be very alert when you see a red traffic-light whether you are driving a car or riding a bicycle. **Hónglǜdēng** *means traffic lights* (*lit.* red green light).

Liànxí 4

Say whether the following statements are **duì** or **bù duì** (true or false)?

	duì/bú duì?	
(*a*) Ānyīn hěn bù gāoxìng.	☐	☐
(*b*) Ben gēn bié rén zhuàng chē le.	☐	☐
(*c*) Nà ge rén shuō shì Ben de cuò.	☐	☐
(*d*) Zhuàng chē yǐhòu, Ben zhǎo le jǐngchá.	☐	☐
(*e*) Ben de chē zhuàng-huài le.	☐	☐
(*f*) Jǐngchá shuō shì Ben de cuò.	☐	☐
(*g*) Ben qù xiū Ānyīn de chē le.	☐	☐

Duìhuà 4

Ben is now at a local police station. He really has had bad luck. Read the dialogue, and find out what his problem is and what he is advised to do.

Jǐngchá Nín yǒu shénme shì?
Ben Wǒde bāo diū le.
Jǐngchá Bāo lǐmiàn yǒu shénme?
Ben Yǒu wǒde hùzhào hé qiánbāo. Qiánbāo lǐ yǒu wǒde xìnyòng kǎ、 sìbǎi duō rénmínbì hé liǎngbǎi měiyuán. O, hái yóu yī ge xiǎo zhàoxiàngjī.
Jǐngchá Nín diū le hùzhào, yīnggāi tōngzhī nǐmen guójiā de dàshǐguǎn.
Ben Wǒ gěi dàshǐguǎn dǎ diànhuà le.
(The policewoman takes down the details of the incident.)
Jǐngchá Nín xiànzài zhù zài nǎr?
Ben Yùlóng Fàndiàn sān-líng-yāo fángjiān.
Jǐngchá Qǐng nín xiān huí qù. Wǒmen **yī** yǒu xiāoxi **jiù** mǎshàng tōngzhī nín.

Linking words (also known as conjunctions) often come in pairs in Chinese so it is good to memorise them as such. There are two examples in this unit.

yīnwei . . . suǒyǐ . . .   because . . . therefore . . .
. . . yī + verb¹ jiù + verb²   as soon as verb¹ happens, then verb² will happen (**Duìhuà** 4)

✔ Liànxí 5

Now you have listened to, or read, **Duìhuà 3** answer the following questions.

(*a*) What was Ben's problem?
(*b*) What was in the bag?
(*c*) How much money had he taken with him?
(*d*) Where was Ben staying?
(*e*) What was he advised to do about the loss of the passport?
(*f*) What did the police say they would do?

✔ Liànxí 6

Make at least one statement about the problems in the following pictures.

Nǐ zuò-cuò chē le.   *You've taken the wrong bus.*

✔ *Xiǎo cèyàn*

You happen to have run into a problem:

(*a*) How would you say it was unlucky?
(*b*) Say that it's not your fault.
(*c*) Say that you think they should go to the police.
(*d*) Say that you've lost your credit card.
(*e*) Something has gone wrong with your bike (or anything), ask if someone can have a look at it.

19

XUÉXÍ ZHŌNGWÉN
Learning Chinese

In this unit you will learn:

- the basic vocabulary to describe the characteristics of a language
- how to talk about your future plans
- how to respond to compliments or forthright remarks

Kaishi yiqian fuxi

- use of **háishi** (6)
- **gēn . . . yíyàng** (6)
- use of **de** after verbs (8)
- **tài – le** (7)
- helping verbs (6)

- be in the middle of doing something (6)
- **gèng** (*even more*) (8)
- verb endings (10)
- **zuì** (*most*) (7)
- **duō** + verb (10)

Which Chinese word describes the language you have been learning in this book? Is it **Hànyǔ**, **Zhōngwén**, **Pǔtōnghuà**, **Guóyǔ** or **Huáyǔ**? Read the passage below and find out.

—— Zhōngwén háishì Hànyǔ? ——

Zhōngwén yìbān zhǐ Hànyǔ. *Zhōng*wén de *Zhōng* shì *Zhōng*guó de *Zhōng*. Wén shì *writing* huòzhě *language* de yìsi. Hànyǔ de hàn shì Hànzú de hàn. Yǔ ʒhi Yǔyán de Yǔ, yě shì *language* de yìsi. Hànyǔ jiù shì Hànzú-rén de yǔyán. Zhōngguó de hěn duō shǎoshù mínzú dōu yǒu zìjǐ de yǔyán.

Hànyǔ yǒu hěn duō zhǒng fāngyán. Shànghǎihuà shì yì zhǒng fāngyán. Shànghǎi-rén shuō Shànghǎihuà. Guǎngdōnghuà yě shì yì zhǒng fāngyán. Guǎngdōng-rén hé Xiānggǎng-rén shuō Guǎngdōnghuà.

Wǒmen xuéxí de Zhōngwén shì Pǔtōnghuà. Pǔtōnghuà bú shì fāngyán, shì guānfāng yǔyán. Táiwān-rén jiào tā Guóyǔ, Dōngnányà de Huá-rén jiào tā Huáyǔ. Guóyǔ hé Huáyǔ jiù shì Pǔtōnghuà. Pǔtōnghuà bú shì Běijīnghuà. Běijīnghuà hé Pǔtōnghuà chàbuduō. Hěn duō Běijīng-rén shuō de Pǔtōnghuà yǒu Běijīng kǒuyīn.

 ────────── # Zhǔyào cíhuì ──────────

Dōngnányà	Southeast Asia
fāngyán	dialect
guānfāng	official
Guóyǔ	national language
Hànzú	Han nationality
Hànzú-rén	the Han people
Huá	another word for China
Huá-rén	overseas Chinese people
kǒuyīn	accent
Pǔtōnghuà	Chinese (Mandarin) (*lit.* common language)
shǎoshù mínzú	national minority
wén	language, writing
yǔ (yán)	language
zhǐ	to refer to

 Liànxí 1

There are several language terms in the passage above. You will find them very useful. Without referring to the vocabulary list, can you match the words with their correct meanings?

(*a*) Pǔtōnghuà   (*i*) Cantonese

(*b*) Guóyǔ   (*ii*) Chinese (spoken by overseas Chinese)

(*c*) Guǎngdōnghuà   (*iii*) Chinese language

(d) fāngyán	(iv) Chinese (spoken in Mainland China)
(e) Zhōngwén	(v) accent
(f) kǒuyīn	(vi) Chinese (spoken by Chinese people in Taiwan)
(g) Huáyǔ	(vii) dialect

✅ Liànxí 2

Fill in the blanks with suitable words. You will find it useful to go back to the passage on the previous page.

(a) Dàbùfen (*most*) Zhōngguó-rén shì ___ rén. Tāmen shuō ___.

(b) Sìchuānhuà bú shì Pǔtōnghuà, shì yì zhǒng ___. Yǒude Sìchuān-rén shuō de Pǔtōnghuà yǒu Sìchuān ___.

(c) Pǔtōnghuà zài Táiwān jiào ___, zài Dōngnányà jiào ___.

(d) Zài Zhōngguó, hěn duō shǎoshù mínzú de rén huì shuō tāmen zìjǐ de ___, yě huì shuō ___.

 ——————— **Zhǔyào cíhuì** ———————

bàng	excellent
bù xíng	not that good
cōngming	clever
dàjiā	everyone
duì . . . yǒu / gǎn xìngqu	to be interested in
duō tīng/shuō/dú/xiě	to listen/speak/read/write more
Éguó-rén	Russian (person)
èrhú	a two-stringed musical instrument
fāngfǎ	method
fānyì	interpreter, translator; to translate
guòjiǎng	to exaggerate, to flatter
Hánguó-rén	Korean (person)
jiǎndān	simple
jièshào	to introduce; introduction
jīngjì	economy
jìzhě	journalist
Kǒngzǐ	Confucius
Lǎozǐ	*an ancient philosopher*
Lǐ Bái	*an ancient poet*
lìshǐ	history
liúlì	fluent
pípa	*a musical instrument*

qiānxū	modest
shēng	tone (e.g. **dì yī/èr shēng** = *the 1st/* *2nd tone*)
shēngdiào	tones
wénxué	literature
xiānsheng	husband
xiě	to write
xìngqu	interest
xuésheng	student
yánjiū	to study, to research
yǔfǎ	grammar
yǔyīn	pronunciation
zhéxué	philosophy
zhǐyào . . . jiù . . .	so long as . . . then . . .
Zhuāngzǐ	*an ancient philosopher*

Duìhuà

Duìhuà 1

Lányīn, a student of Chinese, is talking to Huáyàn, a Chinese student of English, about learning foreign languages. Listen to, or read, the dialogue and find out the secret of Lányīn's success in learning Chinese.

Huáyàn Nǐde Zhōngwén zhèn bàng, shuō-de zhēn liúlì.
Lányīn Nǎli, nǎli, shuō-de bù hǎo.
Huáyàn Nǐde yǔyīn、 shēngdiào dōu fēicháng hǎo.
Lányīn Bù xíng, bù xíng, hái chà-de hěn yuǎn.
Huáyàn Nǐ xué le jǐ nián le?
Lányīn Sān nián le.
Huáyàn Shénme? Zhǐ yǒu sān nián?! Nǐ tài cōngming le.
Lányīn Nǐ guòjiǎng le.
Huáyàn Wǒ xué le liù nián Yīngyǔ le, kěshì shuō-de hái hěn chà.
Lányīn Nǐ zhēn qiānxū.
Huáyàn Nǐ yídìng yào gàosù wǒ nǐde xuéxí fāngfǎ.
Lányīn Hěn jiǎndān. Wǒ xiānsheng shì Zhōngguó-rén.

Liànxí 3

Answer the following questions in Chinese based on **Duìhuà 1**.

(*a*) In what aspects is Lányīn's Chinese good?
(*b*) How long has Lányīn been learning Chinese?

(*c*) How good is Huáyàn's English?
(*d*) How long has Huáyàn been learning English?
(*e*) What does Huáyàn want to know from Lányīn?
(*f*) Who does Lányīn think she owes her success to?

How good is good?

The following table lists the degrees of goodness you have met in descending order.

 ─────────────── **Zhǔyào cíhuì** ───────────────

zuì hǎo	the best
fēicháng hǎo	extremely good/well
búcuò	pretty good/well
(hěn) hǎo	(very) good/well
bú tài hǎo	not very good/well
bù hào	not good/well
(hěn) chà	(very) poor/badly

Note that **hǎo** translates as *good* or *well* depending on whether it is being used as an adjective/verb, when it means *good*, or as an adverb, when it means *well*.

Tā shuō de hěn **hǎo**.   *He speaks very well.*

Duìhuà 2

On the first day of a Chinese summer course the students introduce themselves and talk about their reasons for studying Chinese. Listen to, or read, the dialogue to find out where they are from and why they want to learn Chinese.

Lǎoshī Nǐmen hǎo. Wǒ xìng Táng, shì nǐmen de lǎoshī. Nǐmen kěyǐ jiào wǒ Táng lǎoshī. Wǒ hái bú rènshi nǐmen. Xiān qǐng dàjiā jièshào yíxiàr zìjǐ.

Wèimín Wǒ shì Éguó-rén. Wǒ jiào Bái Wèimín. Bái shì Lǐ Bái de Bái. Wǒ hěn xǐhuan Zhōngguó wénxué. Jiānglái wǒ xiǎng dāng fānyì.

Ānfāng Wǒ xìng Cuī, jiào Cuī Ānfāng. Wǒ shì Hánguó-rén. Wǒ
duì Zhōngguó yīnyuè hěn yǒu xìngqu. Wǒ xiànzài zài
xuéxí èrhú hé pípa.

Wénzhé Wǒ shì Měiguó-rén. Wǒ de Zhōngwén míngzi jiào Shǐ
Wénzhé. Shǐ shì lìshǐ de shǐ, wén shì wénxué de wén,
zhé shì zhéxué de zhé. Wǒ yě xǐhuan Zhōngguó wénxué.
Wǒ gèng xǐhuan Zhōngguó zhéxué. Wǒ yào yánjiū
Kǒngzǐ、Lǎozǐ hé Zhuāngzǐ.

Lányīn Wǒ shì Yīngguó-rén. Wǒ duì Zhōngguó de shǎoshù mínzú
hěn yǒu xìngqu. Wǒ jiānglái xiǎng yánjiū tāmen de lìshǐ
hé yǔyán.

Lǎoshī Nǐ jiào shénme míngzi?

Lányīn O, duìbuqǐ. Wǒ jiào Lányīn. Wǒ hái bù zhīdao jiānglái
zuò shénme, kěnéng dāng jìzhě.

Shānběn Wǒ jiào Shānběn, shì Rìběn-rén. Wǒ xiànzài zài yánjiū
Zhōngguó jīngjì.

Lǎoshī Xièxie dàjiā de jièshào.

🍀 Liànxí 4

Refer to **Duìhuà 2** and fill in the blanks in the sentences below
saying who is who and who is doing what.

(*a*) ____ xuésheng Cuī Ānfāng zài xuéxí ____ hé ____.

(*b*) Lányīn shì ____ -rén. Tā yánjiū ____ de yǔyán hé lìshǐ.

(*c*) Nà ge ____ xuésheng jiào Shānběn. Tā duì ____ yǒu xìngqu.

(*d*) Bái Wèimín xiǎng dāng ____. Lányīn xiǎng dāng ____.

(*e*) Wénzhé de wén shì ____ de wén, zhé shì ____ de zhé. Tā shuō
tā duì ____ yǒu xìngqu, duì ____ gèng yǒu xìngqu.

Liànxí 5

Imagine that you are one of the students in the class (in **Duìhuà 2**)
and try to introduce your teacher and fellow students in Chinese.
You could use some of the sentences in **Liànxí 4**.

🍀 *Duìhuà 3*

Is Chinese difficult? Let's hear what the students in **Duìhuà 2** have
to say.

Lǎoshī Nǐmen juéde Zhōngwén nán bu nán?

Shānběn Hànzì bù nán, yǔyīn hěn nán.

Lānyīn Yīnwei nǐ shì Rìběn-rén, huì xiě Hànzì, suǒyǐ nǐ juéde
Hànzì bù nán. Wǒ juéde Hànzì tài nán le.

Wénzhé Hànzì bù róngyì, kěshì yǔfǎ gèng nán. Wǒ zǒngshì bù
zhīdao shénme shíhou yòng **le**, shénme shíhou bú yòng **le**.

Wèimín Hànyǔ yǔfǎ bù tài nán, shēngdiào zhēn bù róngyì. Wǒ
chángcháng shuō-bù-hǎo dì èr shēng hé dì sì shēng.

Ānfāng Wǒ juéde dì sān shēng zuì nán.

Lǎoshī Zhōngwén bù róngyì, kěshì **zhǐyào** wǒmen duō tīng、duō
shuō、duō dú、duō xiě, wǒmen **jiù** yídìng kěyǐ xué-hǎo.

This is a good time to go back over the Pronunciation Guide and to
practise your tones. If you have the cassette go right back to the
beginning again and repeat all the sounds and tones. Hopefully this
will now seem very easy!

Here's another pair of linking words to add to the ones you met in
Unit 18, ➡️ 213.

Zhǐyào . . . jiù . . .   *if only/as long as . . . then . . .*

No spitting   No smoking   No photography   Danger : Electric Shock

✔️ Liànxí 6

Do you speak other languages? What would you say about them in
terms of pronunciation and grammar? How well do you speak them?
Do you speak them with an accent or not? Try to use some of the
sentences in **Duìhuà 3**. (We have provided sample answers in the
Key to the exercises.)

Here are some phrases you might find useful:

bàng	fēicháng hǎo	hěn hǎo/liúlì
búcuò	tǐng hǎo	hái kěyǐ
bú (tài) hǎo/liúlì	hěn bù hǎo/liúlì	hěn chà

(a) Wǒ huì shuō ___ (hé ___).

(b) Wǒde ___ búcuò. *or* Wǒde ___ shuō-de ___.

(c) Wǒ huì shuō yìdiǎnr ___.

(d) Wǒ shuō___ shuō-de yǒu (yìdiǎnr) ___ kǒuyīn.

(e) ___ (a language) de yǔyīn ___.

☑ Xiǎo cèyàn

How do you say/ask the following in Chinese?

(a) Do you find English pronunciation difficult?

(b) I can only write a few Chinese characters.

(c) I speak a little Chinese but I find tones difficult.

(d) You are modest.

(e) I find it difficult to understand her accent.

(f) Your English/French/German is pretty good.

(g) You are flattering me.

20

LǙXÍNG HÉ TIĀNQI
Travel and weather

In this unit you will

- revise how to get to somewhere
- learn about Chinese festivals
- learn about regional differences
- practise talking about the weather

Kāishǐ yǐqián fùxí

- making comparisons (6)(7)
- cóng . . . dào (9)
- zuì (*most*) (7)
- new situation le (5)
- zěnmeyàng (8)
- gēn . . . yíyàng (6)
- tài . . . le (7)
- helping verbs (5)

- . . . de shíhou (10)
- A lí B yuǎn/jìn (7)
- xiān . . . zài (9)
- . . . yǐhòu (10)
- verb + de (8)
- yǒu diǎnr (8)
- yòu . . . yòu (9)

The passage below, together with the dialogues later in this unit, will help you talk in Chinese about the weather, a topic for all seasons! Can you work out from this passage which seasons Chinese people prefer and why?

Qìhòu hé tiānqi

Zhōngguó hěn dà, dōng、 xī、 nán、 běi de *qìhòu* chángcháng hěn bù yíyàng. Yìbānláishuō, nánfāng de xiàtiān bǐ běifāng de rè, běifāng de dōngtiān bǐ nánfāng de *lěng*.

Zài Zhōngguó, dàbùfen dìfang yǒu sì ge *jìjié*: chūn、xià、 qiū、dōng. *Chūntiān* cóng sānyuè dào wǔyuè. Liùyuè、qīyuè、 bāyuè shì xiàtiān. *Qiūtiān* shì jiǔ、shí hé shíyīyuè. Shí'èryuè dào èryuè shì dōngtiān. Yìbān qī、bāyuè zuì rè; yī、èryuè zuì lěng. Zhōngguó-rén *bǐjiào xǐhuan* chūntiān hé qiūtiān, yīnwéi chūntiān hé qiūtiān bù lěng yě bú rè.

bǐjiào xǐhuan	to prefer
chūn(tiān)	spring
jìjié	seasons
lěng	cold
nánfāng	the south
qìhòu	climate
qiū(tiān)	autumn
yìbānláishuō	generally speaking

Liànxí 1

Follow the sentences in paragraph two in the passage and talk about the seasons in your part of the world or a country or region that you know well. We have given sample answers for Europe in the *Key to the exercises*.

(a) Chūntiān cóng ___ dào ___.
(b) ___、___、___ shì xiàtiān.
(c) Qiūtiān shì ___、___、___.
(d) ___ dào ___ shì dōngtiān.

Liànxí 2

How would you answer these questions that a Chinese person might ask you?

(a) Nǐmen guójiā yǒu jǐ ge jìjié?
(b) Nǎ ge yuè zuì rè? Nǎ ge yuè zuì lěng?
(c) Nǐ bǐjiào xǐhuan nǎ ge jìjié?
(d) Zài nǐmen guójiā běifāng shì bu shì bǐ nánfāng lěng?

Zhǔyào cíhuì

ānpái	arrangement; to arrange
-Wǒ lái ānpái ba.	I'll make the arrangements.
chéngshì	city
cónglái	ever
dàibiǎotuán	delegation
dāng	to be
dù	degree (°C)
fādá	developed
fēngjǐng	scenery
gōngzuò	work; to work
hěn shǎo	seldom
huí guó	return to one's own country
huí lái	to come back
jiàn miàn	to meet
kāi xué	start of term
měi	beautiful
qìwēn	(*weather*) temperature
tè	extremely
Wǔtái Shān	Mount Wutai (*in Shānxī province*)
xiǎng	to miss, long for
(tiānqi) yùbào	(*weather*) forecast

fēng	wind	**guā fēng**	windy (*lit.* blow wind)
yǔ	rain	**xià yǔ**	to rain (*lit.* down rain)
xuě	snow	**xià xuě**	to snow (*lit.* down snow)
nuǎn(huo)	warm	**liáng(kuai)**	cool

  # Duìhuà

Duìhuà 1

Colin, who is studying in Tiānjīn, is ringing his Chinese friend, Sūlán, in Kūnmíng, Yúnnán Province to arrange a meeting between them during the winter vacation.

Colin Zhè jǐ tiān Tiānjīn tè lěng, kěshì fēngjǐng zhēn měi. Zuótiān xià xuě le.

Sūlán Xuě dà ma?

Colin Bù xiǎo. Tiānqi yùbào shuō, míngtiān hái yào xià xuě.

Sūlán Kūnmíng cónglái bú xià xuě. Wǒ zhēn xiǎng qù Tiānjīn kàn xuě.

Colin Nǐ nàr tiānqi zěnmeyàng?

Sūlán Bù nuǎnhuo. Jīntiān de qìwēn shì shíwǔ dù.

Colin Shénme? Shíwǔ dù? Gēn Tiānjīn de chūntiān yíyàng nuǎnhuo.

Sūlán Kěshì wǒ juéde lěng. Jīntiān shàngwǔ xià le xiǎo yǔ.

Colin Wǒ zuì xǐhuan xiǎo yǔ. Kěshì Tiānjīn dōngtiān hěn shǎo xià yǔ.

Sūlán Nǐ lái Kūnmíng kàn yǔ, wǒ qù Tiānjīn kàn xuě, zěnmeyàng?

Colin Zhēn shì ge hǎo zhǔyì! Wǒ lái ānpái ba.

Sūlán Děngyiděng! Nàme wǒmen zài nǎr jiàn miàn ne?

✔ Liànxí 3

Are these statements about **Duìhuà 1 duì** or **bú duì**?

	duì/bú duì	
(a) Tiānjīn zuótiān xià le xiǎo xuě.	☐	☐
(b) Kūnmíng jīntiān xià le xiǎo yǔ.	☐	☐
(c) Sūlán bù xǐhuan kàn xuě.	☐	☐
(d) Kūnmíng tiānqi bù lěng, kěshì Sūlán juéde lěng.	☐	☐
(e) Colin rènwéi tāmen yīnggāi zài Kūnmíng jiàn miàn.	☐	☐

✔ Liànxí 4

Zhèi liǎng tiān tiānqi zěnmeyàng?

Read the following statements, and decide whether each is true. If not, negate it.

Example: Zuótiān xià yǔ le.
   (a) Duì. (*ie.* Zuótiān xià yǔ le.)
   (b) Bú duì. Zuótiān méi xià yǔ.

(a) Jīntiān tiānqi hěn nuǎnhuo.

(b) Jīntiān zǎoshang guā fēng le.

(c) Jīntiān wǎnshang yǒu dà yǔ.

(d) Jīntiān èrshí dù.

(e) Zuótiān tiānqi tè rè.

(f) Zuótiān shàngwǔ xià le xiǎo xuě.

(g) Zuótiān xiàwǔ fēng bú dà.

📷 *Duìhuà 2*

The students in Unit 19 are discussing where they plan to go during the holiday.

Lǎoshī	Jiàqī nǐmen dǎsuàn qù nǎr?
Shānběn	Wǒ xǐhuan dà chéngshì. Wǒ xiān qù Shànghǎi, ránhòu qù Guǎngzhōu. Shànghǎi hé Guǎngzhōu de jīngjì zuì fādá.
Lányīn	Wǒ bù xǐhuan dà chéngshì. Wǒ yào qù Yúnnán hé Guìzhōu. Nàr yǒu hěn duō shǎoshù mínzú.
Wénzhé	Yúnnán hé Guìzhōu dōu zài Zhōngguó de nánfāng, xiàtiān yídìng hěn rè. Wǒ qù Shānxī de Wǔtái Shān. Nàr yídìng hěn liángkuai.
Wèimín	Zhè ge jiàqī wǒ yǒu gōngzuò. Wǒ qù Tiānjīn gěi yí ge dàibiǎotuán dāng fānyì.
Lǎoshī	Ānfāng, nǐ ne?
Ānfāng	Wǒ zhēn xiànmù nǐmen. Kěshì wǒ yào huí Hánguó. Wǒ tài xiǎng wǒ bàba、 māma le. Kāi xué de shíhou wǒ zài huí lái.

--- **Cultural tip** ---

The Chinese Calendar

In China there are two different calendars in use. One is identical to our Western calendar and the other is the traditional or lunar calendar. Chinese calendars include both!

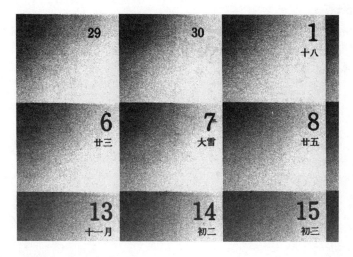

Major Chinese Festivals

The most important Chinese festival is **Chūnjié** the *Spring Festival* or the *Chinese Lunar New Year,* which falls on the first day of the first lunar month. The Lunar New Year itself may occur as early as January 21st and as late as February 21st. It is the major festival in China (rather like Christmas in the West) and most people try to get home to celebrate it with their families even if it means travelling long distances.

Firecrackers are set off on New Year's Eve and New Year's Day to warn off evil spirits even though many Chinese have probably forgotten the origin of this custom.

Other major festivals are the *Lantern Festival*, the *Pure Brightness* or *Grave Sweeping Festival*, the *Dragon Boat Festival* and the *Mid-Autumn Festival*, which was originally to pay homage to the full moon.

You could visit your local library to find out more about these festivals: what their origins are, when they occur and how they are celebrated. Most overseas Chinese communities observe these festivals too.

You could learn a lot about Chinese traditions. It would also give you an insight into the traditional Chinese way of life which has helped to shape their language.

☑ Liànxí 5

Match the sentences in Column A with their English equivalents in Column B.

Column A	Column B
(a) Nàr xiàtiān yídìng hěn liángkuai.	(i) During the holidays I plan to travel.
(b) Dà chéngshì de jīngjì hěn fādá.	(ii) There are many minorities there.
(c) Nàr yǒu hěn duō shǎoshù mínzú.	(iii) I will come back again when term starts.
(d) Jiàqī wǒ dǎsuàn qù lǚxíng.	(iv) The economy in big cities is developed.
(e) Kāi xué de shíhou wǒ zài huí lái.	(v) It must be cool there in the summer.

☑ Liànxí 6

Now cover up Column B in **Liànxí 5** and say what the sentences in Column A mean in English. Once you have done that, cover up Column A and say what the sentences in Column B mean in Chinese.

Duìhuà 3

Listen to the dialogue and find out how these students plan to travel to the places they are going to visit during the holiday. Go straight to **Liànxí 7** without reading the dialogue below. If you haven't got the cassette, read the dialogue, and then do **Liànxí 7**.

Lǎoshī	Nǐmen zěnme qù?
Wèimín	Tiānjīn bù yuǎn. Wǒ zuò huǒchē qù. Liǎng、sān ge xiǎoshí jiù dào le.
Lányīn	Yúnnán lí Běijīng hěn yuǎn. Wǒ kěyǐ zuò huǒchē, yě kěyǐ zuò fēijī. Wǒ hái méi yǒu juédìng.
Lǎoshī	Fēijī bǐ huǒchē kuài duōle, kěshì yě guì duōle.
Wénzhé	Wǔtái Shān bù yuǎn yě bú jìn. Wǒ xiān zuò huǒchē, zài zuò chángtú qìchē.
Lǎoshī	Shānběn, nǐ yào qù liǎng ge dìfang. Nǐ zěnme qù?
Shānběn	Wǒ xiān zuò fēijī dào Shànghǎi, zài zuò huǒchē qù Guǎngzhōu.
Ānfāng	Wǒ bù xǐhuan zuò fēijī, kěshì wǒ zhǐ néng zuò fēijī huí guó.
Lǎoshī	Hǎo. Zhù dàjiā jiàqī yúkuài.

走马看花

Chinese proverb: **Zǒu mǎ kàn huā**
Look at flowers while riding on horseback – gain a superficial understanding

✔ Liànxí 7

How will the students in **Duìhuà 3** get to their destinations?

(*a*) Wèimín zuò ＿＿ qù Tiānjīn.
(*b*) Lányīn zuò ＿＿ huòzhě ＿＿ qù Yúnnán.
(*c*) Wénzhé zuò ＿＿ hé ＿＿ qù Wǔtái Shān.
(*d*) Shānběn zuò ＿＿ qù Shànghǎi, zuò ＿＿ qù Guǎngzhōu.
(*e*) Ānfāng zuò ＿＿ huí Hánguó.

✔ Liànxí 8

Make complete sentences with the words or phrases given. You will have to supply a missing word in each case. Pay attention to the word order.

Example: Lúndūn/ fēijī/ lái/ tā/ bù
Tā bú zuò fēijī lái Lúndūn.

(a) tā/ qù/ Shànghǎi/ huǒchē/ míngtiān
(b) lái/ wǒde péngyou/ wǒ jiā/ gōnggòng qìchē
(c) qù gōngyuán/ zìxíngchē/ bù/ wǒ
(d) mǎi dōngxi/ chē/ tāmen/ chángcháng/ qù
(e) dìtiě/ huí jiā/ xiànzài/ wǒ

Liànxí 9

Your Chinese friend, Yànmíng, is asking you about the holiday you plan to take.

Yànmíng   Nǐ dǎsuàn qù shénme dìfang?
(a) **You**   (*Say you want to go to Hong Kong and Macao.*)
    Yànmíng Nǐ zěnme qù?
(b) **You**   (*Say you will fly to Hong Kong and then go to Macao by boat.*)
    Yànmíng Nàr de tiānqi zěnmeyàng?
(c) **You**   (*Say it's hot there in August.*)
    Yànmíng Xià bu xià yǔ?
(d) **You**   (*Say sometimes it rains.*)
    Yànmíng Nǐ qù jǐ tiān?
(e) **You**   (*Say you haven't decided yet.*)

Liànxí 10

Read the following passage and then answer the questions.

Běijīng de Jìjié

Běijīng de dōngtiān yòu *cháng* yòu lěng; xiàtiān yòu cháng yòu rè. Běijīng de chūntiān hěn duǎn yě hěn nuǎnhuo, kěshì chángcháng guā fēng.

Běijīng zuì hǎo de jìjié shì qiūtiān. Qiūtiān bù lěng yě bú rè. *Báitiān* hěn nuǎnhuo, zǎoshang hé wǎnshang hěn liángkuai. Qiūtiān *qíngtiān* duō, *yīntiān* shǎo. Bù cháng guā fēng, yě hěn shǎo xià yǔ.

cháng	long	**qíngtiān**	sunny (day)
báitiān	daytime	**yīntiān**	cloudy (day)

(*a*) Běijīng de xiàtiān hěn duǎn, shì bu shi?
(*b*) Běijīng de dōngtiān shì bu shì hěn lěng?
(*c*) Běijīng de chūntiān zěnmeyàng?
(*d*) Běijīng de chūntiān shì zuì hǎo de jìjié ma?
(*e*) Wèishénme Běijīng-rén hěn xǐhuan qiūtiān?

✔ *Xiǎo cèyàn*

The following pictures show what the weather was, is and will be like. Make two statements about each of them in relation to what time it is now. It's 10 a.m. Friday.

Example: Jīntiān zǎoshang xià dà yǔ le.
(Jīntiān zǎoshang) qìwēn (shì) qī dù.

(a) **xīngqīsì shàngwǔ**   20°c

(b) **xīngqīsì wǎnshang**   5°c

(c) **xīngqīwǔ shàngwǔ**   12°c

(d) **xīngqīwǔ xiàwǔ**   18°c

(e) **xīngqīliù**   3°c

(f) **xià xīngqīyī**   0°c

Bào shàng shuō jīntiān bú huì xià yǔ.
But the paper said it wouldn't rain today.

21

TÁN GǍNXIǍNG
Experiences, feelings and reflections

In this unit you will learn:

- how to talk about things that happened in the past
- how to ask people about their impressions
- how to express regret
- how to express satisfaction
- how to write a thank you note

Kāishǐ yǐqián fùxí

- measure words (4) (7)
- numbers from 100 to 1000 (7)
- verb + **guo** (9)
- helping verbs (6)
- **gèng** (*even more*) (8)
- verb + **de** (8)
- reduplicated verbs (5)

- **zuì** (*most*) (7)
- verb endings (10)
- . . . **de shíhou** (10)
- new situation **le** (5)
- **shì bu shì** (3)
- **tài . . . le** (7)
- sentence **le** (4)
- **gěi** (*for*) (6)

With China opening up more and more, she attracts more and more visitors: students, tourists and business people. What do the students study? What are the tourists interested in? Why are business people going to China? Read the passage overleaf to find out.

Qù Zhōngguó Xuéxí, Lǚyóu hé Gōngzuò

Měi nián yǒu hěn duō wàiguó-rén qù Zhōngguó xuéxí. Tāmen xuéxí Zhōngguó de yǔyán、 wénxué、 *wénhuà*、 lìshǐ、 *zōngjiào*, děngděng. Zài Zhōngguó de *yìbǎi duō suǒ dàxué* lǐ, yǒu jǐ qiān ge wàiguó *liúxuéshēng*.

Qù Zhōngguó lǚyóu de wàiguó-rén *yuè lái yuè* duō. *Tāmen hěn duō rén* duì Zhōngguó de wénhuà hé lìshǐ gǎn xìngqu. Hěn duō rén qù-guo Zhōngguó hěn duō cì.

Zhè jǐ nián qù Zhōngguó gōngzuò de wàiguó-rén yě yuè lái yuè duō. Zài Zhōngguó de *wàizī qǐyè* hé *hézī qǐyè* yě yuè lái yuè duō. Hěn duō gōngsī dōu xiǎng zài Zhōngguó kuòdà *shēngyi*.

dàxué	university
hézī qǐyè	joint venture
kuòdà	to expand
liúxuéshēng	overseas student
lǚyóu	to travel
shēngyi	business
suǒ	(*measure word for schools, and so on*)
tāmen hěn duō rén	many of them (*lit.* they many people)
yìbǎi duō	more than a hundred
yuè lái yuè ...	more and more ...
wàizī qǐyè	foreign enterprise
wénhuà	culture
zōngjiào	religion

Here's another pair of linking words to add to your list: **yuè lái** ... **yuè** ...

yuè lái yuè duō — *more and more*
yuè lái yuè hǎo — *better and better*
yuè lái yuè kuài — *quicker and quicker*

If you replace **lái** with another adjective/verb you get:

yuè **kuài** yuè **hǎo** — *the quicker the better*
yuè **duō** yuè **hǎo** — *the more the better*

Liànxí 1

How would you say the following?

(a) More and more Chinese come to Britain to study.
(b) Many of them are interested in the history and culture of Britain.
(c) Every year many foreign students come to Britain to study English.
(d) More and more English companies want to expand their business in China.

Zhǔyào cíhuì

bāo	to wrap; to make (*jiǎozi*)
chángshòu (miàn)	long life (*noodles*)
chī-de-guàn	to be used to the food
chī-bu-guàn	to be not used to the food
dǒng	to understand
duì X yǒu shénme yìnxiàng?	what is your impression of X?
duì shénme (zuì) mǎnyì?	(*most*) satisfied with what?
fāzhǎn	to develop
jiàoxué	teaching
jiǎozi	(*Chinese*) dumplings
jiùshi	it's just that
mǎnyì	satisfied
měi(-jíle)	(extremely) beautiful
nàli/nàr	there
nánshuō	difficult to say
qìngzhù	to celebrate
shān qū	mountain(ous) area
tán(yi)tán	to talk (a bit) about
tèsè	feature, characteristics
tīng-bu-dǒng	to be unable to understand (*verbal speech*)
tóngshì (men)	colleague(s)
tóngxué (men)	fellow student(s)
xià ge	next
xuéxiào	school
yìnxiàng	impression
yíqiè	everything
yìzhí	all the time
yǒuhǎo	friendly

Duìhuà

Duìhuà 1

The group of students you met in Units 19 and 20 are now all safely back in college. What do they think of the places they have just visited? Let's find out.

Lǎoshī Tóngxuémen, nǐmen jiàqī guò-de hǎo ma?

Xuésheng Hěn hǎo.

(chorus) Bú tài hǎo.

Fēicháng hǎo.

Hái kěyǐ.

Lǎoshī Qǐng měi ge rén dōu tányitán, hǎo ma?

Wénzhé Wǒ qù le Wǔtái Shān. Nàli yíqiè dōu hǎo, jiùshi fàn . . .

Lǎoshī Fàn zěnme le?

Wénzhé Fàn hěn hǎochī, kěshì tāmen bù chī ròu. Wǒ zuì ài chī ròu, suǒyǐ wǒ yǒu shíhou juéde è.

Wèimín Nǐ yīnggāi gēn wǒ yìqǐ qù Tiānjīn. Wǒmen de dàibiǎotuán měi tiān dōu yǒu yànhuì.

Lǎoshī Lányīn, shàoshù mínzú de fàn nǐ chī-de-guàn ma?

Lányīn Kāishǐ de shíhou chī-bu-guàn, hòulái jiù chī-de-guàn le. Nèixiē shǎoshù mínzú de rén fēicháng yǒuhǎo.

Lǎoshī Nàr shì bu shì hěn rè?

Lányīn Wǒ qù de dìfang zài shān qū, suǒyǐ bú tài rè. Nàr de fēngjǐng měi-jíle.

Lǎoshī Shānběn, nǐ duì Shànghǎi hé Guǎngzhōu yǒu shénme yìnxiàng?

Shānběn Zhè liǎng ge chéngshì de jīngjì dōu fāzhǎn-de hěn kuài. Kěxī wǒ tīng-bu-dǒng Shànghǎihuà hé Guǎngdōnghuà.

Lǎoshī Zhè liǎng zhǒng fāngyán dōu bù róngyì dǒng. Ānfāng, nǐ bàba、 māma dōu hǎo ma?

Ānfāng Dōu hěn hǎo, xièxie nín. Wǒ bàba、 māma shuō xià ge jiàqī tāmen yào lái Zhōngguó. Wǒmen yìqǐ zài Zhōngguó lǚyóu.

Dàjiā Nà tài hǎo le!

✳ Xuéxí jìqiǎo

Keep reading all the dialogues in the book whenever you have a spare moment: better still listen to the cassette whenever you can.

Practise covering up the English words in the **Zhǔyào cíhuì** and see how many of the Chinese words you know, then do the reverse. You can go back to the beginning of the book and do this right the way through for useful revision.

Liànxí 2

Where did you go on your last holiday? Here are some questions a Chinese person might ask you:

(a) Nǐ de jiàqī guò-de hǎo bu hǎo?
(b) Nǐ qù le duō cháng shíjiān?
(c) Nàli de tiānqi zěnmeyàng?
(d) Nàli de fàn nǐ chī-de-guàn ma?
(e) Nàli de fēngjǐng měi bu měi?

Liànxí 3

Nǐ duì shénme gǎn/yǒu xìngqu?

State whether you are interested in the following things.
Example: Zhōngguó lìshǐ

(i) Wǒ duì Zhōngguó lìshǐ gǎn/yǒu xìngqu.
(ii) Wǒ duì Zhōngguó lìshǐ bù gǎn xìngqu *or*
(iii) Wǒ duì Zhōngguó lìshǐ méi (yǒu) xìngqu.

(a) liúxíng (*popular*) yīnyuè
(b) Yìdàlì fàn
(c) jīngjù
(d) shōují (*collect*) yóupiào
(e) Déguó diànyǐng

Liànxí 4

Are you used to the following food or drinks?

If you are, say **Wǒ chī/hē-de-guàn** X. If you are not, say **Wǒ chī/hē-bu-guàn** Y. Remember you can also put the noun (the sort of thing) at the beginning of the sentence for emphasis.

tángcù yú   *sweet and sour fish*
(i) Wǒ **chī-de-guàn** tángcù yú.
(ii) Tángcù yú wǒ **chī-bu-guàn**.

suānlà tāng   *hot and sour soup*
(i) Suānlà tāng wǒ **hē-de-guàn**.
(ii) Wǒ **hē-bu-guàn** suānlà tāng.

Can you start with **tángcù yú** and **suānlà tāng**? And then:

(*a*) Yìndù (*Indian*) fàn?
(*b*) tián pútáojiǔ?
(*c*) dòufu (*tofu*)?
(*d*) Kěkǒukělè?
(*e*) mángguǒ (*mango*)?
(*f*) kāfēi?

Duìhuà 2

Mr Ford has lived and worked in China for nearly 12 years. He is interviewed by a Chinese journalist on his 60th birthday. What is he most satisified and dissatisfied with?

Jìzhě Fútè xiānsheng, zhù nín shēngrì kuàilè!
Ford Xièxie, xièxie.
Jìzhě Nín zài Zhōngguó jǐ nián le?
Ford Chàbuduō shí'èr nián le.
Jìzhě Nín yìzhí zài dàxué gōngzuò ma?
Ford Duì. Wǒ fēicháng xǐhuan dāng lǎoshī.
Jìzhě Zài Zhōngguó nín duì shénme zuì mǎnyì?
Ford Dāngrán shì wǒde gōngzuò. Wǒmen xuéxiào de jiàoxué yuè lái yuè hǎo.
Jìzhě Nàme nín duì shénme zuì bù mǎnyì?
Ford Wǒ duì hěn duō shìqing bù mǎnyì. Kěshì hěn nánshuō duì shénme zuì bù mǎnyì.
Jìzhě Nín dǎsuàn zěnme qìngzhù nínde shēngrì?
Ford Zǎoshang wǒ tàitai gěi wǒ zuò le Zhōngguó de chángshòu miàn. Wǎnshang tóngshìmen lái wǒ jiā bāo jiǎozi.
Jìzhě Nínde shēngrì guò-de zhēn yǒu Zhōngguó tèsè.
Ford Wǒ xiànzài yǐjīng shì bàn ge Zhōngguó-rén le.

Do you remember meeting two phrases using **duì** in Unit 10?

A **duì** shēntǐ (bu) hǎo.   *A is (not) good for the health/body.*
Y **duì** X (bù) hǎo   *Y is/(not) good to X.*

Here are some more useful phrases with **duì**:

Nǐ **duì** X yǒu shénme yìnxiàng?   *What impression have you of X?*

Wǒ **duì** X de yìnxiàng hěn hǎo.   *I have a very good impression of X.*

Nǐ **duì** shénme (zuì) bù mǎnyì?   *What are you (most) dissat-*
   isfied with?

A **duì** B bù mǎnyì.   *A is not satisfied with B.*

A **duì** B **zuì** bù mǎnyì.   *A is* most*dissatisfied with B.*

Cultural tip

It is very common for elderly people (the Chinese tend to regard people of 60 and over as elderly!) to eat 'long-life noodles' (**chángshòu miàn**) on their birthdays!

miàntiáo
noodles

Shuǐjiǎo
boiled dumplings

On special occasions such as birthdays and the Chinese New Year the family (plus close friends or colleagues) might make Chinese ravioli (**bāo jiǎozi**) together. It is a very companionable activity which also requires some skill. Beginners can usually spot which **jiǎozi** are theirs when it comes to eating them as they tend to be the unsightly ones or the ones which have burst!

✅ Liànxí 5

Your Chinese friend is asking you about your visit to China. This passage is a brief account of your visit.

You visited China on a package tour for two weeks. You visited Beijing, Shanghai, and Guilin. You liked all three places, but for different reasons. There were many parks in Beijing which you liked a lot. Shanghai was developing very fast, which impressed you. But there were too many people there and it was very crowded. The scenery at Guilin was extremely beautiful.

Now answer your friend's questions:

Friend Nǐ zài Zhōngguó duōshao tiān?
(*a*) **You** _____
Friend Nǐ qù le shénme dìfang?
(*b*) **You** _____
Friend Nǐ duì Shànghǎi yǒu shénme yìnxiàng?
(*c*) **You** _____
Friend Nàme Běijīng ne?
(*d*) **You** _____
Friend Nǐ duì Guìlín de yìnxiàng zěnmeyàng?
(*e*) **You** _____

Liànxí 6

Listen to the thank-you message on Lanyin's answerphone. Then decide whether the statements below are **duì** or **bú duì**. Read the new words before you listen to the message.

zhēn kěxī	what a pity	**dāngmiàn**	face to face
bāngzhù	help	**gǎnxiè**	to thank (*formal*)
tèbié	especially	**wèn XX hǎo**	say hello to XX

(*a*) Xiǎo Qīng jīntiān shàngwǔ qù Lányīn de xuéxiào le.
(*b*) Xiǎo Qīng dāngmiàn gēn Lányīn shuō le zàijiàn.
(*c*) Xiǎo Qīng qù-guo Lányīn de jiā.
(*d*) Xiǎo Qīng méi jiàn-guo Lányīn de bàba he māma.

Lányīn,

Nǐ hǎo! Wǒ shì Xiǎo Qīng. Jīntiān xiàwǔ wǒ qù nǐde xuéxiào zhǎo nǐ, kěshì nǐ bú zài. Zhēn kěxī, wǒ bù néng dāngmiàn gēn nǐ shuō 'zàijiàn'.

Zhè cì lái Yīngguó fǎngwèn, wǒ guó-de zhēn yúkuài. Nǐ gěi le wǒ hěn duō bāngzhù. Wǒ fēicháng gǎnxiè nǐ. Tèbié gǎnxiè nǐ qǐng wǒ qù nǐde jiā chī fàn. Wǒ gěi nǐ he nǐ bàba, màma tiān le hěn duō máfan.

Xīwàng nǐ jiānglái yǒu jīhuì yě qù Zhōngguó fǎngwèn. Zhù nǐ shēntǐ jiànkāng, shēnghuó yúkuài, gōngzuò shùnlì, wànshì rúyì!

Wèn nǐ bàba, māma hǎo! Zàijiàn!

☑ *Xiǎo cèyàn*

What would you say to a Chinese person to convey the following?

(a) Say you are not used to eating hot/spicy dishes.
(b) Ask her if she is interested in opera (**gējù**).
(c) Say there are more and more people going abroad for holidays.
(d) Ask her what is her impression of Britain (the US and so on).
(e) Ask her what she is (most) satisfied and/or not satisfied with.
(f) Wish her Happy Birthday!

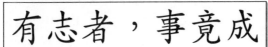

Chinese proverb: **Yǒu zhì zhě, shì jìng chéng**
Where there's a will, there's a way.

Zhùhè nǐ! Congratulations!

You have completed *Teach Yourself Beginner's Chinese* and are now a competent speaker of basic Chinese. You should be able to handle most everyday situations on a visit to China and to communicate with Chinese people sufficiently to make friends.

If you would like to extend your ability so that you can develop your confidence, fluency and scope in the language, whether for social or business purposes, why not take your Chinese a step further with *Teach Yourself Chinese*?

Chūkǒu *Exit*

— KEY TO THE EXERCISES —

Unit 1

1 (*a*) Nǐ hǎo! (*b*) Xièxie. (*c*) Bú
yòng xiè. 2 (*a*) Nǐ hǎo! (*b*) Bú
yòng xiè. (*c*) Xièxie. (*d*) Zàijiàn!
3 (*a*) Nǐ hǎo! (*b*) Lǐ tàitai hǎo
ma? (*c*) Lǐ xiānsheng zài ma?
(*d*) Xièxie (nǐ). 4 (*a*) Xièxie.
(*b*) **Bú yòng** xiè. (*c*) **Zài**jiàn.
(*d*) **Míngtiān** jiàn. (*e*) Qǐng **jìn**.
(*f*) **Qǐng** zuò. (*g*) **Wǒ/Tā hěn**
hǎo. (*h*) **Nǐ/Tā** hǎo **ma**? 5 (*a*) =
(*iv*), (*b*) = (*iii*), (*c*) = (*ii*), (*d*) = (*i*).

Xiǎo cèyàn:
(*a*) Lǐ xiānsheng, nǐ hǎo! or, Nǐ
hǎo, Lǐ xiānsheng! (*b*) Nǐ tàitai
hǎo ma? (*c*) Duìbuqǐ. (*d*) Xièxie
nǐ. (*e*) Bú yòng xiè. (*f*) Zàijiàn.

Unit 2

Shìshi (*a*) Qǐng jìn. (*b*) Nǐ hǎo.
(*c*) Qǐng zuò. (*d*) Míngtiān jiàn.
1 (*a*) shénme; jiào. (*b*) huì; shuō.
(*c*) shì; rènshi. 2 (*a*) Tāmen shì
Lǐ xiānsheng、Yīng tàitai. (*b*) Tā
jiào Lǐ Jīnshēng. (*c*) Duì. Tā xìng
Yīng. (*d*) Bù. Tā xìng Lǐ. (*e*) Wǒ
(bú) rènshi tāmen. 3 (*a*) Wáng.
(*b*) Lányīng. (*c*) a little bit. (*d*)
Chinese teacher. (*e*) No, she
doesn't. (*f*) She's beautiful.

(*g*) Yes. 4 (*a*) Tā jiào Zhào Huá.
Tā shì jǐngchá. (*b*) Zhè shì Liú
Guāng. Tā shì sījī. (*c*) Nà shì Guō
Jié. Tā shì dàifu. (*d*) Tā jiào Lǐ
Mínglì. Tā shì lǎoshī. (*e*) Zhè shì
Zhōu Jiābǎo. Tā shì xuéshēng.
(*f*) Nà shì Wú Zébì. Tā shì chūshī.
5 (*a*) bú duì, (*b*) bú duì, (*c*) bú
duì, (*d*) bú duì, (*e*) bú duì, (*f*)
duì. 6 (*a*) Nǐ huì shuō Yīngwén
ma? Nǐ huì bu huì shuō Yīngwén?
(*b*) Nǐmen shì lǎoshī ma? Nǐmen
shì bu shì lǎoshī? (*c*) Xiǎo Zhèng
zài ma? Xiǎo Zhèng zài bu zài?
(*d*) Lǐ xiānsheng jīntiān lái ma?
Lǐ xiānsheng jīntiān lái bu lái?
(*e*) Wáng Fāng yǒu Yīngwén míngzi
ma? Wáng Fāng yǒu mei yǒu Yīngwén míngzi? (*f*) Lín lǎoshī jiào
Lín Péng ma? Lín lǎoshī jiào bu jiào
Lín Péng?

Xiǎo cèyàn:
(*a*) Nín guì xìng? Nǐ xìng shénme?
(*b*) Wǒ jiào xxx. (*c*) Wǒ méi yǒu
Zhōngwén míngzi. (*d*) Wǒ bú rènshi tā. (*e*) Méi guānxi. (*f*) Wǒde
péngyou bú shì lǎoshī.

Unit 3

Shìshi (*a*) Nǐ hǎo. Wǒ jiào X.
Nǐ jiào shénme? or Nín guì xìng?

(*b*) Nǐ/Nín yǒu háizi ma? Nǐ/Nín yǒu mei yǒu háizi?
1 (*a*) shì/bú shì, (*b*) shì/bú shì, (*c*) shì/bú shì, (*d*) shì/bú shì, (*e*) shì/bù zhīdào, (*f*) shì/bù zhīdào. **2** *Speaker 1*: Nǐ hǎo! Wǒ jiào Chén Lìmǐn. Wǒ shì Xiānggǎng-rén. Wǒ zhù zài Xiānggǎng Lì Yè Lù 8 hào. Wǒde diànhuà hàomǎ shì 507 1293. *Speaker 2*: Nǐ hǎo! Wǒ jiào Wú Yìfēi. Wǒ shì Shānghǎi-rén. Wǒde diànhuà hàomǎ shì 874 3659. Wǒ zhù zài Shànghǎi Nánjīng Lù 9 hào. *Speaker 3*: Wǒ jiào Guō Wànjí. Wǒ shì Fǎguó-rén. Wǒ zhù zài Běijīng Hépíng Lù 6 hào. Wǒde diànhuà hàomǎ shì 724 6274. **4** (*a*) Běijīng Cháoyáng Lù èr hào, Lǐ Mínglì lǎoshī. (*b*) Sūzhōu Lónghǎi Lù jiǔ hào, Dōngfāng Fàndiàn sān-bā-sì fángjiān, Zhào Huá xiānsheng. (*c*) Nánjīng Xīchéng Qū Hépíng Lù wǔ hào, Zhào Jiābǎo xiǎojie. **5** (*a*) (*iii*), (*b*) (*vii*), (*c*) (*i*), (*d*) (*v*), (*e*) (*ii*), (*f*) (*iv*), (*g*) (*vi*).

Xiǎo cèyàn:
(*a*) Tā shì shéi? (*b*) Nǐ zhù (zài) nǎr? (*c*) Wǒ bú zhù (zài) Lúndūn. (*d*) Nǐde diànhuà hàomǎ shì duōshao? (*e*) Diànhuà shì shénme yìsi? (*f*) Zhè shì wǒde fēijī piào.

Unit 4

Shìshi (*a*) Nǐ zhù zài shénme fàndiàn? (Nǐ zhù zài) jǐ hào fángjiān? (*b*) Zhè shì wǒde míngpiàn.
1 (*a*) èrshíjiǔ, (*b*) qīshíyī, (*c*) sānshí'èr. **2** (*a*) èrshíyī, (*b*) qīshí, (*c*) liùshíliù, (*d*) sìshíbā (*e*) sānshí, (*f*) liùshí, (*g*) shíwǔ, (*h*) sānshísān. **3** Dīng Fèng is married. She's got two children, a son and a daughter. Her son is called Dīng Míng and is 12 this year. Her daughter's name is Dīng Yīng. She

is 14 years old. **4** (*a*) Méi yǒu. (*b*) Méi yǒu. (*c*) Bú shì (Tā bú shì lǎoshī.) (*d*) Wǒ méi yǒu háizi. (*e*) Wǒ méi yǒu dìdi. **5** (*a*) Are you married? = (*iv*) (*b*) How old is she? = (*iii*) (*c*) What's Mr Wang, the teacher, called? = (*i*) (*d*) Have you any children? = (*v*) (*e*) Has Mrs Li a daughter? = (*ii*) **6** Wǒ jiào Mǎlì, jīnnián shíqī suì. Wǒ méi yǒu jiějie, méi yǒu mèimei. Wǒ yǒu yí ge gēge, yí ge dìdi. Wǒ gēge jiào Hēnglì. Tā èrshí suì. Wǒ dìdi jiào Bǐdé. Tā shíwǔ suì. Wǒmen dōu shì xuésheng.

Xiǎo cèyàn:
(*a*) Nǐ hǎo! (*b*) Nǐ jiào shénme? (*c*) Nǐ duō dà? (*d*) Nǐ yǒu xiōngdì jiěmèi ma? (*e*) Xièxie (nǐ). (*f*) Zàijiàn!

Unit 5

Shìshi (*a*) Chén xiānsheng, nǐ hǎo ma? Nǐ jiào shénme míngzi? Nǐ huì bu huì shuō Yīngwén? Nǐ zhù zài nǎr? Nǐ jié hūn le ma? Nǐ yǒu háizi ma? Nǐ(de) háizi jǐ suì/duō dà? Nǐde diànhuà hàomǎ shì duōshao/shénme? Nǐ rènshi bu rènshi X? Nǐ shì Běijīng-/Shànghǎi-/Guǎngdōng-rén ma? Nǐ bàba\ màma dōu zài (Běijīng) ma? (*b*) liùshísì, èrshíjiǔ, wǔshíqī, sānshíbā, shí'èr, jiǔshíwǔ, sìshí, èr, qīshísān, shí.
1 (*a*) yīyuè yī hào, (*b*) shí'èr yuè èrshíwǔ hào, (*c*) sānyuè bā hào, (*d*) shíyuè yī hào. **3** (*a*) September 9th (*b*) Sunday morning, (*c*) Thursday, November 28th, (*d*) 10. 45a.m. Saturday, (*e*) 3.30p.m. Friday, July 6th, (*f*) 11a.m. Monday, December 31st. **4** (*a*) Wǔ diǎn yí kè; wǔ diǎn shíwǔ fēn. (*b*) Chà wǔ fēn wǔ diǎn; sì diǎn wǔshíwǔ fēn. (*c*) (Hái yǒu) sìshí fēnzhōng.

(*d*) Zǎoshang wǔ diǎn líng wǔ fēn. (*e*) Wǔ diǎn líng qī fēn.

Xiǎo cèyàn:
(*a*) Sānyuè sānshí hào. (*b*) Xīngqīsì. (*c*) Sì diǎn èrshíqī fēn (*d*) Sì diǎn sān kè **or** chà yí kè wǔ diǎn. Dī sān zhàntái. (*e*) Sì diǎn wǔshí fēn **or** Wǔ diǎn chà shí fēn. Dì yī zhàntái.

Unit 6

Shìshi 1 Wǒ yào xīngqīsì shàngwu jiǔ diǎn bàn de huǒchē piào. 2 (*a*) yī-jiǔ-jiǔ-qī nián yīyuè liù hào (*b*) èr-líng-líng-líng nián sānyuè èrshíyī hào (*c*) yī-jiǔ-sì-sān nián bāyuè shíwǔ hào
1 (*a*) Tā zài mǎi dōngxi. (*b*) Tāmen zài kàn zájì. (*c*) Tā zài huàn qián. (*d*) Tā zài dǎ tàijí. (*e*) Tāmen zài kàn diànyǐng. (*f*) Tā zài tīng yīnyuè. 3 (*a*) bù yíyàng (gāo), (*b*) yíyàng (dà), (*c*) bù yíyàng (zhòng), (*d*) bù yíyàng (gāo), (*e*) yíyàng (zhòng), (*f*) yíyàng (dà). 4 (*a*) Bú duì. Xǔ bǐ Hú gāo. (*b*) Bú duì. Hú bǐ Qū zhòng. (*c*) Bú duì. Tāmen yíyàng dà. (*d*) Duì. (*e*) Duì. 5 (*a*) Xīngqītiān, (*b*) Xīngqīsì xiàwǔ, (*c*) Xīngqīsān wǎnshang, (*d*) shàngwǔ, (*e*) Xīngqīliù.

Xiǎo cèyàn:
(*a*) Nǐ míngtiān xiǎng zuò shénme? (*b*) Xiǎo Mǎ gēn tā jiějie yíyàng gāo. (*c*) Wǒ juéde zájì bǐ jīngjù yǒu yìsi. (*d*) Xiǎo Zhào, jīntiān wǎnshang nǐ xiǎng qù nǎr? (*e*) Lǐ xiǎojie, nǐ xiǎng qù kàn diànyǐng háishi tīng yīnyuèhuì?

Unit 7

Shìshi (*a*) Nǐmen xiǎng tīng yīnyuèhuì háishi kàn xì? (*b*) Nǐmen xǐhuan (tīng) Xīfāng yīnyuè ma?

Nǐmen xǐhuan bu xǐhuan (tīng) Xīfāng yīnyuè? (*c*) Zài Xīfāng dāngrán tīng Xīfāng yīnyuè.
1 (*a*) wǔ máo èr (fēn), (*b*) liǎng/èr kuài liǎng/èr máo wǔ, (*c*) shí'èr kuài qī máo liù, (*d*) jiǔshíjiǔ kuài jiǔ máo jiǔ, (*e*) èr/liǎngbǎi líng wǔ kuài wǔ máo sì. (*f*) bā kuài líng qī (fēn). 2 (*a*) Píngguǒ sìshíwǔ biànshì yí bàng. (*b*) Pútao liùshíjiǔ biànshì yí bàng. (*c*) Cǎoméi jiǔshíjiǔ biànshì yì hé. (*d*) Xiāngjiāo wǔshí'èr biànshì yí bàng. 3 (*a*) **Xīhóngshì zěnme** mài? (*b*) **Báicài** yì jīn **duōshao** qián? (*c*) **Tǔdòu duōshao** qián yì jīn? 4 **Cassette**: (*a*) Yú zěnme mài? Qī kuài líng jiǔ yì jīn. (*b*) Cǎoméi duōshao qián yì hé? Qī kuài sì yì hé. (*c*) Báicài yì jīn duōshao qián? Yí kuài èr yì jīn. (*d*) Pútao guì bu guì? Bú guì. Yí kuài jiǔ yì jīn. (*e*) Wǒ mǎi liǎng jīn tǔdòu. Sān kuài èr. 5 (*a*) Tài dà le! (*b*) Tài rè le! (*c*) Tāde qián tài duōle! (*d*) (Piào) tài guì le! (*e*) Fǎwén tài nán le! 6 (*a*) Pútao bǐ píngguǒ guì (yìdiǎnr). (*b*) Xiǎo Wáng bǐ Lǎo Lǐ gāo yìdiǎnr. (*c*) Běijīng bǐ Lúndūn rè duōle. (*d*) Bái xiānsheng bǐ Bái tàitai dà deduō. 7 (*a*) jiù, (*b*) jiù, (*c*) cái, (*d*) jiù, (*e*) cái.

Xiǎo cèyàn:
(*a*) Zhǐ yào wǔ fēnzhōng jiù dào. (*b*) Yào/děi wǔshí fēnzhōng cái dào. (*c*) Zài wǒ jiā wǒ bàba zuì dà. (*d*) Diànyǐngyuàn lí wǒ jiā bù yuǎn. (*e*) Xiāngjiāo sìshíjiǔ biànshì yí bàng.

Unit 8

Shìshi 1 No, she didn't. One was too big, one was too small, and one was too expensive. 2 He said his

apples were a little bigger, his grapes were much sweeter, his strawberries were a lot fresher, and his things were the best.
1 (*a*) (*v*), (*b*) (*vi*), (*c*) (*iv*), (*d*) (*i*), (*e*) (*ii*), (*f*) (*vii*), (*g*) (*iii*).
2 (*a*) yí jiàn bái chènyī, (*b*) yí jiàn huáng dàyī, (*c*) yì táo làn xīfú, (*d*) yì tiáo lǜ qúnzi, (*e*) yì shuāng hēi xié, (*f*) yì tiáo hóng kùzi. **3** Xiǎo Cài is wearing a white shirt, a blue skirt, and a pair of red leather shoes. Xiǎo Zhào is wearing a blue silk shirt, black trousers, and green cloth shoes. Lǎo Fāng is wearing a black suit, a white shirt, and a pair of black leather shoes. **4** (*a*) Lǎo Mǎ chuān yì shuāng hēi píxié、yí jiàn lán chènyī. (*b*) Xiǎo Qián chuān yí jiàn hóng chènyī、(yì tiáo) hēi kùzi、yì shuāng bùxié. (*c*) Liú xiānsheng chuān yí tào huī xīfú、huáng chènyī、zōng píxié. **5** (*a*) Lǐ xiānsheng Déwén (*German*) shuō-de fēicháng hǎo. (*b*) Zhāng tàitai jiàqī guò-de bù tài hǎo. (*c*) Cháo xiǎojie Yīngwén xué-de kuài-jíle. (*d*) Mǎlì yòng kuàizi (*chopsticks*) yòng-de bù zěnmeyàng. (*e*) Hēnglì shuō Rìyǔ (*Japanese*) shuō-de hěn qīngchu. **6** (*a*) Zhāng Tóng de bīngxiāng méi yǒu Mǎ Fēng de bīngxiāng guì, yě méi yǒu Mǎ Fēng de bīngxiāng dà. (*b*) Mǎ Fēng méi yǒu Zhāng Tóng gāo. Zhāng Tóng méi yǒu Mǎ Fēng dà, yě méi yǒu tā zhòng. (*c*) Mǎ Fēng de zì méi yǒu Zhāng Tóng de zì qīngchu.

Xiǎo cèyàn:
(*a*) Nǐde Yīngwén shuō-de zhēn hǎo. (*b*) Zhè jiàn chènyī yǒu yìdiǎn(r) xiǎo. (*c*) Nǐde jiàqī guò-de zěnmeyàng? (*d*) Yīnggélán bǐ Ài'ěrlán dà. (*e*) Fǎguó méi yǒu Déguó dà.

Unit 9

Shìshi 1 (*a*) Jiǔshíjiǔ kuài. (*b*) Sān zhāng zúqiú piào. **2** (*a*) Fǎguó de dōngxi bǐ Yīngguó de (dōngxi) guì. Fǎguó de dōngxi méi yǒu Yīngguó de (dōngxi) guì. Fǎguó de dōngxi gēn Yīngguó de (dōngxi) yíyàng guì. (*b*) Nǎli, nǎli, shuō-de bù hǎo. (or Xièxie.) **2 Cassette:** First walk southwards. When you get to East Sea Road, turn east. Pass two blocks and you will find the cinema on the south side of the road opposite the department store. The answer is F. **3** Wǎng xī zǒu, guò liǎng ge lùkǒu, wǎng běi guǎi. Fàndiàn jiù zài lù de dōngbianr. **4** B = school. C = shop; D = Donghai Park; E = Bank of China **8** (*a*) Fǎguó hé Yìdàlì. (*b*) Sì tiān. (*c*) Gēn tāde Fǎguó péngyou. Tāmen kāi chē qù. (*d*) Yí gè xīngqī. (*e*) Zuò fēijī. (*f*) Kāi chē. **Cassette:** Mr White is going on holiday soon. He is going to two places. He'll first go from London to Paris by train. He plans to stay in Paris for four days. After that he and his French friend will drive to Italy. They will stay in Italy for a week. Lastly he will fly back to London from Italy. His friend will drive back to France.

Xiǎo cèyàn:
(*a*) Qù Zhōngguó Yínháng zěnme zǒu? (*b*) Zuò shí lù (gōnggòng) qìchē. (*c*) Zuò wǔ zhàn. (*d*) Wǒde péngyou méi (yǒu) qù-guo Zhōngguó. (*e*) Kuài (yào) xià yǔ le.

Unit 10

Shìshi 1 (*a*) Wǒ xiān zuò fēijī qù Xiānggǎng. Zài nàr zhù liǎng tiān. (*b*) Ránhòu (cóng Xiānggǎng) zuò

huǒchē qù Shànghǎi. (c) Wǒ dǎsuàn bāyuè shí hào (cóng Shànghǎi) zuò fēijī qù Běijīng. **2** Nǐ qù-guo Shànghǎi ma? Nǐ qù-guo Shànghǎi méi you?
1 Cassette: Mr. Jones ordered **yúxiāng ròusī** (fish flavoured shredded meat), **zhàcài tāng** (preserved vegetable soup) and **Wǔxīng píjiǔ** (Fivestar beer). **2** (a) yì wǎn chǎomiàn, (b) sì píng pútáojiǔ, (c) wǔ tīng kěkǒukělè, (d) liù zhī yān, (e) liǎng wǎn tāng, (f) sān zhāng piào. **4** (a) Fúwùyuán, qǐng jié zhàng. (b) Chī-hǎo le. Xièxie. (c) Nǐ suàn-cuò le ba. (d) Méi guānxi. **5** (a) bù, (b) méi, (c) méi, (d) bù.

Dà cèyàn:
1 1066, 1462, 1798, 1914, 1945, 2000. **2** (a) Tāmen shì bu shì jiěmèi? Tāmen shì jiěmèi ma? (b) Tāde chǎomiàn hǎochī bu hǎochī? Tāde chǎomiàn hǎochī ma? (c) Míngtiān tā tàitai qù bu qù mǎi dōngxi? Míngtiān tā tàitai qù mǎi dōngxi ma? (d) Nǐ rènshi bu rènshi tā? Nǐ bú rènshi tā ma? (e) Xiǎo Lǐ yǒu mei yǒu yì tiáo hóng kùzi? Xiǎo Lǐ yǒu yì tiáo hóng kùzi ma? **3** (a) Y, (b) X, (c) Y, (d) X. **4** (a) = (v), (b) = (i), (c) = (ii), (d) = (vi), (e) = (iii), (f) = (iv) **5** (a) Méi qù-guo. (b) Qù Měiguó le. (c) Huì shuō. (d) Qù-guo. (e) Bù chōu le. (f) Chī-guo. (g) Qù Zhōngguó hé Rìběn.

Unit 11

1 (a) 2, (b) 6, (c) 10, (d) 5, (e) 11, (f) 24, (g) 83, (h) 69, (i) 57, (j) 36. **2** (a) 三 (b) 八 (c) 十 (d) 十五 (e) 四十二

(f) 九十八 (g) 六十七 **3** (a) 天 (b) 三 (c) 六 (d) 四 **4** (a) 天／日, (b) 期 (c) 期 (d) 星 (e) 星 **5** (a) 3 November, (b) 16 June (c) 11 July (d) 14 October (e) 29 August **6** (a) 十二月二十五日 (b) 三月八日 **7** (a) 1918, (b) 1937 (c) 1949 (d) 1995 (e) 1642 **8** (a) 9:15, (b) 12:25, (c) 6:30 (d) 3:50, (e) 7:45 **9** (a) 六点二十分, (b) 差一刻十二点,（十一点三刻, 十二点差一刻）(c) 十点十分, (d) 四点四十八分, (e) 七点半。

Unit 12

1 (a) lǚguǎn, lǚdiàn, fàndiàn, bīnguǎn. (b) **Lǚ** means *travel*. **Diàn** and **guǎn** both mean *house*. **Fàn** means *food*. **Bīn** means *guest*. (c) No. (d) It says there are all kinds of reasons. (e) Chinese people can stay in any hotel. **2** (a) Duì. (b) Bú duì. (c) Duì. (d) Duì (UK); Bú duì (USA). (e) Duì. **3** (a) Wǒ shì sān-líng-yāo fángjiān de (*your name*). Wǒde fángjiān tài xiǎo le. Néng bu néng huàn yì jiān dà yìdiǎn de? (b) Shuāngrén fángjiān duōshao qián yì tiān? (c) Tài guì le. Hái yǒu, wǒde fángjiān lǐ zěnme méi yǒu diànshì? (d) Zúqiú sài bàn ge xiǎoshí yǐhòu jiù kāishǐ le! **4** (a) Nǐ néng bu néng gěi wǒ sòng lái yìdiǎnr chī de/ yìdiǎnr hē de/ yì bēi chá, jiā nǎi, bù jiā táng/ liǎng ge sānmíngzhì, yí ge nǎilào de/ yí ge huǒtuǐ de? (b) Nǐ néng bu néng dǎ diànhuà jiàoxǐng wǒ/ gěi wǒ dǎ diànhuà/ gěi wǒ mǎi yì píng jiǔ/ zài gěi wǒ yì tiáo tǎnzi/ yì juǎn wèishēng zhǐ/ yí kuài dà yìdiǎnr de xiāngzào/ yí ge rèshuǐpíng? **5** (a) Dōngfāng, (b) pretty good,

(c) not at all good, (d) not polite, (e) three times. **6** (a) Wǒ xīwàng nǐmen hái yǒu fángjiān. (b) Yì jiān shuāngrén fángjiān, yì jiān dānrén fángjiān. (c) Sān、 sì tiān. Wǒ míngtiān gàosu nǐ wǒmen shénme shíhou zǒu, kěyǐ ma? (d) Bù, wǒmen yǐjīng chī le.

Xiǎo cèyàn:
(a) Bāo zǎocān ma? (b) Wǔfàn shì jǐ diǎn? Wǔfàn shì shénme shíhou? (c) Fángjiān lǐ yǒu diànshì ma? (d) Nǐmen yǒu méi yǒu (yì jiān) dà yìdiānr de dǎnrén fángjiān? (e) Yì tiān/wǎnshang duōshao qián?

Unit 13

1 (a) ruǎnwò, (b) yìngzuò, (c) ruǎnzuò, (d) yìngwò, (e) tóuděng, (f) èrděng, (g) passenger train, (h) special express, (i) train, (j) express, (k) express. **2** (a) trains no. 13, no. 21 and no. 161. (b) tèkuài, (c) No. (d) sānbǎi wǔshíyī cì, *or* sān-wǔ-yāo cì, (e) No. **3 Qǐng wèn, hái yǒu:** (a) jīntiān wǎnshang de diànyǐng piào, (b) shíyuè sì hào de fēijī piào, (c) yāo-wǔ-sān cì de huǒchē piào, (d) qù Tiānjīn de huǒchē piào. **Wǒ mǎi:** (e) sān zhāng jīntiān wǎnshang de diànyǐng piào, (f) sì zhāng shíyuè sì hào de fēijī piào, (g) wǔ zhāng yāo-wǔ-sān cì de huǒchē piào, (h) liù zhāng qù Tiānjīn de huǒchē piào. **4** (a) Yǒu liǎng zhǒng (huǒchē) piào: tóuděng hé èrděng. (b) Tóuděng piào bǐ èrděng piào guì. (c) Zài Yīngguó huǒchē yòu kuài yòu shūfu. **or** Yīngguó de huǒchē yòu kuài yòu shūfu. **6** (a) Nǐ néng bu néng gàosu wǒ tā zhù nǎr? (b) Nǐ néng bu néng gàosu wǒ nǐde diànhuà

hàomǎ? (c) Nǐ néng bu néng gàosu wǒ tā nǚ'ér duō dà le? (d) Nǐ néng bu néng gàosu wǒ tāmen yào zhù duō cháng shíjiān? **7** (a) Zuò huǒchē qù Xī'ān duōshao qiān? (b) Cóng Lúndūn dào Shànghǎi zuò fēijī děi duō cháng shíjiān? (c) Zuò chūzūchē qù Hépíng Bīnguǎn, děi duōshao qián? (d) Cóng Rìběn dào Zhōngguó zuò chuán yào/děi duō cháng shíjiān?

Xiǎo cèyàn:
(a) = (iii), (b) = (iv), (c) = (v), (d) = (vii), (e) = (ii), (f) = (i), (g) = (vi).

Unit 14

1 (a) Zhōngguó-rén qǐ-de hěn zǎo ma? (b) Zǎoshang nǐ qù nǎr? (c) Lǎo rén zài gōngyuán zuò shénme? (d) Nǐ(men) zài hú lǐ yóuyǒng ma? **3** (a) Wǒ xǐhuan zuò huǒchē, gèng xǐhuan zuò fēijī, zuì xǐhuan zuò chuán. (b) Wǒ bù xǐhuan qí mǎ, gèng bù xǐhuan qí zixíngchē, zuì bu xǐhuan qí mótuóchē. (c) Wǒ bù xǐhuan zuò chūzūchē, gèng bù xǐhuan zuò dìtiě, zuì bù xǐhuan zuò gōnggòng qìchē. (d) Wǒ xǐhuan kàn jīngjù, gèng xǐhuan kàn diànshì, zuì xǐhuan kàn diànyǐng. (e) Wǒ xǐhuan tīng liúxíng yīnyuè, gèng xǐhuan tīng xiàndai yīnyuè, zuì xǐhuan tīng gǔdiǎn yīnyuè. **4** qiūtiān,/lǚxíng,/ hái,/ méi,/ háishi,/ yòu,/ yòu,/ piányi,/ zìyóu,/ bù,/ bàn,/ dìng/mǎi,/ zhǎo/ dìng. **5** (a) Xiǎo Wáng, hǎo jiǔ bú jiàn. (b) Nǐ zuìjìn zài zuò shénme? (c) Nǐ jié hūn le ma? (d) Nǐ zài děng shéi? (e) Wǒ qù yóuyǒng. (f) Zàijiàn! **6 A** yì pái èrshíwǔ hào; èr pái wǔ hào; sān pái èrshíliù hào. **B** èrshísì pái èrshísì hào; èrshíwǔ pái sì hào; èrshíliù pái èrshísān hào. C Lóushàng shíyī pái liù hào; lóushàng shí'èr pái èrshíbā hào; lóushàng shísān pái èrshíyī hào. 7 (a) A pái shí'èr hào, (b) J pái sānshíqī hào, (c) lóushàng F pái sìshí hào, (d) K pái èr hào. 8 (a) Shíyuè èrshíwǔ hào xīngqīliù wǎnshang liù diǎn、bā diǎn hé shí diǎn. Diànyǐng jiào (is called) Dōngtiān. Diànyǐng piào sì bàng wǔ yì zhāng. (b) Shíyuè èrshíwǔ hào xīngqīliù wǎnshang qī diǎn yí kè. Huàjù jiào 《Wǒmen niánqīng de shíhou》. Huàjù piào yì zhāng liù bàng、qī bàng wǔ. (c) Shíyuè èrshíliù hào xīngqītiān wǎnshàng qī diǎn bàn. Bālěi 《Tiān'é Hú》. Piào yì zhāng bā bàng、shí bàng hé shí'èr bàng. (d) Shíyuè èrshíliù hào xīngqīrì wǎnshang bā diǎn. Gējù 《Kǎmén》. Yì zhāng piào shíwǔ bàng、èrshí bàng hé èrshíwǔ bàng.

Xiǎo cèyàn:
(a) Go to see a film. (b) No, because she had already seen it. (c) Chinese music or Western music. (d) No. (e) To go dancing.

Unit 15

1 (a) Nǐ kěyǐ zài yóujú jì xìn hé bāoguǒ. (b) Yīngguó de yóujú xīngqīliù xiàwǔ he xīngqītiān bù kāi mén. (c) Zài Yīngguó xìnxiāng shì hóngsè de, bú shì lüsè de. (d) Zài Yīngguó bú yòng qù yóujú dǎ chángtú diànhuà. 2 (a) Zhè ge bāoguǒ jì dào Měiguó, duōshao qián? (b) Dōu shì shū. (c) Yào duōshao/jǐ tiān? (d) Wǒ xiǎng mǎi míngxìnpiàn. Duōshao qián yí tào? (e) Wǒ yào yí tào dà de, liǎng tào xiǎo de. (f) Gěi nín qīshí kuài. (g) Xièxie. Zàijiàn. 3 (a) Qǐng wèn, kěyǐ zài zhèr dǎ (ge) diànhuà ma? Qǐng wèn,

kěyǐ zài zhèr jì (ge) bāoguǒ ma? Qǐng wèn, kěyǐ zài zhèr dǎ (ge) diànbào ma? (b) Qǐng gěi wǒ nǐde diànhuà hàomǎ. Qǐng gěi wǒ tāde chuánzhēn hàomǎ. Qǐng gěi wǒ nǐde hùzhào. Qǐng gěi wǒ tāmende dìzhǐ. (c) Qǐng dào nèibiān huàn qián. Qǐng dào wàibiān dǎ diànhuà. 4 (a) Hépíng Bīnguǎn. (b) Bái Huá xiānsheng. (c) There is no such extension number. (d) The caller had got the number wrong. 5 (a) Duì. (b) Duì. (c) Bú duì. (d) Bú duì. 6 (a) Qǐng wèn, jīntiān yīngbàng hé rénmínbì de duìhuànlǜ shì duōshao? (b) Qǐng wèn, jīntiān měiyuán hé rénmínbì de duìhuànlǜ shì duōshao? (c) Qǐng wèn, jīntiān mǎkè hé rénmínbì de duìhuànlǜ shì duōshao? (d) Qǐng wèn, jīntiān fǎláng hé rénmínbì de duìhuànlǜ shì duōshao? (e) Qǐng wèn, jīntiān rìyuán hé rénmínbì de duìhuànlǜ shì duōshao? (f) Qǐng wèn, jīntiān gǎngbì hé rénmínbì de duìhuànlǜ shì duōshao? 7 (a) yìbǎi bǐ bābǎi sìshí; yìbǎi měiyuán huàn bābǎi sìshí yuán. (b) yìbǎi bǐ yìbǎi líng bā; yìbǎi gǎngbì huàn yìbǎi líng bā yuán. (c) yìbǎi bǐ yìqiān sānbǎi èrshí; yìbǎi yīngbàng huàn yìqiān sānbǎi èrshí yuán. (d) yìbǎi bǐ yìbǎi liùshíwǔ; yìbǎi fǎláng huàn yìbǎi liùshíwǔ yuán. (e) yìbǎi bǐ wǔbǎi liùshí'èr; yìbǎi mǎkè huàn wǔbǎi liùshí'èr yuán. (f) yíwàn bǐ qībǎi bāshí'èr; yíwàn rìyuán huàn qībǎi bāshí'èr yuán. 8 (a) Wǒ xiǎng huàn yìbǎi yīngbàng de rénmínbì. (b) Wǒ xiǎng huàn èrbǎi měiyuán de rénmínbì. (c) Wǒ xiǎng huàn sānbǎi mǎkè de rénmínbì. (d) Wǒ xiǎng huàn sìbǎi fǎláng de rénmínbì. (e) Wǒ xiǎng huàn wǔbǎi gǎngbì de rénmínbì. (f) Wǒ xiǎng huàn liùwàn rìyuán de rénmínbì.

Xiǎo cèyàn:
(a) Zhè zhāng míngxìnpiàn jì dào Yīngguó duōshao qián? (b) Wǒ xiǎng mǎi yí tào yóupiào. (c) Jīntiān yīngbàng hé rénmínbì de duìhuànlǜ shì duōshao? (d) Wǒ xiǎng huàn yìbǎi wǔshí yīngbàng de rénmínbì. (e) Wǒde fēnjī shì èr-yāo-yāo-wǔ.

Unit 16

1 (a) hē jiǔ, chī rè fàn、rè cài, hē tāng, (b) hē tāng, chī zhèngcān, chī shuǐguǒ, (c) wǎn/kuàizi, (d) dāochā/pánzi, (e) Zhōngguórén. 2 (a) Zhè shì gěi nǐ de (yì hé) qiǎokèlì. Zhè hé qiǎokèlì shì gěi nǐ de. (b) Zhè shì gěi nǐ de (yì píng) jiǔ. Zhè píng jiǔ shì gěi nǐ de. (c) Zhè shì gěi nǐ de (liǎng zhāng) diànyǐng piào. Zhè liǎng zhāng diànyǐng piào shì gěi nǐ de. (d) Zhè shì gěi nǐ de (yì hé) lǜ chá. Zhè hé lǜ chá shì gěi nǐ de. (e) Zhè shì gěi nǐ de (yì běn) shū. Zhè běn shū shì gěi nǐ de. 3 (a) Zhè shì gěi wǒ jiějie de (yì hé) qiǎokèlì. Zhè hé qiǎokèlì shì gěi wǒ jiějie de. (b) Zhè shì gěi tā tàitai de (yì hé) lǜchá. Zhè hé lǜchá shì gěi tā tàitai de. (c) Zhè shì gěi tā shūshu de (yì běn) shū. Zhè běn shū shì gěi tā shūshu de. (d) Zhè shì gěi tā nán péngyou de (yì píng) jiǔ. Zhè píng jiǔ shì gěi tā nán péngyou de. (e) Zhè shì gěi nǐmende péngyou de (liǎng zhāng) diànyǐng piào. Zhè liǎng zhāng diànyǐng piào shì gěi nǐmende péngyou de. (f) Zhè shì gěi tāmen gōngsī de (yì fú) huà. Zhè fú huà shì gěi tāmen gōngsī de. 4 (a) Gān bēi! (b) Wǒ chī-bu-xià le. (c) Zhēn xiāng a! (d) Wǒ zìjǐ lái. (e) Zhù nǐ wànshì rúyì! 5 (a) Wǒ gāi zǒu le. (b) Hái zǎo ne. Zài zuò yìhuǐr ba. (c) Gěi

nǐmen tiān máfan le. (d) Méi shénme (máfan). (e) Bú yòng le. Qǐng huí qù ba. (f) Lùshang xiǎoxīn. (g) Màn zǒu. Màn zǒu. 6 (a) = (iii), (b) = (i), (c) = (v), (d) = (ii), (e) = (vi), (f) = (iv).

Xiǎo cèyàn:
(a) Wishing you good health! To your good health! (b) Wishing you a happy life! (c) Wishing you every happiness! (d) May your work go smoothly/well! (e) Wishing you success! To your success! (f) To our friendship! (g) To our cooperation!

Unit 17

1 (a) Duì. (b) Duì. (c) Duì. (d) Bú duì. 2 (a) Wǒ tóu déng. (b) Wǒ yǒu (yì) diǎnr késou. (c) Wǒ yě juéde shì gǎnmào. (d) Wǒ méi chī-guo Zhōngyào. Zhōngyào yǒu xiào ma? (e) Hǎo ba. (Xíng.) Wǒ shìshi ba. 3 (a) before/twice/one ball, (b) after/4 times/3 tablets, (c) one hour after meal/3 times/one spoonful, (d) twice (early morning and evening)/2–3 tablets. 4 (a) quite a few, (b) all sorts of, (c) headaches, (d) was scared. 6 (a) = (iv), (b) = (v), (c) = (i), (d) = (iii), (e) = (vi), (f) = (ii).

Xiǎo cèyàn:
(a) Nǐ nǎr bù shūfu? (b) Wǒ xiǎng shìshi zhēnjiǔ. (c) Wǒ juéde wǒ gǎnmào le. (d) Wǒ méi chī-guo Zhōngyào. (e) Wǒ yǒu shíhou tóu téng.

Unit 18

1 (a) Zài Yīngguó kāi chē hé qí zìxíngchē dōu zǒu lù de zuǒbiān. (b) Zhè gēn zài Rìběn hé Ài'ěrlán yíyàng, gēn zài Ōuzhōu dàlù bù yíyàng. (c) Měiguó shì shìjiè shàng

qìchē zuì duō de guójiā. (*d*) Zài Xīfāng zū qìchē bù nán. 2 (*a*) Wǒ xiǎng zū yí liàng chē. (*b*) Yǒu. Shì Yīngguó de (jiàzhào). (*c*) Wǒ xiǎng zū yí liàng xiǎo de (*or* xiǎo chē. (*d*) Kěyǐ. (*e*) Liǎng tiān. (*f*) Nǐmen shōu bu shōu xìnyòng kǎ? 3 (*a*) Kāi chē shàng bān yào/děi yí ge xiǎoshí. (*b*) Bǔ chēdài yào/děi duōshao qián? (*c*) Zuò gōnggòng qìchē dào Xiāngshān zěnme qù? (*d*) Zū zìxíngchē yào/děi sānshí kuài. 4 (*a*) Bù duì. (*b*) Duì. (*c*) Duì. (*d*) Duì. (*e*) Duì. (*f*) Bú duì. (*g*) Bú duì. 5 (*a*) He'd lost his bag. (*b*) His passport, wallet, credit card, some money, and a small camera. (*c*) More than 400 yuan and 200 US dollars. (*d*) Yulong Hotel. (*e*) Report its loss to his Embassy. (*f*) Inform him once they'd got any news. 6 (*a*) Tāde chédài huài le. (*b*) Tāde chē huài le. (*c*) Tāde bāo diū le. (*d*) Tāmen zhuàng chē le. (*e*) Tā tóu déng. (*f*) Tāde chē dēng huài le.

Xiǎo cèyàn:

(*a*) Zhēn dǎoméi! (*b*) Bú shì wǒde cuò. (*c*) Wǒ xiǎng tāmen yīnggāi qù zhǎo jǐngchá. (*d*) Wǒde xìnyòng kǎ diū le. (*e*) Wǒde zìxíngchē huài le. Nín néng bu néng bāng wǒ kàn(yi)kan?

Unit 19

1 (*a*) = (*iv*), (*b*) = (*vi*), (*c*) = (*i*), (*d*) = (*vii*), (*e*) = (*iii*), (*f*) = (*v*), (*g*) = (*ii*). 2 (*a*) Hànzú, Hànyǔ; (*b*) fāngyán, kǒuyīn; (*c*) Guóyǔ, Huáyǔ; (*d*) yǔyán, Hànyǔ. 3 (*a*) Fluent with good pronunciation and tones. (*b*) Three years. (*c*) Not good (according to himself). (*d*) Six years. (*e*) Her learning

method(s). (*f*) Her husband. 4 (*a*) Hánguó, pípa, èrhú; (*b*) Yīngguó, shǎoshù mínzú; (*c*) Rìběn, Zhōngguó jīngjì; (*d*) fānyì, jìzhě; (*e*) wénxué, zhéxué, wénxué, zhéxué. 6 (*a*) Wǒ huì shuō **Déwén** (hé **Fǎwén**). (*b*) Wǒde Rìyǔ búcuò *or* Wǒde **yìdàlìyǔ** shuō-de bú tài **liúlì**. (*c*) Wǒ huì shuō yìdiǎnr **Éyǔ**. (*d*) Wo shuō **Zhōngwén** shuō-de yǒu (yìdiǎnr) Měiguó kǒuyīn. (*e*) **Fǎyǔ** de yǔyīn hěn nán.

Xiǎo cèyàn:

(*a*) Wǒ juéde Yīngwén (de) yǔyīn hěn nán. (*b*) Wǒ zhǐ huì xiě jǐ ge/ yìxiē Hànzì. (*c*) Wǒ huì shuō yìdiǎnr Zhōngwén, kěshì wǒ juéde shēngdiào hěn nán. (*d*) Nǐ hěn qiānxū. (Nǐ tài qiānxū le.) (*e*) Wǒ juéde tāde kǒuyīn hěn nán dǒng. (*f*) Nǐde Yīngyǔ/Fǎyǔ/Déyǔ búcuò. (*g*) Nǐ guòjiǎng le.

Unit 20

1 (*a*) sānyuè, wǔyuè (*b*) liùyuè, qīyuè, bāyuè (*c*) jiǔyuè, shíyuè, shíyīyuè (*d*) shí'èryuè, èryuè. 3 (*a*) Bú duì. (*b*) Duì. (*c*) Bú duì. (*d*) Duì. (*e*) Bú duì. 5 (*a*) = (*v*), (*b*) = (*iv*), (*c*) = (*ii*), (*d*) = (*i*), (*e*) = (*iii*). 7 (*a*) huǒchē; (*b*) huǒchē, fēijī; (*c*) huǒchē, chángtú qìchē; (*d*) fēijī, huǒchē; (*e*) fēijī. 8 (*a*) Tā míngtiān zuò huǒchē qù Shànghǎi. (*b*) Wǒde péngyou zuò gōnggòng qìchē lái wǒ jiā. (*c*) Wǒ bù qí zìxíngchē qù gōngyuán. (*d*) Tāmen chángcháng kāi/zuò chē qù mǎi dōngxi. (*e*) Wǒ xiànzài zuò dìtiě huí jiā. 9 (*a*) Wǒ xiǎng qù Xiānggǎng hé Àomén. (*b*) Wǒ (xiān) zuò fēijī qù Xiānggǎng, zài zuò chuán qù Àomén. (*c*) Bāyuè nàr/nàli hěn rè. (*d*) Yǒu shíhou xià yǔ. (*e*) Wǒ hái

méi juédìng(ne). **10** (*a*) Shì.
(*b*) Shì. (*c*) Hěn duǎn yě hěn nuǎnhuo, kěshì chángcháng guā fēng.
(*d*) Bú shì. (*e*) Qiūtiān bù lěng yě
bú rè. Qíngtiān duō, yīntiān shǎo. Bù
cháng guā fēng, yě hěn shǎo xià yǔ.

Xiǎo cèyàn:
(*a*) Zuótiān shàngwǔ xià yǔ le,
qìwēn èrshí dù. (*b*) Zuótiān wǎnshang guā fēng le, qìwēn wǔ dù.
(*c*) Jīntiān shàngwǔ shì qíngtiān,
qìwēn shí'èr dù. (*d*) Jīntiān xiàwǔ
yǒu xiǎo yǔ, qìwēn shíbā dù. (*e*)
Míngtiān yīntiān, qìwēn sān dù.
(*f*) Xià xīngqīyī yǒu/xià xuě, qìwēn
líng dù.

Unit 21

1 (*a*) Yuè lái yuè duō de Zhōngguó-
rén lái Yīngguó xuéxí. (*b*) Tāmen
hěn duō rén duì Yīngguó de lìshǐ
hé wénhuà yǒu xìngqu. (*c*) Měi
nián hěn duō wàiguó xuésheng lái
Yīngguó xuéxí Yīngwén. (*d*) Yuè
lái yuè duō de Yīngguó gōngsī
xiǎng zài Zhōngguó kuòdà shēngyi.
5 (*a*) Liǎng ge xīngqī. (*b*) Wǒ qù
le Běijǐng、Shànghǎi hé Guìlín. (*c*)
Shànghǎi fāzhǎn-de hěn kuài. (*d*)
Běijǐng yǒu hěn duō gōngyuán. Wǒ
hěn xǐhuan tāmen. (*e*) Guìlín de
fēngjǐng měi-jíle. **6** (*a*) Bú duì.
(*b*) Bú duì. (*c*) Duì. (*d*) Bú duì.

Xiǎo cèyàn:
(*a*) Wǒ chī-bu-guàn là de cài. (*b*)
Nǐ duì gējù yǒu/gǎn xìngqu ma?
(*c*) Yuè lái yuè duō de rén qù wàiguó dù jià. (*d*) Nǐ duì Yīngguó de
yìnxiàng zěnmeyàng? (*e*) Nǐ duì
shénme zuì mǎnyì, shénme zuì bù
mǎnyì? (*f*) Zhù nǐ shēngrì kuàilè!

VOCABULARY
Chinese – English

The number after each vocabulary item indicates the unit in which it first appears.

ài *love; to love, to like very much* **16**

Ài'ěrlán *Ireland* **3**

àiren *husband/wife* **10** (used in P.R.C.)

ānjìng *quiet* **12**

ānpái *arrangement, to arrange* **20**

ānquán *safe* **9**

Àomén *Macao* **9**

ba particle indicating suggestion **3**

bàba *dad, father* **4**

bǎi *hundred* **7**

báijiǔ *strong alcohol* **16**

bái(sè) (de) *white* **7**

bàn *half* **5**

bàn *to handle* **14**

bāng *to help* **5**

bàng *excellent* **19**

bāo *bag* **18**

bāo *to include; to make* (jiǎozi) **21**

bāoguǒ *parcel* **15**

bēi *a cup of* **10**

běi *north* **9**

běifāng *the north* **14**

bǐ *compared to* **6**

biān *side* **9**

biǎo *form* **12**

bié *don't* **9**

bié rén *other/another person* **18**

biéde *other* **12**

bǐjiào *relatively* **12**

bǐjiào xǐhuan *to prefer* **20**

bìng *illness* **17**

bīngqílín *ice-cream* **10**

bìngrén *patient* **17**

bù *not* **1**

bǔ chēdài *to mend a tyre* **18**

bú kèqi *you are welcome* **4**

bú xiàng *not look it* **4**

bú xiè *not at all* **17**

bù xíng *not that good* **19**

bú yòng xiè *not at all* (lit. *no need thank*) **1**

bù zěnmeyàng *not so good* **8**

búcuò *pretty good, not bad* **7**

búguò *but, however* **12**

bùtóng de *different* **16**

cái *not ... until, only then* **16**

cài *dish* **10**

càidān *menu* **10**

cānjiā *to attend* **17**

cāntīng *restaurant, canteen* 12
cǎoméi *strawberry* 7
cèsuǒ *toilet* 12
chá *to look up* (something) 15
chá *tea* 16
chà *lacking, short of* 5
chàbuduō *similar* (lit. *different not much*) 15
chǎng measure word for a show 14
chàng (gē) *to sing (a song)* 14
chàng jīngjù *to sing Peking opera* 14
cháng(chang) *to taste* 16
chángcháng *often* 16
Chángchéng *the Great Wall* 10
chángshòu (miàn) *long life* (noodles) 21
chángtú *long distance* 15
chángtú qìchē *coach* 8
chǎo *noisy* 12
chǎomiàn *stir-fried noodles* 10
chāozhòng le *exceeded the weight limit* 15
chē *vehicle* (bus, bike, car) 6
chēdài *tyre* 18
chèng *scales* 15
chéng lǐ *in the city, in urban areas* 18
chénggōng *success, successful* 16
chéngshì *city* 18
chēzhàn *bus/train stop or station* 9
chī *to eat* 10
chī (yào) *to take* (medicine) 17
chī-bǎo le *to eat one's fill* 10
chī de *something to eat* 12
chī fàn *to eat, eating* 16
chī sù *to be vegetarian* 10
chōu (yān) *to smoke* (a cigarette) 10
chuán *ship, boat* 9
chúfáng *kitchen* 16
chūntiān *spring* 20
Chūnjié *the Spring Festival, Chinese New Year* 5

chūzūchē *taxi* 9
cí *word* 9
cì measure word for trains 12
cì *time, occasion* 12
cóng *from* 9
cónglái *ever* 20
cōngming *clever* 19
cún qián *to deposit money* 15
cuò *fault* 18

dà *big, old* 4
dǎ diànhuà *to telephone* 12
dàbùfen *majority* 16
dàgài *approximately* 13
dàibiǎotuán *delegation* 20
dàjiā *everyone* 16
dāng *to be* 20
dāngrán *of course* 2
dānrén/shuāngrén fángjiān *single/double room* 12
dānwèi *work unit* 17
dànyuànrúcǐ *I hope so* (four-character phrase) 14
dào *to; to arrive, to go to* 5
dāochā *knife and fork* 16
dǎ pái *to play cards* 14
dàshǐguǎn *embassy* 18
dǎsuàn *to plan* 9
dǎ tàijíquán *to do Tai Chi* 6
dàxiǎo *size* 8
dàxué *university* 21
de possessive indicator 2
...deduō *much*... 7
Déguó *Germany* 3
děi *to need, must; it takes* 13
dēng *lights* 18
děng *to wait* 13
děngděng *etc.* 14
...de shíhou (*the time*) *when*... 13
dì for ordinal numbers 5
diǎn *o'clock* 5
diǎn *to count* 15
diànbào *telegram* 15
diànchē *tram* (lit. *electric vehicle*) 18

diànhuà *telephone* 3
diànshì *television* 9
diànyǐng *film, movie* 6
dìdi *younger brother* 4
dìfang *place* 9
dìng *to book* (a ticket) 6
dìqū *district* 15
dìtiě *underground* 18
diū *to lose* 18
dōng *east* 9
dǒng *to understand* 21
Dōngnányà *South-East Asia* 19
dǒngshìzhǎng *managing
    director* 16
dōngtiān *winter* 14
dōngxi *thing, object* 6
dōu *all, both* 5
dòufu *beancurd, tofu* 10
dù *degree* (°C) 20
duì *yes, correct* 3
duì *to, for* 10
duìbuqǐ *excuse me* 1
duìfu *to cope with* 18
duìhuànlǜ *exchange rate* 15
duìmiàn *opposite* 9
dù jià *to take a holiday* 9
duō *many, more* 10
duōshao? *how much, how many,
    what's the number of?* 3
duō cháng? *how long?* 7
duō yuǎn? *how far?* 7
dùzi *tummy, stomach* 17

è *hungry* 10
Éguó-rén *Russian* (*person*) 19
èrděng *second-class* (ticket) 13
èrhú *a two-stringed musical
    instrument* 19
érzi *son* 4

fā *to send* 15
fādá *developed* 20
fā chuánzhēn *to send a fax* 15
fā fēng *mad* 9
Fǎguó *France* 3
fàn *food, meal* 12
fàn hòu *after meals* 17

fàn qián *before meals* 17
fàndiàn *hotel* 3
fàng *to put* 15
fāngbiàn *convenient* 14
fāngfǎ *method* 19
fángjiān *room* 3
fǎngwèn *visit; to visit*
    (formal) 16
fāngyán *dialect* 19
fānyì *interpreter, translator* 19
fǎnzheng *no way, in any case* 9
fāzhǎn *to develop* 21
fēicháng *extremely* 8
fēijī *plane* 3
fēn(zhōng) *minute* 5
fēnchéng *to divide/to be divided
    into* 17
fēng measure word for
    letters 15
fēng *wind* 20
fēngjǐng *scenery* 20
fèngzhǎo *chicken feet* 16
fù qián *pay* (money) 10
fù zhàng *to pay bills* 15
fūren *wife* (formal), *madam* 16
fúwù *service* 12
fúwùtái *reception* 12
fúwùyuán *assistant, housestaff* 6
fúyòng fāngfǎ *instruction* (for
    taking medicine) 17

gān bēi! *cheers!* 16
gānjìng *clean* 10
gǎnmào *to have a cold* 17
gàosu *to tell* 12
gāoxìng *happy* 18
gè measure word 4
gēge *elder brother* 4
gěi *for; to give* 16
gēn *and, with, to follow* 6
gèng *even more* 8
gèzhǒng gèyàng de *all kinds* 12
gōnggòng qìchē *bus* (lit. *public
    together steam vehicle*) 18
gōngjīn *kilogram* 6
gōngsī *company* 16

gōngyuán *park* **14**
gōngzuò *to work, work* **20**
guā fēng *windy* (lit. *blow
  wind*) **20**
guǎi *to turn* **18**
guān (mén) *to close* (door) **5**
guānfāng *official* **19**
Guǎngdōng *Canton*
  (province) **3**
guì *expensive; honourable* **2**
guò *to pass, spend* (of time) **8**
-guo *have ever done* (verbal,
  suffix) **9**
guójì *international* **15**
guójiā *country* **18**
guòjiǎng *to exaggerate, to
  flatter* **19**
guóyǔ *national language* **19**

hái *still* **5**
hái kěyǐ *just so so* **8**
háishi *or* (used in question
  forms) **6**
háishi *would be better* **9**
hǎiyùn (to post) *by sea* **15**
háizi *child/children* **2**
hángkōng (to post) *by air* **15**
Hánguó-rén *Korean*
  (person) **19**
Hànzì *Chinese characters* **17**
Hànzú *Han nationality* **19**
Hànzú-rén *the Han people* **19**
hǎo *good, well* **1**
hào *number* **3**
hǎochī (de) *delicious, tasty* **10**
hǎokàn *nice-looking* **15**
hàomǎ *number* (often used for
  telephone, telex, fax numbers
  and car registration plates) **3**
hǎoxiàng *to seem* **18**
hē *to drink* **10**
hé *and* **4**
hé *box* **16**
hē de *something to drink* **12**
hēi(sè) (de) *black* **7**
hěn *very* **1**

hépíng *peace* **3**
héshì *suitable* **8**
hézī qǐyè *joint venture* **21**
hézuò *cooperation, to
  cooperate* **16**
hóng(sè) (de) *red* **7**
hòu *later* **16**
hòulái *later* **18**
hòutiān *the day after
  tomorrow* **13**
hú *lake* **14**
Huá *another word for China* **19**
huá bīng *to skate* **14**
Huá-rén *overseas Chinese
  people* **19**
huài *broken, not working; bad* **18**
huán *to return something to* **12**
huàn *to change* **9**
huàn qián *to change money* **6**
huáng(sè) (de) *yellow* **7**
huānyíng *to welcome* **16**
huì *can, be able to* **2**
huì *meeting* **5**
huí guó *to return to one's own
  country* **20**
huí lái *to come back* **20**
huí qù *to go back* **16**
huò(zhě) *or* (used in
  statements) **16**
huǒchē *train* **5**
huódòng *activity* **14**
huǒtuǐ *ham* **12**
hùshi *nurse* **17**
hùzhào *passport* **12**

jǐ *how many?* (usually less than
  10) **4**
jǐ *crowded* **7**
jǐ *several, a few* **17**
jì *to post* **15**
jǐ hào? *which number?* **3**
jiā *home* **9**
jiā *to add* **12**
jià(qī) *holiday, vacation* **8**
jiān measure word for
  rooms **12**

jiàn   measure word for clothes **7**

jiàn miàn *to meet* **20**

jiǎndān *simple* **19**

jiānglái *in (the) future* **15**

jiànkāng *health, healthy* **16**

jiǎo *corner* **15**

jiào *to call, to be called* **2**

jiāotōng *transport traffic* **18**

jiàoxǐng *to (call to) wake up* **12**

jiàoxué *teaching* **21**

jiǎozi *(Chinese) dumplings* **21**

jiè (yān) *to give up (smoking)* **10**

jié hūn *to marry* **4**

jié zhàng *to have the bill* **10**

jiějie *elder sister* **4**

jiěmèi *sisters* **4**

jiémù *programme, performance* **14**

jièshào *to introduce; introduction* **19**

jīhuì *opportunity* **14**

jì(jié) *seasons* **20**

-jíle *(suffix) extremely* **10**

jīn *half a kilogram* **7**

jìn *to enter* **1**

jìn *near* **7**

jǐn(yi)jǐn *to tighten* **18**

jīngcǎi *wonderful (display, show)* **14**

jǐngchá *policeman* **18**

jīngjì *economy* **19**

jīngjù *Peking opera* **6**

jīnglǐ *manager* **12**

jīnnián *this year* **4**

jīntiān *today* **1**

jīròu *chicken (meat)* **12**

jiù *just; only* **7**

jìzhě *journalist* **19**

juéde *to feel, to think* **8**

juédìng *to decide* **14**

júzizhī *orange juice* **10**

kāfēi *coffee* **12**

kāi *to drive* **13**

kāi (huì) *to have (a meeting)* **5**

kāi (mén) *to open (a door)* **5**

kāi xué *to start a term* **20**

kāishǐ *to start, start* **5**

kāishuǐ *boiled water* **17**

kàn *to look at, watch* **5**

kàn bìng *to see a doctor* **17**

kàn(yi)kàn *to have a look* **5**

kàn-jian *to see* **16**

kē *department (in a hospital)* **17**

kěkǒukělè *Coca-Cola* **10**

kěnéng *possible, possibly* **15**

kèqi *polite* **16**

késou *cough, to cough* **17**

kètīng *sitting room* **16**

kěxī *it's a pity* **5**

kǒuyīn *accent* **19**

kǔ *bitter* **17**

kuài   Chinese unit of money **7**

kuài *fast* **8**

kuàizi *chopsticks* **10**

kuòdà *to expand* **21**

là *hot, spicy* **10**

lā dùzi *to have diarrhoea* **17**

lái *to come* **1**

lái *I'll have (colloquial)* **10**

lán(sè) (de) *blue* **7**

lǎo *old* **14**

lǎoshī *teacher* **1**

le   grammatical marker **4**

lèi *tired, tiring* **9**

lěng *cold* **20**

lí *distance from* **7**

lì *pill* **17**

liǎng *two (of anything)* **4**

liàng   measure word for vehicles (inc. bicycles) **18**

liáng(kuai) *cold, cool* **16**

liànxí *to practise; exercise* **14**

líng *(brakes) work well* **18**

lìng yí gè *another* **18**

línghuó *flexible* **15**

línyù *shower* **12**

lìshǐ *history* **19**

liúlì *fluent* **19**

liúxuéshēng *overseas student* **21**

lóushàng *upstairs* **14**

lù *road, street* **3**
lǜ(sè) (de) *green* **7**
lǚguǎn *hotel* **12**
Lúndūn *London* **3**
lùxiàng(dài) *video (tape)* **15**
lǚxíng *to travel; travel* **14**
lǚxíngtuán *tourist group* **14**
lǚyóu *to travel* **21**

ma question particle **1**
máfan *(to) trouble* **12**
mǎi *to buy* **6**
mài *to sell* **7**
mǎlù *road* **9**
māma *mum, mother* **4**
màn *slow* **8**
mǎnyì *satisfied* **21**
mànzǒu *take care* (as in *goodbye*;
    lit. *walk slowly*) **16**
màoxiǎn *adventurous; to take the
    risk* **9**
máoyī *woollen pullover* **7**
mápó dòufu *spicy beancurd/
    tofu* **10**
mǎshàng *at once* **18**
méi *no, not, (have not)* **2**
měi *every* **8**
měi *beautiful* **20**
méi guānxi *it's OK, it doesn't
    matter* **2**
Měiguó *USA* **3**
méi shénme *it's nothing, don't
    mention it* **9**
měi tiān *every day* **8**
méi wèntí *no problem* **6**
mèimei *younger sister* **4**
měiyuán *US dollar* **12**
mén *door* **5**
míngbai *to understand* **13**
míngnián *next year* **5**
míngpiàn *namecard* **3**
míngtiān *tomorrow* **1**
míngtiān jiàn *see you
    tomorrow* **1**
míngxìnpiàn *postcard* **15**
míngzi *name* **2**

mínzú *nationality* **19**
mō(mo) *to feel, touch* **8**
mùqián *at present, currently* **15**

ná *to take, to fetch* **17**
nǎr?/nǎli? *where?* **3**
nǎ/něi *which?* **7**
nǎ/něi zhǒng? *which kind?* **13**
nà/nèi *that* **7**
nǎi *milk* **12**
nǎilào *cheese* **12**
nǎli nǎli *not really* (response to a
    compliment) **8**
nàme *in that case, then* **6**
nán *male* **2**
nán *difficult* **6**
nán *south* **9**
nánfāng *the south* **20**
nánkàn *ugly* **8**
nánshuō *difficult to say* **21**
nàr/nàli *there* **9**
ne question particle **2**
nèibiān *over there* **15**
néng *to be able to, can* **12**
nǐ *you* (singular) **1**
niánqīng *young* **14**
nǐde *your*
nǐmen *you* (plural) **1**
nín *you* (polite form) **2**
niúròu *beef* **12**
nǚ'er *daughter* **4**
nuǎn(huo) *warm* **20**

Ōuzhōu dàlù *Continental
    Europe* **18**

pà *afraid* **9**
pái *row* (of seats) **14**
pàng *fat* **10**
péngyou *friend* **2**
piàn(r) *tablets* **17**
piányi *cheap* **8**
piào *ticket* **3**
piàoliang *beautiful* **2**
píjiǔ *beer* **16**
píngguǒ *apple* **7**
píng(zi) *bottle* **17**

pípa *a musical instrument* 19
pútao *grapes* 7
pútáojiǔ *wine* 10
pǔtōnghuà *common language, Chinese (Mandarin)* 19

qí *to ride* 9
qǐ *to get up* 14
qiān *thousand* 7
qián *money* 6
qián *front, ahead* 9
qiánbāo *purse/wallet* 18
qiānxū *modest* 19
qiānzhèng *visa* 14
qiǎokèlì *chocolate(s)* 16
qìchē *vehicle, bus* 9
qìhòu *climate* 20
qǐng *to invite; please* 1
qīng cài *vegetables* 10
qìngzhù *to celebrate* 21
qīutiān *autumn* 14
qìwēn *(weather) temperature* 20
qū *district, area* 3
qù *to go to* 5
qǔ qián *withdraw money* 15

ràng *to let, allow* 10
ránhòu *afterwards* 6
rè *hot* 10
rén *person* 3
rénmen *people (in general)* 16
rénmín *the people (of a country)* 19
rénmínbì Chinese currency 13
rènshi *to recognise, to know (people)* 2
rènwéi *to think, believe* 14
Rìběn *Japan* 3
róngyì *easy* 6
ròu *meat* 10
ruǎnwò *soft sleeper* 13
ruǎnzuò *soft seat* 13
rúguǒ *if* 12

sàn bù *to stroll* 14
sānmíngzhì *sandwich* 12
shān *mountain* 21

shàng *on* 5
shàng *to board* (a vehicle) 13
shàng cì *last time* 10
shàngwǔ *morning* 5
shǎo *few; less* 10
shǎoshù (mínzú) *(national) minority* 19
shéi /shuí? *who?* 2
shéide? *whose?* 18
shēnfènzhèng *identity card* 18
shēng *tone* (eg. *dì yī/èr shēng* the first/second tone) 19
shēngdiào *tones* 19
shēngyi *business* 21
shénme shíhou? *when, what time?* 12
shénme yàng de? *what kind?* 12
shénme? *what?* 2
shēntǐ *health, body* 10
shì *to be* 2
shìchǎng *market* 7
shīfu title used when addressing a craftsman (lit. *master*) 18
shìhé *to suit* 7
shíjiān *time* 5
shìjiè (shàng) *(in the) world* 18
shìqing *matter, issue, thing* 16
shìshi *to try* 7
shōu *to accept, receive* 10
shǒu *hand* 18
shòu *thin* 14
shōujù *receipt* 15
shū *book* 15
shūfu *comfortable* 9
shuǐ *water* 12
shuì *to sleep* 13
shuǐguǒ *fruit* 16
shuō *to speak, to say* 2
shūshu *uncle* 16
sì jì *four seasons* 20
sòng lái *to send over* (to the speaker) 12
sòng qù *to send over* (away from the speaker) 12
suàn-cuò le *calculated wrongly* 10

Sūgélán *Scotland* 3
... suì ... *years old, age* 4
suíbiàn *casually* 10
suǒ measure word for schools,
    houses, etc. 21
suǒyǐ *so, therefore* 13
suǒyǒude *all* 16

tā *she, he, it* 1
tāde *his, her, its* 1
tài ... le! *too* ...! 7
tàitai *Mrs, wife* 1
tāmen *they, them* 21
tán *to talk, to chat* 14
tán liàn'ài *to be in love, go steady*
    (lit. *talk love*) 14
tán(yì)tán *to talk (a bit)*
    about 21
tāng *soup* 10
táng *sugar* 12
tānzi *stall* 10
tè *extremely* (colloquial) 20
tèkuài *special express (train)* 13
téng *pain; painful* 17
tèsè *feature, characteristic* 21
tiān *day* 9
tián *to fill* (in a form*)* 12
tián (de) *sweet* 7
tiānqi *weather* 10
tiánshí *dessert* 16
tiào wǔ *to dance* 14
tiáojiàn *condition* 12
tiē *to stick to* 15
tīng *to listen to, (attend*
    concert) 6
tīng measure word for cans (of
    drink) 10
tǐng *quite, fairly* 14
tīngshuō *I heard, I am told* 9
tóngshì(men) *colleague(s)* 21
tóngxué(men) *fellow*
    student(s) 21
tōngzhī *to inform* 18
tóu téng *headache* 17
tóuděng (piào) *first-class*
    (ticket) 13

tóupán *starter* 16
tuìxiū *to retire* 9

wàiguó *foreign country* 16
wàiguó-rén *foreigner* 16
wàizī qǐyè *foreign enterprise* 21
wǎn *bowl* 10
wǎn'ān *good night* 12
wán(r) *(Chinese medicine)*
    ball 17
wǎnfàn *dinner, supper* 12
wǎng *in the direction of* 9
wǎnshang *evening* 5
wèi measure word for person
    (polite) 2
wèi *for* (formal) 16
wèi ... gān bēi! *to* ... (used in a
    toast) 16
Wēi'ěrshì *Wales* 3
wèishēng *hygiene, hygienic* 10
wèishénme? *why?* 12
wēixiǎn *dangerous* 9
wèizi *seat* 14
wēn *warm* 17
wén *language, writing* 19
wèn *to ask* 1
wénhuà *culture* 21
wèntí *question, problem* 6
wénxué *literature* 19
wǒ *I, me* 2
wǒmen *we, us* 2

xī *west* 9
xià chē *to get off (a vehicle)* 9
xià qí *to play chess* 14
xià xuě *to snow* (lit. *down*
    snow) 20
xià yǔ *to rain* (lit. *down*
    rain) 8, 20
xià(yí)ge *next* 9
xiān *first* 6
xiàndàihuà (de) *modern* 16
xiāng *fragrant* 16
xiǎng *would like to; to think* 6
xiǎng *to miss, long for* 20
xiàng *to (look) like* 4
Xiānggǎng *Hong Kong* 9

zhǐ *only* 10
zhǐ *to refer to* 19
zhǐ yào *only need/cost* 8
zhīdao *to know* 5
zhíjiē *direct(ly)* 17
zhíkuài *express (train)* 13
zhìliàng *quality* 8
zhīpiào *cheque, check* 10
zhǐyào . . . jiù . . . *so long as . . . then . . .* 19
zhǒng *kind, sort* (measure word) 17
Zhōngguó *China* 3
Zhōngguóchéng *Chinatown* 16
Zhōngguó-rén *Chinese* 3
Zhōngwén *Chinese (language)* 2
Zhōngyào *Chinese medicine* 17
Zhōngyī *Chinese medical (doctor)* 17
zhōumò *weekend* 5
zhù (nǐ) *to wish (you)* 5
zhù (zài) *to live (in/at a place)* 3
zhuǎn *to change to (extension)* 15
zhuàng *to collide* 18
zhuàng-huài(le) *damage(ed)* 18

zhuānkē *special, specialised; speciality* 17
zhúyì *idea* 8
zì *(Chinese) character* 12
zìjǐ *oneself* 14
zìrán *natural* 14
zìxíngchē *bicycle* 9
zìxíngchē dào *bicycle lane* 18
zìyóu *free, freedom* 7
zōngjiào *religion* 21
zǒngshì *always* 18
zǒu *to leave* 12
zǒu (lù) *to walk, on foot* 7
zū *to hire, to rent* 18
zuì *the most* 7
zuìhòu *last* 16
zuìjìn *recent, recently* 14
zuǒ *left* 18
zuò *to sit* 1
zuò *to do* 6
zuò (fàn) *to cook* 16
zuò chē *to take the bus* 6
zuò kè *to be a guest* 16
zuò qìgōng *to do qigong* 6
zuǒshǒu *left-hand* 16
zúqiú *football* 8

VOCABULARY
English–Chinese

afternoon xiàwǔ
afterwards ránhòu
all + noun suǒyǒude + noun
all, both dōu
already yǐjīng
also yě
always zǒngshì
apple píngguǒ
arrangement; to arrange ānpái
to ask wèn
assistant, housestaff fúwùyuán
autumn qiūtiān

bag bāo
bank yínháng
banquet yànhuì
bathroom xǐzǎojiān
to be shì
to be at/in zài
beautiful měi, piàoliang
because yīnwei
beer píjiǔ
before yǐqián
bicycle zìxíngchē
big dà
black hēi(sè) (de)
blue lán(sè) (de)
to board (a vehicle) shàng (chē)
boiled water kāishuǐ
book shū
to book (a ticket) dìng (piào)

both dōu
bottle píngzi
breakfast zǎocān/zǎofàn
broken, not working; bad huài
bus gōnggòng qìchē
business shēngyi
to buy mǎi

to call, to be called jiào
camera zhàoxiàngjī
can, be able to néng
can, know how to huì
car qìchē
cash xiànjīn
certainly, definitely yídìng
to change huàn
to change money huàn qián
cheap piányi
cheers! gān bēi!
cheque, check zhīpiào
child/children háizi
China Zhōngguó
Chinese (language) Zhōngwén
Chinese characters Hànzì
chocolate(s) qiǎokèlì
to choose xuǎnzé
chopsticks kuàizi
city chéngshì
clean gānjìng
clever cōngming
to close (door) guān (mén)

coach *(vechicle)* chángtú qìchē
coffee kāfēi
cold lěng
cold, cool liáng(kuai)
colleague tóngshì
to come lái
to come back huí lái
comfortable shūfu
company gōngsī
concert yīnyuèhuì
convenient fāngbiàn
to cook zuò (fàn)
cough; to cough késou
country guójiā
credit card xìnyòng kǎ
crowded jǐ
cup(ful) bēi

dad, father bàba
dangerous wēixiǎn
daughter nǚ'ér
day tiān
to decide juédìng
delicious, tasty hǎochī (de)
difficult nán
dish cài
to do zuò
doctor yīshēng, dàifu
don't bié
door mén
double room shuāngrén fángjiān
downstairs lóuxià
to drink hē
to drive kāi

early zǎo
east dōng
easy róngyì
to eat chī
economy jīngjì
elder brother gēge
elder sister jiějie
embassy dàshǐguǎn
English *(language)* Yīngwén
to enter jìn
every měi
everyone dàjiā

everything yíqiè
excuse me duìbuqǐ
expensive; honourable guì
extremely fēicháng, tè

far yuǎn
fast kuài
fat pàng
fault cuò
to feel, to think juéde
few; less shǎo
to fill *(in a form)* tián (biǎo)
film, movie diànyǐng
first xiān
fish yú
food, meal fàn
football zúqiú
for; to give gěi
foreign country wàiguó
foreign enterprise wàizī qǐyè
form biǎo
free; freedom zìyóu
friend péngyou
friendly yǒuhǎo
friendship yǒuyì
from cóng
fruit shuǐguǒ

to get off the bus xià chē
to go back huí qù
to go to qù, dào
good; well hǎo
goodbye zàijiàn
green lǜ(sè) (de)
guest kèren

half bàn
hand shǒu
happy gāoxìng
to have yǒu
to have a cold gǎnmào
to have diarrhoea lā dùzi
he/she/it tā
headache tóu téng
health, body shēntǐ
health; healthy jiànkāng
to help bāng

here, this place zhèr
to hire, to rent zū
his, her, its tāde
holiday, vacation jià(qī)
home jiā
to hope; hope xīwàng
hospital yīyuàn
hot rè
hot, spicy là
hotel fàndiàn, bīnguǎn, lǚguǎn
hour xiǎoshí
how far? duō yuǎn?
how is it? how about it?
  zěnmeyàng?
how much? how many? duōshao?
how? zěnme?
hundred bǎi
hungry è
husband xiānsheng, àiren

I, me wǒ
idea zhúyì
identity card shēnfènzhèng
if rúguǒ, yàoshi
illness bìng
to inform tōngzhī
interest xìngqu
interesting yǒu yìsi
international guójì
interpreter, translator; to interpret,
  translate fānyì
to introduce; introduction jièshào
to invite; please qǐng

joint venture hézī qǐyè

key yàoshi
kilogram gōngjīn
knife and fork dāochā
to know (a fact) zhīdao
to know (people) rènshi

language yǔyán
last zuìhòu
later, after yǐhòu
to leave; to walk zǒu
left zuǒ

to let, allow ràng
letter xìn
letter box xìnxiāng
light(s) dēng
to (look) like xiàng
to like xǐhuan
to listen to tīng
a little yìdiǎn(r)
little, young, small xiǎo
to live (in/at a place) zhù (zài)
to look at, watch kàn
to look for zhǎo
to lose diū
to love; love ài

male nán
many; more duō
to marry jié hūn
meaning yìsi
meat ròu
medicine yào
to meet jiàn miàn
meeting huì
menu càidān
minute fēn(zhōng)
Miss, young lady xiǎojie
money qián
month yuè
morning shàngwǔ
morning (early) zǎoshang
most zuì
mountain shān
Mr; husband; gentleman xiānsheng
Mrs; wife tàitai
mum, mother māma
music yīnyuè

near jìn
to need, must; it takes děi
new xīn
news, information xiāoxi
next xià(yí)ge
nice looking hǎokàn
no, not, (have not) méi
noisy chǎo
north běi
not bù

not bad, pretty good búcuò
now xiànzài
number hào
number (telephone, telex, fax)
  hàomǎ
nurse hùshi

o'clock diǎn(zhōng)
of course dāngrán
often chángcháng
old lǎo
on shàng
only zhǐ
opportunity jīhuì
opposite duìmiàn
other biéde

pain; painful téng
park gōngyuán
passport hùzhào
to pay (money) fù qián
peace hépíng
person rén
pharmacy yàofáng
place dìfang
to plan dǎsuàn
plane fēijī
platform zhàntái
policeman jǐngchá
polite kèqi
possible; possibly kěnéng
to post jì
post office yóujú
postcard míngxìnpiàn
to practise; exercise liànxí
prescription yàofāng
pretty good búcuò
pound (money) (Yīng)bàng
purse/wallet qiánbāo

question, problem wèntí
quiet ānjìng
to put fàng

rain yǔ
to rain xià yǔ
real; really zhēn
really zhēnde

reason yuányīn
receipt shōujù
recent; recently zuìjìn
to recognise, to know (people)
  rènshi
red hóng(sè) (de)
to rest xiūxi
to return something (to)
  huán (gěi)
right (the opposite of left) yòu
road, street lù
room fángjiān

safe ānquán
same yíyàng
sandwich sānmíngzhì
satisfied mǎnyì
seat wèizi
to see kàn-jiàn
to see a doctor kàn bìng, kàn
  yīshēng
to seem hǎoxiàng
to sell mài
service fúwù
she, he, it tā
ship, boat chuán
a short while, after a moment
  yìhuǐ(r)
sightseeing yóulǎn
simple jiǎndān
to sing (a song) chàng (gē)
single room dānrén fángjiān
to sit zuò
size dàxiǎo
to sleep shuì
slow màn
to smoke (a cigarette)
  chōu (yān)
to snow xià xuě
so, therefore suǒyǐ
some yìxiē, yǒude
sometimes yǒu shíhou
son érzi
soup tāng
south nán
to speak, to say shuō

sports; to take exercise
  yùndòng
spring chūntiān
stamp yóupiào
to start kāishǐ
station, (bus) stop (chē) zhàn
still hái
to stroll sàn bù
student xuésheng
to study, to learn xué(xí)
success; successful chénggōng
sugar táng
summer xiàtiān
surname xìng
sweet tián (de)
to swim yóuyǒng

to take a holiday dù jià
to take the bus zuò chē
to take, to fetch ná
to talk, chat tán
taxi chūzūchē
tea chá
teacher lǎoshī
telephone diànhuà
to telephone dǎ diànhuà
television diànshì
to tell gàosu
to thank; thank you xièxie (nǐ)
that nà/nèi
there nàr/nàli
these/those zhèixiē/nèixiē
they, them tāmen
thin shòu
thing, matter, issue shìqing
thing, object dōngxi
to think, believe rènwéi
to think, to assume yǐwéi
this zhè/zhèi
this year jīnnián
thousand qiān
ticket piào
time shíjiān
time, occasion cì
tired, tiring lèi
to; to arrive, to go to dào

today jīntiān
together yìqǐ
toilet cèsuǒ
tomorrow míngtiān
too ...! tài ... le!
train huǒchē
transport, traffic jiāotōng
to travel; travel lǚxíng, lǚyóu
to try shìshi
to turn guǎi
two (of anything) liǎng

underground, subway dìtiě
to understand dǒng, míngbai
university dàxué
upstairs lóushàng
to use yòng
US dollar měiyuán
usually yìbān

vegetables qīng cài
vehicle (bus, bike, car) chē
very hěn
visa qiānzhèng
visit; to visit (formal) fǎngwèn

to wait děng
to walk, on foot zǒu lù
to want (to), need, will yào
to want to, would like to;
  miss xiǎng
warm nuǎn(huo)
water shuǐ
we, us wǒmen
weather tiānqi
week xīngqī
weekend zhōumò
to welcome; welcome huānyíng
west xī
what kind? shénme yàng de?
what? shénme?
when, what time? shénme
  shíhou?
where? nǎr?/nǎli?
which number? jǐ hào?
which? nǎ/něi?

white bái(sè) (de)

who? shéi/shuí?

whose? shéide?/shuíde?

why? wèishénme?

wife tàitai, àiren

wife (formal); madam fūren

wind fēng

wine pútáojiǔ

winter dōngtiān

to work; work gōngzuò

to write xiě

... year (of age) ... suì

yellow huáng(sè) (de)

yes, correct duì

you (singular) nǐ

you (polite form) nín

you (plural) nǐmen

young niánqīng

younger brother dìdi

younger sister mèimei

your (singular) nǐde

your (plural) nǐmende